Clothed in Nothingness

Clothed in Nothingness
Consolation for Suffering

❖

Leonard M. Hummel

Fortress Press
Minneapolis

Cover art: *Woman with Strands of Hair* © Noma/Images.com, Inc.
Cover design: Marti Naughton
Interior design: Beth Wright

Library of Congress Cataloging-in-Publication Data

Hummel, Leonard M.
    Clothed in nothingness : consolation for suffering / Leonard M. Hummel.
        p.   cm.
    Includes bibliographical references and index.
    ISBN 0-8006-3455-1 (pbk. : alk. paper)
    1. Suffering—Religious aspects—Lutheran Church—Case studies.
    2. Consolation—Case studies.
    BT732.7 .H86 2003
    248.8/6 21

                                                                    2002156694

The paper used in this publication meets the minimum requirements of American
National Standard for Information Sciences — Permanence of Paper for Printed
Library Materials, ANSI Z329.48-1984.

Manufactured in the U.S.A.
07   06   05   04   03   1   2   3   4   5   6   7   8   9   10

Contents

❯•❮

Preface

⋙·⋘

This book investigates the sources of consolation for suffering found in religious experience—by analyzing the role of tradition in lived religion. That is, how do a group's learned beliefs and practices affect their actual religious experience? How do people make sense of their traditions when they suffer? In difficult times, members of a tradition may embrace—or ignore—a wide assortment of inherited beliefs and practices. In doing so, they may also reform their tradition.

In this book we will look at a particular religious tradition, Lutheranism, and at the lived religion of seven Lutheran "co-researchers" with whom I talked at length. These people had experienced a variety of negative events in their personal lives: the death of a loved one, a divorce, a serious illness. An analysis of their stories suggests a theology for consolation. We will inquire into the influence of their tradition on their lived religious experience.

While I believe this book has relevance beyond the theological academy, it belongs primarily in the fields of pastoral and practical theology. Along with Bonnie Miller-McLemore, I understand the starting point of pastoral theology to be human suffering.[1] As a practical theologian, I seek to understand the relationships between religious beliefs and practices, especially those that relate to the causes of human suffering and to its care.

However, the passions of others have accompanied me in writing this book. For example, I have been inspired by conversations with members of the Constructive Theology Workgroup.[2] In our struggle to develop a new text for the field of constructive (systematic) theology, Workgroup members have raised concerns relevant to pastoral theology. Amy Plantinga Pauw contends that "the carrying on of tradition is a messy, subversive business. . . . Doing constructive Christian theology involves confronting the deep hurts the tradition has inflicted on us and others, as well as the hope, vision and comfort it has provided."[3] While Pauw points to both these blessings and curses, Joerg Rieger argues that theology must begin with a study of "contexts which hurt," that is, with the sources of human suffering: "What I am suggesting, therefore, is to do theology more self-consciously out of the (unsystematic) messiness of life, which includes a give-and-take of messy life and messy traditions. . . . Difference must not be displaced in favor of an easy synthesis."[4]

Constructive theologians' focus on human suffering may seem like a subversion of theological tradition, since God alone is manifestly the defining subject and definitive object of that discipline. That is to say, these theologians' tack might seem to lead toward an idolatrous confusion of the penultimate—that which is weak, finite, and human—with the divine. However, I propose that human suffering is an ultimate concern of God and, therefore, that any theologian who attends to it as such is not only giving an account of God but also doing the work of the Lord.[5]

I believe pastoral theologians may take heart at our colleagues' intense concern for lived religion and human suffering. However, like the proverbial ships in the night, systematic and pastoral theologians may pass one another without signaling—in this case, because they have each set sail for the other's harbor. Some pastoral theologians believe that they have tabernacled too long in a wilderness of social scientific studies (anthropology, psychology, and sociology) and now yearn for what seems to be the promised land of theology. However, were they to draw near to that land, they might see fewer colleagues to befriend than they anticipated, because many constructive theologians now are seeking the wisdom in that wilderness behind them.

I also found inspiration in the Convocation of Lutheran Teaching Theologians where *tentatio* (suffering) was articulated as a subject matter of theology and a defining experience for a theologian. In his conference paper, "Characteristically Lutheran Leanings in Pedagogy," Mark U. Edwards notes a predilection for what is finite, fragile, and human: "Lutheranism . . . leans toward the case method, because it leans towards understanding the world in terms of concrete and historically situated particulars, which can, with the help of prudential reason, be brought into dialogue with principles and convictions." The tradition also tends to raise more questions than are answered or answerable: "The Lutheran should favor pedagogy that recognizes the ambiguity and messiness involved in all knowledge and in life generally. Further, there is wisdom in recognizing that most important things in the world are not clear-cut, that shades of gray are more common than stark blacks or whites."[6]

A preference for "historically situated particulars" has drawn my focus to a small number of case studies within a single tradition—the suffering of seven Lutherans. I believe we can learn much by investigating what Anton Boisen called "living human documents." I hope to demonstrate that examining what is small is not only a beautiful practice but a necessary art—an art not to be lost in our important pastoral meta-analyses of the systemic sources of suffering, precisely because it may put even more flesh on those analyses. Similarly, I hope that this book points to the riches that await the pastoral theological study of particular religious ways of being in the world—that is, of specific religious traditions. While I believe that a person who knows only one religious tradition actually knows none, I also believe that the following tautology has practical import: a person who does not know any one tradition well indeed does not know any well. Accordingly, in this book, I focus on one tradition, only one of many, without attempting to show how that tradition relates to all of the many or how those many may all be one.

In response to my observation that neither Luther nor the Lutheran confessions presents a systematic theology of consolation, one Lutheran colleague quipped, "No surprise!" It will also come as little surprise to those familiar with the Lutheran tradition as described by Edwards that this book does not offer a systematic pastoral theology of consolation. Rather, it focuses quite simply, and I believe quite profoundly, on understanding the experience of suffering among seven Lutherans. Therefore, while I conclude with what I judge to be some coherent observations, I also conclude with at least as many ambiguities and unanswered—or unanswerable—questions.

Accordingly, let the reader beware: This is not a manual for, nor a model of, the provision of consolation for suffering—from a Lutheran perspective or any other. I do not recommend any of the particular beliefs or practices of the co-researchers—or those who cared for them—as a means to console others, no matter how similar their suffering seems to be. Also, in addressing a number of pastoral issues, I have left a greater number unaddressed. For example, I have rendered Luther's devil as a bodiless superego, an overbearing conscience that gives no respite. But I have not attempted to determine which of Luther's many other late-medieval worldviews about care and consolation may be translated into our thought-world, and which are more or less untranslatable.

A word about the structure of the book: Because concerns about tradition, lived religion, and human suffering are not limited to professionals in the fields of pastoral, historical, and systematic theology, I have attempted not to overburden this book with professional concerns. At the same time, since many in those fields have addressed relevant matters, I have opened a dialogue with a number of them throughout the text, but most directly in the endnotes.

I write this book not only as a pastoral theologian but also as a pastor of the Evangelical Lutheran Church in America. That is, I write as one who cares about, and has an insider's perspective on, this tradition and its lived religion. To a large degree, I also write as one who believes that much in this tradition is right, true, and, not least of all, consoling. I easily echo the words of one of the co-researchers, Charles, who said of the Lutheran tradition: "You handle it and let yourself be handled by it and it works." At the same time, I write as one who finds much in it unsettling. Furthermore, throughout the book, I detail the difficulty of determining the boundaries of this tradition and, consequently, who is in it and who is not in it. I experience myself very much within this tradition but also, at certain points, outside it.

Luther constructed his theology of consolation out of many late-medieval practices, including that of needy people meditating on the lives of saints past. Among these needy were travelers, people with tuberculosis, and—perhaps surprisingly, perhaps not—scholars. In his theology, Luther broadened the company of saints who could help those in need to include living persons who transmit consolation and discipline. Furthermore—and as we shall see, at the core of his pastoral theology—Luther understood the consolation contained by this companionship to be the very consolation of God.

What was true for Luther was true for me as I wrote this book. In my scholarly need, I experienced the words of criticism and support from those who read all or portions of my book as the very words of God. Consequently, the following acknowledgments are expressions of thanks but also of my gratitude for grace.

To Michael West at Fortress Press for his thoughtful comments and guidance through this, my first book; members of the Constructive Theology Workgroup for their keen interest in these issues and for the enthusiasm their work lent to mine; Chris Schlauch for his continued support and encouragement; Deanna Thompson at Hamline University for her unflagging interest in this work; Marcia Bunge at Valparaiso University for her characteristically helpful, pointed questions and comments; Sharon Thornton at Andover Newton Theological Seminary for graciously permitting me to review her own book manuscript; Luther scholar Jane Strohl at Pacific Lutheran Theological Seminary for her careful readings of my dissertation and its metamorphosis into this book; Rod Hunter at Emory University for helping me situate this book in our common guild of pastoral and practical theology; my spouse, Elizabeth Sponheim, for her careful reading of the manuscript and consequently crystal-clear suggestions for its form and content; Carter Lindberg at Boston University for having reviewed my chapter on consolation in the early Lutheran tradition in its dissertation form; again to Ken Pargament for his permission to use in my dissertation scales he developed for religious coping research and to my colleagues at Vanderbilt University Divinity School: James Byrd, for his guidance as I sought to present an accurate portrayal of the complexities of the Baptist tradition and its possible impact on the life of a former Baptist co-researcher; Paul DeHart for his reviewing and making recommendations for my chapter on the theology of consolation in the early Lutheran tradition as well as reviewing my translations of cited German texts; Jay Geller for also reviewing these German translations; Victor Anderson for his careful comments about African American Christianity as I examined the life of an African American Lutheran; Patout Burns for lending me insights into Stoicism and the consoling writings of the early church fathers; my research assistants, Yohan Ka, Katharine Baker, and Vincent Wynne, for their tremendous labor in preparing this manuscript for publication; to the Vanderbilt Divinity School faculty secretary, Arliene Dearing, for her assistance; and to both former Dean Jack Forstman and Dean James Hudnut-Beumler for carving out time for me to research and write. My deans knew I had an interesting but hard task ahead of me.

Most of all, I acknowledge and am grateful for what I have learned from conversing with, and analyzing the reports of, the co-researchers whose accounts I set forth in this book. Without their cooperation in this work and their trust that it would come to a good end, the work itself would not have been possible. I dedicate this book to them and wish them God's blessings.

What is this book about? It is about a tradition that is justified and sinful at the same time. It is about the suffering of some specific members of this tradition and the ways one may view their suffering through its lens. It asks what threads of their tradition's "living human web" are woven into their lives. It also asks what other threads may be discerned in their lives and what they themselves are weaving.

For whom is this book written? It is for all who want to understand how sufferers seek solace in the theology and practice of a particular tradition. I invite the reader on a journey to see how a tradition can help and how it can hurt. We will explore the degree to which one should, or can, discern a tradition informing people's lives.

> Therefore our life is simply contained in the bare Word; for we have Christ, we have eternal life, eternal righteousness, help and consolation. But where is it? We neither possess it in coffers nor hold it in our hands, but have it only in the bare Word. Thus has God clothed his object in nothingness.[7]

This book is for all who wish to understand what these words of Martin Luther mean—in a tradition and in its lived religion.

1.
Backgrounds and Orientations

❧·❦

In the following case study excerpts, two co-researchers reflect on how they coped with and sought consolation for a significant negative event in their lives. I have attempted to protect the confidentiality of all co-researchers and other individuals by removing or altering insignificant but possibly telltale biographical details. These vignettes raise questions that are also the central questions of the book itself.

Tradition in Lived Religion: Two Vignettes

Ruth is a thirty-nine-year-old divorced businesswoman with an eight-year-old son and two-year-old daughter. The daughter of an African American Baptist father and a German Lutheran mother, Ruth sometimes refers to herself as an "Afro-Saxon." Her divorce came about primarily because "the marriage had been quite abusive. As a result of my husband's persistent pattern of physical abuse, I was at first unable to finish my course work at a very prestigious university." Ruth feared the "punishment of God" for having filed for a divorce, and this fear led to her belief that God had indeed punished her through the proceedings and verdict of the divorce court. "I'm not getting any money and I'm risking my job being here with this idiotic lawyer and this wicked man. And now the judge says to me I'm going to force you to have your children visit with this very wicked man because he took the time to come here and tell me that that's what he wants. Lord, what is this? And I cried and I said, 'Lord, can you give me some faith?'"

Abandoned by her husband, Ruth also felt abandoned by God. "I get to the point where I say, 'Okay, Lord, you know you've brought me this far and we're out here in the wilderness and instead of giving me the extra money that I need to take care of these children, I'm going further into debt.'" Ruth also related her fear of her husband to her fear of God. Furthermore, she identified Luther's refrain throughout his commentary on the Ten Commandments in his Small Catechism that the faithful are to "fear, love, and trust God" as something that binds those fears together.

> I love and fear God. And you can't have that tension in a relationship. You can't be afraid of someone and also trust them deeply. You can accept discipline from someone that you love, and be in fear of their anger and their wrath, and not also really, really trust them. Because if they're just random in their anger, it makes you crazy. It can make you nuts. That's what abused women go through. They love this man who any Friday night could come home with flowers or a gun.

Later, Ruth calmly remarked, "I'm such a Lutheran . . . I love the liturgy and I love Bach. I love the way the catechism contemplates God because it is exactly my experience."

Charles, a sixty-nine-year-old retired pastor of the Evangelical Lutheran Church in America, is also "such a Lutheran." Reared and ordained in the Lutheran Church–Missouri Synod, Charles descends from a long line of renowned orthodox Lutheran theologians—that is, those who have attempted to norm their beliefs and practices according to those set forth in the complete Book of Concord. Charles shared that "after a lifetime of relatively good health," he experienced a cascade of life-threatening medical disorders requiring many treatments, major surgeries, and multiple hospitalizations. He noted that throughout his illnesses he received consolation from a number of sources, including a gift, a book authored by a non-Christian. Charles felt he found wisdom in that book, whose author "was once Episcopalian, then he became a nonbeliever, then he went into Zen. But he's a very spiritual person. I have no spooky ideas about spirituality."

Later in the conversation, Charles claimed that he did not seek consolation by attributing his illness to the will of God. "How come I got the heart attack? The physician said, 'You're male, you're white, you're sixty years old or older, you live too stressful a life.' I said, 'Bingo! And I'm also a Westerner.' Now was the will of God in all of that—God chose me to have this? No. God doesn't work that way." Charles saw a connection between his "Lutheran worldview," finding solace in a generically spiritual, manifestly nonbiblical book, and in not speculating on the will of God. He pointedly referred to Luther's theology of the cross to explain this connection. "I don't ever see Him [God]. I don't know where He is. The book itself was a gift. And I think to look for God means you're not going to find Him. Because God is found in the—this is the way I think—God is found in the cross."

As I listened to Ruth and Charles, I heard themes consistent with what one may very broadly call the Lutheran tradition—arguably distinguished by the "red thread" of Luther's writings and the Book of Concord. I also heard themes consistent with that tradition's understanding of consolation—the grace that God brings to strengthen the faithful who suffer with illness, dying, grief, terrible hardship, or religious doubt. Accordingly, I wondered what in this tradition might lead one of its members to attribute her suffering to God and another not to do so. How is it that Charles found consolation in sources outside of Lutheran orthodoxy yet considers his doing so to be consonant with his tradition? How is it that Luther's Small Catechism mediates both dread and comfort to Ruth?

I also found myself confronted with other, broader questions that arise both inside and outside the Lutheran tradition: Where is God when one suffers? How may one be consoled when one suffers? What actions may one, in faith, take or not take to overcome suffering?

This book explores these and other questions, examining the theology of consolation for suffering as formulated in the early Lutheran tradition and as practiced by some contemporary Lutherans. Situated in the urgent theological concern for what is and is not helpful in tradition and in lived religion, this book describes how the theology of consolation in this tradition may have informed the beliefs and practices of those who suffer, and may be reformed in light of those beliefs and practices. In conclusion, it offers insights to theologians and pastoral caregivers of various traditions about what consolation for suffering means in this context. Additionally, it contributes to ongoing theological inquiries into the normativity of tradition in lived religion. This book, therefore, addresses specifically the relationship between tradition and lived religion of consolation within Lutheranism, and, more broadly, within any Christian tradition.

Tradition and Lived Religion

Tradition: Literally, the term means that which is handed down or handed over. Tradition is not a dimension limited to those religions that tout it, but is that dimension of all faiths denoting those shared ways of being religious that have been passed on. To be sure, some religions that call themselves "traditional" may have more distinctive beliefs and practices than those that do not, but all religions engage in the process of "traditioning," handing over styles of belief and practice.[1]

Tradition has been, and is, the subject of much theological thought. In his famous epitome of nineteenth-century liberal theology, *The Essence of Christianity,* Adolf von Harnack used many metaphors to describe its essence—for example, distinguishing between "what is traditional and what is peculiar, between the kernel and the husk."[2] Von Harnack employed another metaphor to link what is thought to be both essential and traditional in religion: "It [the gospel] would still be traceable like a red thread in the center of a web, and somewhere or other it would emerge afresh, and free itself from its entanglements."[3] Although von Harnack liberally judged many historical expressions of the gospel to be entangling extras, he believed that it is by "handing on" that the red thread of this gospel moves from one group of persons to another. As reflected in the debate between von Harnack and Abbé Loisy, Catholics have been more prone to identify the historical unfolding of tradition with its essence. Accordingly, one may define tradition as not only that which is handed on, but also as the process of handing on itself.[4]

As we shall see, von Harnack's metaphor of a "red thread" has itself appeared like a red thread in later studies of the Lutheran tradition, and even in studies of Luther's theology of consolation, to describe something that persists through time and space. However, whether any tradition does in fact endure its own traditioning has been questioned. In Kathryn Tanner's words, the view that "whatever the time or place, the same beliefs and practices therefore form a red thread to be found in all ways of living that are genuinely Christian . . . loses plausibility when historical investigation shows how difficult it is to exempt any Christian belief and practice from substantial change across differences of time and place."[5] Tanner even more pointedly notes that what is judged as traditional may not have been the tradition in the past: "What is labeled 'tradition' always has links to a preferred course of Christian behaviors now."[6] Not only Christian theologians but also cultural anthropologists have raised concerns about the reification of tradition: "We take issue with the naturalistic conception of tradition. We suggest that there is no essential, bounded tradition; tradition is a model of the past and is inseparable from the interpretation of tradition in the present."[7] The myriad ways in which a religious tradition informs the present and, conversely, in which the present reshapes tradition, is the subject matter of lived religion studies.

In his introduction to a series of essays on lived religion in the United States, David D. Hall describes how those essays developed from studies in "popular religion"—"the space that emerged between official or learned Christianity and profane (or pagan) culture."[8] While acknowledging what popular religious studies have demonstrated— that laity have agency and extra-ecclesial activities have integrity— scholars who examine lived religious experience do not structure their studies around an opposition between tradition and practice. Rather, they investigate something even "messier" than popular religion: the ways in which persons both have, and do not have, agency over their own traditions and practices. While American studies in lived religion are relatively recent, European sociologists of religion and practical theologians have attended to this study for many decades.[9]

Pietism, especially Lutheran pietism, is one of a number of sources for these European studies of lived religion, and is the one source that bears most directly on the present investigation. In his seminal treatise *Pious Desires,* the Lutheran Pietist Philip Jakob Spener (1635–1705) proposed, "The people must have impressed upon them and must accustom themselves to believing that *it is by no means enough to have knowledge of the Christian faith, for Christianity consists rather of practice (praxis).*"[10] "Life, not doctrine" became a rallying cry for this religious cause, which has since been accused of anti-intellectualism—although the Pietists pioneered critical-historical studies of the Bible—and individualism, even though Pietism nurtured both social reform, in such places as Halle, and social thinkers such as the Blumhardts.

Although Hegel aligned himself later in life with the conservative orthodox theologians against the Pietists, Alan Olson has argued that Hegel's Pietist heritage pervasively informed his life work.[11] For example, Hegel seems to betray his Pietist background when he proposes that God becomes God only by participating in the struggles of humanity. Pietism also seems to be at work in Hegel's call for traditions to make a difference in lived religion: "It was the principal contention of Pietists that . . . subjective belief must be capable of translation into the objective or actual well-being of the life of community."[12] His assertion that what is true *(wahr)* is real *(wirklich),* and what is real is true, also evinces the influence of the Pietist tradition. Olson notes that "the fundamental question in Pietism has to do with making real or *wirklich* what is asserted as being formally and materially true—that is, *wahr*—in action or in life as lived."[13]

This book asks the following question: To what degree is that which is said to be *true* in the Lutheran tradition *real* in the lived religion of seven Lutherans who sought consolation for their suffering? A full answer requires a look at some features of consolation in the broader tradition and lived religion of Christianity.

Consolation in Christian Tradition and Lived Religion

To analyze the various epochs of pastoral care in the history of the church, William Clebsch and Charles Jaekle constructed an elaborate grid of the forms this care has assumed. They located "consolation" in one of the five subsets of "sustaining ministry," which itself stands beside three other pastoral functions—healing, reconciling, and guiding.[14] However, I believe that the many dimensions involved in the provision and reception of consolation are hard to parcel out of these other pastoral practices—past or present. Rather, I believe Thomas Oden is closer to capturing the use and meaning of consolation throughout the Christian tradition in claiming that it designates any pastoral response to questions about the will of God for human suffering.[15] Reflecting on Luther in particular, but with relevance to Christian caregivers throughout history, Gerhard Ebeling describes consolation as the comfort God brings for the suffering of religious doubt, personal and interpersonal turmoil, illness, preparation for death, or the pain of grief.[16] While to many moderns, the term *consolation* denotes a paltry gift in lieu of success—a "consolation prize"—both Ebeling and Martin Treu note that in Luther's time, consolation (*consolatio* in Latin, *Trost* in German) did not have such associations, but connoted a gift from God to sufferers that strengthens them.[17]

Before and after Luther's time, theologies about, and ministries of, consolation have had a rich history in the Christian tradition and lived religion. As John McNeill has noted, Christian thought and practice draws not only on Wisdom literature and Talmudic writings, but on classical philosophy in general, and the moral reflections of the Latin Stoics in particular.[18] For example, the Roman statesman Cicero (106–43 B.C.E.) wrote numerous treatises on how to bear adversity. In the turbulent world of the late Republic, Cicero upheld *gravitas* (dignity) as a virtue to be cultivated and exercised not just by politicians but by all persons. Arguably the most influential of the Stoics for later Christian thought was Seneca (4 B.C.E.–65 C.E.) who, in his epistles of consolation during the turmoil of the early Empire, exhorted those who suffered to will themselves to be "beyond hope and fear." "The sage is neither elated by prosperity nor depressed by adversity. His endeavor is to rely mainly on himself and to seek his own satisfaction from within himself. . . . Never have I trusted Fortune, even when she seemed to be at peace. . . . No one is crushed by adverse Fortune who has not first been beguiled by her smile."[19]

In writing moral treatises in the form of letters to those who suffered, Seneca created a literary genre that pastoral theologians from the early church fathers to Henri Nouwen have adopted. Seneca also established a moral philosophy that shaped much subsequent Christian theology on consolation. For example, Clebsch and Jaeckle comment on the consoling letters of John Chrysostom: "Christian faith molded the form of Chrysostom's pastoral concern, but its content he took over entire from Stoicism."[20] Both the literary template and the thought-world of Stoic philosophy can be seen in Cyprian's letter to those fearing the ravages of a plague: "We should consider, dearly beloved brethren—we should ever and anon reflect that we have renounced the world, and are in the meantime living here as guests and strangers. Let us greet the day which assigns each of us to his own home, which snatches us hence, and sets us free from the snares of the world, and restores us to paradise and the kingdom."[21]

In her comprehensive study of Luther's letters of consolation, Ute Mennecke-Haustein has argued that this classical tradition influenced Luther's writings.[22] She has also detailed the close connection between his manuals of consolation and those of later medieval pastoral theologians such as Jean Gerson. After Luther, orthodox theologians such as Gerhard, and Pietist theologians such as Francke, developed the theory and practice of consolation in Lutheranism. Others such as Jeremy Taylor (1613–1667) added to the Protestant tradition of consolation by offering advice to the dying: "Be content that the time which was formerly spent in prayer, be now spent in vomiting. . . . Do not think, that God is only to be found in great prayer, or a solemn office: he is moved by a sigh, by a groan, by an act of love."[23] For Taylor, the approach of death was the ultimate test of the soul.

In most histories of pastoral care, stories of persons without power or prestige are not told. That is also the case with the history of consolation in Christian tradition and practice. And just as one must often turn to atypical sources to hear less dominant voices for a more complete history of pastoral care, one must make a similar turn for a fuller history of consolation. One such source is provided by George Eliot (Mary Ann Evans) in her novel *Adam Bede*. Through her portrayal of the lay Methodist ministry of Dinah Morris (modeled to a degree after that of Eliot's aunt Elizabeth Evans) in rural England around 1800, Eliot expanded that history. A poised, passionate preacher of the God of love and the love of God, Dinah tended to many in their deepest needs: for example, she ministered to Adam's mother after the sudden death of her alcoholic husband ("God didn't send me to you to make light of your sorrow, but to mourn with you, if you will let me")[24] and to a young woman who had been seduced, impregnated, abandoned, and finally was awaiting execution for infanticide (". . . some one who has been with you through all your hours of sin and trouble. It makes no difference—whether we live or die, we are in the presence of God").[25] In a conversation with Adam's brother, Seth, after their father's death, Dinah summarized her theology: "Infinite Love is suffering too—yes, in the fullness of knowledge it suffers, it yearns, it mourns. . . . Is not the Man of Sorrow there in that crucified body wherewith he ascended? And is He not one with Infinite Love itself?"[26]

In a recent work, Peter Hodgson formulates his understanding of Dinah Morris's ministry: "She provided comfort without consolation; by her sympathetic deeds and truthful speech, she manifested God's presence in the world."[27] Why comfort without consolation? Because Hodgson believes that consolation offers only a thin gruel—a paltry secondary gain—for life's primary losses. In its stead, Eliot espoused a clear-eyed, practical religion that would do without the palliatives of most religious teachings about suffering. Similarly, her religion had no room for a God who accuses humanity of the failings born of its finitude. For these reasons, some read Eliot's religion to be no religion—to be instead a Feuerbachian reduction of theology to anthropology that substitutes the activity of God with the ministry of humanity. Hodgson understands Eliot otherwise, proposing that her broad-minded thought-world has a place for a loving God. Hodgson elaborates on his own understanding of the "suffering God," which Eliot claims we need in the midst of our own suffering, by turning to the words of Hegel: "'God himself is dead,' it says in a Lutheran [Good Friday] hymn, expressing an awareness that the human, the finite, the fragile, the weak, the negative are themselves a moment of the divine, that they are within God himself, that finitude, negativity, otherness are not outside of God and do not, as otherness, hinder unity with God."[28]

Accordingly, one may ask this question: Is it possible for Lutherans to separate the activity of God from the ministry of humanity? While not the focus of this book, this question will be considered in the final chapter, following an investigation of some Lutherans' lived religion.

But what is the Lutheran tradition that provides a source for Hegel's reflections on the pains of finitude, for the accusations that Ruth suffered during her divorce, and for Charles's consolation when he was sick?

The Lutheran Tradition

In discussing religion and health in the Lutheran tradition, Carter Lindberg observes, "In spite of Martin Luther's insistence 'that people make no reference to my name; let them call themselves Christians, not Lutherans,' the churches rooted in the Reformation initiated by this German monk usually identify themselves as Lutheran."[29] However, it was not Luther's writings themselves, but the publication in 1580 of the Book of Concord (whose contents are often referred to as "the Lutheran confessions") that formally established Lutheranism as a distinct movement within the broader Christian tradition. The church leaders who assembled this book—a collection of confessional statements, occasional theological treatises, and catechisms— sought to establish boundaries of faith and practice for those Christians who called themselves Lutherans (or "evangelicals," as they and many non-Lutherans frequently referred to themselves then, and sometimes do today).

While the Book of Concord has been the touchstone for the Lutheran tradition, the influence of Luther on that tradition is manifest even in the contents of this book: He authored both its small and large catechisms and one of its theological expositions, the Smalcald Articles. Furthermore, the force of his beliefs about such weighty matters as justification, election, and sin may be felt throughout its remaining four writings. Thus the tradition that often bears Luther's name was indeed shaped by him from whom "a theology came into being which was not merely new by normal standards but overwhelmed the force of fifteen hundred years of tradition."[30] Accordingly, Luther's writings and the Book of Concord are usually linked as constitutive elements of the early Lutheran tradition.

Employing a variant translation of a von Harnack metaphor, Lindberg argues that throughout its five hundred year history, "both Luther and the Lutheran Confessions run like a *red line* through the tradition" (emphasis added).[31] That is, throughout these centuries, theologians and church leaders typically have harkened back to Luther and the Book of Concord to guide, if not ground, evangelical Lutheran beliefs and practices. The orthodox theologians of the seventeenth century did so—in fact, they and their descendants are distinguished by their insistence in doing so—but so did a number of eighteenth-century Pietists and many Lutherans of various stripes in the ensuing centuries. In more recent times, many theologians continue to refer to the texts of the early Lutheran tradition as tantamount to the Lutheran tradition itself. For example, at the 2001 conference of the Association of Teaching Theologians of the Evangelical Lutheran Church in America, participating scholars were asked to "mine the Lutheran tradition for pedagogical possibilities." All the papers presented referred primarily to the early Lutheran tradition—especially the works of Luther—in articulating those possibilities. In a recently published collection of essays on the Lutheran tradition, though Luther is mentioned only in passing, themes from his theology clearly shape the essays.[32]

In their work on the Lutheran confessions, Hendrix and Gassman claim that these confessions are "essential elements and criteria" of Lutheran identity.

> All Lutheran churches in the world have accepted the Book of Concord or some of its texts, including in every case the Augsburg Confession and Luther's Small Catechism. In their church constitutions, under the norm of Holy Scripture and together with ecumenical creeds, the Lutheran confessions are described as the true witnesses to the gospel, as pure expositions of the Word of God, or in similar terms. They are generally described as authoritative guides for the proclamation, teaching, and life of the Lutheran churches. At their ordination future pastors commit themselves to the confessions.[33]

In this summary, Hendrix and Gassman further specify the ways in which Lutheranism is both firmly within, and yet distinct from, the broader Christian tradition. First, the authors of the Lutheran confessions advanced beliefs that they judged to be in harmony with the Apostles', Nicene, and Athanasian Creeds. That is, even as they attempted to establish themselves as a distinct confessing movement, the authors judged themselves to be members of the one, holy, catholic, and apostolic Church. However, the Roman Catholics gathered at the Council of Trent did not judge them to be so, precisely because of the teachings contained in the Lutheran confessions. Conversely, Lutherans, at the time of Trent and afterward, typically have judged the beliefs and practices of all other Christians to be false to the degree that they vary from those advanced in the Book of Concord.

Second, the confessions clearly claim that they are under the norm of holy scripture.[34] "Scripture Alone" was the Lutheran battle cry against all human authority—including tradition— in religious matters. Luther himself claimed that only scripture, which "drives" or "produces" Christ, should be the impetus for faith and practice. However, some Lutherans have subsequently argued that the Lutheran confessions are normative not *insofar as (quatenus)* they are pure expositions of scripture but precisely *because (quia)* they are. Furthermore, to the frequent bafflement and bother of non-Lutherans, scripture alone has been viewed through Luther's and the confessions' interpretative lens of law and gospel. This singularly Lutheran hermeneutical circle has produced many spinoffs.[35]

Thus the most significant mark of the Lutheran tradition is a concern that all beliefs and practices be normed according to the confessions. This attentiveness to "purity" and "correctness" shows itself even—or perhaps most especially—in investigations of Lutheran pastoral care. For example, in the foreword to *Luther als Seelsorger* ("Luther as Pastor"), a German bishop writes: "We hope that the publication of these lectures on such important themes of pastoral care—*which are correct according to a Reformation understanding*— will supply a new and helpful direction for pastoral care" (emphasis added).[36]

The statement above, and that noted earlier from Gassman and Hendrix, illustrate how the Lutheran confessions have been constitutive for much of the Lutheran tradition. However, Gassman and Hendrix also note that its early writings are not the sum of the Lutheran tradition. "Lutheran identity is a lived, dynamic reality that cannot be equated with this collection of texts. This identity is shaped and sustained by fundamental theological and pastoral convictions, which are based in the confessional texts but which are also shaped and nourished by the tradition and living faith of the Lutheran Church."[37]

Here Hendrix and Gassmann broaden the definition of the Lutheran tradition to include the subsequent expressions of Lutheran lived religion. Others have argued much the same thing: "The people called Lutheran, just by the way they go about things, become documents for understanding the tradition."[38] While he highlights the "red line" in Lutheranism, Lindberg also suggests that other threads have been woven into this tradition: "There is diversity as well as strong confessional loyalty and identity in the Lutheran tradition. This diversity reflects not only differing cultural and historical contexts ranging from European state and folk churches to Third World indigenous churches, but also such variables as sex, race, education, and socioeconomic status."[39]

There is diversity not only in that theology but also within the tradition itself, for not all Lutherans signed on to the Formula of Concord, the final work of the Book of Concord, and not all Lutherans ascribe to it now.[40] Furthermore, within Lutheranism's five-hundred-year history, there have been significant variations on the early tradition's theology of consolation. In this study, I will occasionally note some of these variations in Lutheran orthodoxy and Lutheran Pietism, but I will not investigate any of them in detail. A critical exploration of the development of the theology and practice of consolation throughout the history of Lutheranism, with close attention to the theology and practice of its lived religion, would further both the field of Lutheran studies and the field of pastoral theology. Such a study is long overdue.

The Location of This Book in Practical and Pastoral Theology

In considering how some members of a tradition have become a part of and reshaped their tradition through their search for consolation in suffering, this book belongs in the fields of practical theology and pastoral theology. I locate it among other investigations into human suffering and, in particular, those investigations that employ historical theology. What is the role of historical analysis in such a practical and pastoral theology?

When he proposed a new shape for the discipline of practical theology in the early 1800s, Friedrich Schleiermacher detailed a prominent place for historical analysis. In his first edition of *The Brief Outline of Theology*, he envisioned practical theology as the crown of the entire theological enterprise, which also included philosophical and historical theology—the crown not in the sense of a regent over those two domains but as the final flourishing of that enterprise, with philosophical theology as its root and historical theology as its trunk. In other words, both philosophical and historical theology had practical theology—the art of the maintenance and perfection of the church—as their goal.[41] However, theology could achieve its practical end only through the medium (trunk) of historical theological study.

Since Schleiermacher made this proposal, few practical theologians in the United States have adopted it. Why is this the case? Until recently, the dominant influence of the social sciences over the discipline rendered tradition-specific, historically sensitive studies suspect of confessionalism. More recently, some have read Schleiermacher's practical theology as a facile application of the truths of philosophical and historical theology. However, as Bonnie Miller-McLemore has noted, all theologies are inevitably confessional—that is, located in and addressing themselves to some social and historical circumstance.[42] Furthermore, I agree with Henning Luther that Schleiermacher did not advocate the mechanical application of theology to everyday life, but rather the thoughtful study of the ways in which the theology of everyday life reforms the theology of the church and academy.[43]

In the practical theological studies of Pamela Couture, I find a model for how one may thoughtfully attend to the predicaments of lived religion through historical theological research. For example, in *Blessed Are the Poor? Women's Poverty, Family Policy and Practical Theology*, Couture blends contemporary social science and historical studies to recommend remedies for a prominent form of suffering in the United States. In order to challenge the individualistic assumptions of most American public policies for poor women, she turns to the thought and practices of Luther, Wesley, and a broadly construed tradition of American women peopled by Abigail Adams, Susan B. Anthony, and Elizabeth Cady Stanton.[44] In her article "Feminist, Wesleyan, Practical Theology and the Practice of Pastoral Care," Couture again highlights religious tradition and the experience of women as sources for constructing practical theology: "One aim of practical theology is to seek truth through lived faith."[45]

Among pastoral theologians, one finds only a few studies attending to historical theology. Working nearly alone, Thomas Oden has attempted to represent—to make present again—the past writings and reflections of the "classical theologians." For example, in his *Pastoral Theology: Essentials for Ministry*, Oden cites and quotes many great thinkers in Christian history including Gregory Nazianzus, Gregory the Great, Luther, and Calvin.[46] However, Oden simply restates these teachings without proposing how one may either reconcile the tensions within them or appropriate them for contemporary pastoral practice. Ironically, while he excoriates pastoral theologians for their lack of historical knowledge, and for falling captive to the "objectivity" of the social sciences, Oden himself seems to have fallen prey to what Gadamer calls "historical objectivism."[47]

Another attempt to consider both the history of religious teachings and their pastoral implications may be found in the recent work of a theologian who is not, at least in name, a pastoral theologian. In *By the Renewing of Your Minds: The Pastoral Function of Christian Doctrine* (1997), Ellen Charry claims, "This study examines primary Christian doctrines and teachings from the Apostolic era through the Reformation in order to argue that a central theological task is to assist people to come to God."[48] Charry considers many of the same theologians studied by Oden but avoids the "historical objectivism" to which Oden seems subject. She writes: "Needing to listen to them [these classic texts] is not to be confused with agreeing with them."[49] Furthermore, her book's dedication to "'Donald,' Inmate 242386, in a state prison somewhere in the United States," suggests that she seeks to understand how these classic texts may be understood in light of contemporary religious concerns. However, like Oden, Charry does not suggest how traditional materials may be appropriated for use by contemporary thinkers or pastoral caregivers—or how they may be related to the lived religion of persons such as Donald.

More recently, Andrew Purves has conducted a thoughtful historical theological study of six major figures in church history and demonstrated the pastoral depth of their lives' work.[50] Purves, like Oden, upholds the classical tradition in order "to allow these classical texts to provoke us into critical thinking by disturbing our calm, culture-bound assumptions concerning ministry, and in so doing suggest avenues for exploration."[51] However, Purves does not lay out these avenues. Nor does he explain how these classical texts, which are as culture-bound as any contemporary assumptions, may challenge those assumptions. In his careful consideration of these great theologians of the past, and of our present cultural and religious dilemmas, there seems to be a link missing in Purves's pastoral theology.

While tradition has not been the subject matter of much pastoral theology, pastoral theologians have been singularly attentive to something much like lived religion. Anton Boisen's proposal that pastoral theologians should study "the living human document"—the life histories of those who suffer—seems to have become part of the assumptive world of pastoral theology.[52] In effect, this proposal has meant that the transcription and analysis of case studies according to various dimensions—psychological, social, and theological—are a primary means of instruction in this discipline. And while historical theological analysis of the living human document has been a rarity, I find that Miller-McLemore's revision of this concept as the "living human web" suggests that what is historical and contextual is not peripheral, but very much central, to a pastoral theology for persons who suffer.[53] Indeed, attending to the "living human document" and the "living human web" are central to that purpose.

The Purpose of This Book Elaborated

This study of consolation in Lutheranism has two primary sources: the texts of the early Lutheran tradition and some examples from contemporary Lutheran lived religion, which itself has extended the tradition. That is, I investigate the relationship between the normative theology of this tradition and the lived religion of some of its members.

On the one hand, it is not obvious that there is, has been, or even could be a relationship between the two. One is a set of texts and theologies. The other is a set of lives.

On the other hand, it is obvious that there must be some kind of relationship. As I shall show, the texts of the early Lutheran tradition address the problem of human suffering. Furthermore, these texts exist only by traditioning—by being passed on to others who sometimes read them as addressing their suffering. That is, these texts have been received into the life-world of many members of the tradition—not only pastors like Charles who must publicly ascribe to them, but also laypersons like Ruth. Consequently, the effects of this tradition on the lived religion of Lutherans may, with careful study and consideration, be surmised.

In this book, I am not attempting to write a pastoral theology from the perspective of the doctrine of justification or a theology of the cross.[54] Nor, in my use of historical theology to examine the normative teachings of the Lutheran tradition, am I trying to construct a pastoral theology based on Luther and the Lutheran confessions. Rather, this book is an effort to understand the experience of suffering and consolation in the lived religion of a few members of the Lutheran tradition. In doing so, I bring the lens of tradition to their experiences to determine what that lens clarifies and what it obscures. I am building on Schleiermacher's notion that the purpose of historical theology is to help the church better understand its everyday religious practices. I am also building on Jane Strohl's claim that

> to reach maturity, to understand why certain constructions of reality have become part of one's person, each of us must explore our family history and the domestic dynamics and external forces that have shaped it. It is no different with a religious community whose values and behaviors make claims upon us. One must know the history and come to terms with it, not just of one's immediate household of faith but of the extended kin as well.[55]

Referencing the Lutheran philosopher Johann Gottfried Herder, Marcia Bunge notes that "every text should be read on its own terms in light of its original language, author and audience. Thus interpretation is not simply empathy; it is a philological, historical, and rational task."[56] The importance of Bunge's observation for this book is this: Pastors and pastoral theologians must labor to understand the forces at work in the lives of religious persons. Those lives are as complicated as any historical text—they are living human documents that require careful attention if we are to pastor properly.

Accordingly, I use a form of the case study method to engage in the hard, fascinating work of trying to understand those lives. In doing so, I hope to offer a style of inquiry that others may wish to modify and adopt. To the degree that I enable the reader to better understand these seven Lutherans and, thereby, to participate in a process by which he or she may better understand and care for others of any tradition, I will have achieved a primary purpose of this book.

Our Path in This Book

The next chapter surveys the theology of consolation proposed in the normative texts of Lutheranism—the works of Luther and the Book of Concord. I explicate the pastoral implications of the central concepts of the early Lutheran tradition: justification by faith and the theology of the cross. I also describe the various "means of consolation," those ecclesial practices by which God strengthens the faithful, and the various responses (or reflexes) that the faithful are consequently enjoined to exercise in the world in response to having been consoled. I conclude this chapter by noting how, in this tradition, the finite actions of ministry may contain the consolation of the infinite God.

Chapter three, "Significant Negative Events in Seven Lives," describes first some of the procedures used to analyze the case histories of seven Lutherans who suffered a variety of "negative events," and then presents the case histories themselves. It concludes with further comments on my analytical methods and on the problems and possibilities of the use of tradition as a lens to view lived religion. Is the Lutheran tradition something that can be "mined" like iron or gold, as we teaching theologians were enjoined to do at our recent conference? Or is tradition a more malleable substance? Or is it nothing substantial at all?

The two chapters that follow analyze the lived religion of these seven co-researchers. In chapter four, I do so under the rubric "Beliefs." Here, using the principles of justification by faith and the theology of the cross, I look at the convictions of these seven while they suffered. In some of these cases, we shall see how their lived religion reflects tensions in the theology of their tradition. In chapter five, I analyze the co-researchers' lived religion under the rubric "Practices." Consonant with their tradition, nearly all of the co-researchers claimed that the quality of their relationship with other persons was a significant feature in their experiencing or not experiencing consolation. I also found that much of their suffering was the product of social forces for which they experienced only minimal support.

In the final chapter, I use the results of my empirical analysis to revisit the issue of the normativity of tradition in lived religion. Having noted the pitfalls and possibilities of using tradition as a lens to analyze lived religion, I compare my own findings with that of two counterparts: one author representing the pastoral theology of the Wesleyan tradition, and another representing that theology in the Reformed tradition. I conclude by explicating the meaning of the consolation of God as an object "clothed in nothingness."

2.
Consolation in the Early Lutheran Tradition

❖·❖

In the previous chapter, I briefly outlined the argument that the works of
Luther and the Lutheran confessions (authored by Luther and others) constitute what has been called the early Lutheran tradition,
and that this tradition has influenced the subsequent course of
Lutheran theology and practice. I noted that Lindberg's use of the
"red line" (or "red thread") metaphor to describe this continuity
within Lutheranism is at odds with Kathryn Tanner's contention
that this metaphor "loses plausibility" given the changes that occur in
the transmission of beliefs and practices.[1] A primary question of this
book is the degree to which the "red thread" of the early Lutheran tradition's teaching and praxis for consolation appears to be intact, missing, broadened, fragmented, twisted, discolored, highlighted, or
woven with other threads in the beliefs and practices of seven contemporary Lutherans who sought consolation for their suffering.

I also noted that, while the term *consolation* may now have pejorative connotations, Christian theologians have typically understood it
as that gift from God that fortifies sufferers. That is certainly what it
meant in the early Lutheran tradition.

But more precisely, how did the concept of consolation function
in the early Lutheran tradition, and in that function, what else did it
come to mean? The purpose of this chapter is to answer that question. To be sure, Luther himself nowhere detailed his theology of

consolation.[2] Nor does the Book of Concord address this pastoral matter in a systematic way. Yet as I shall demonstrate, Luther and the confessions present a complex but nevertheless coherent account of how persons who suffer may receive consolation. Rather than explaining consolation thematically—that is, in association with related concepts such as tribulation, conscience, and suffering—I will unpack its meaning by showing its use within the major themes of the Lutheran tradition: justification, the theology of the cross, the means of grace, and Christian living. Having analyzed the theology of consolation via the most distinctive features of the early Lutheran tradition, I will conclude by reviewing the most distinctive features of that theology.

Theologies of Consolation: Justification and the Cross

Justification: God's Right Relationship with Humanity

Luther and the Lutheran Reformation. "In matters concerning the cure of souls, the German Reformation had its beginning."[3] Specifically, Luther's protest against the administration of indulgences was the spark that ignited the ensuing ecclesiastical and theological firestorm. The history of indulgences in Luther's time is complex.[4] Typically, penitents received papal-authorized documents that, in exchange for payment of money, assured them that after death, they (or some designated already deceased loved one) could journey out of purgatory to heaven. For sure, some show of faith—active contrition—was required for this to come about, but inevitably that contrition included the purchase of penance. Like all ecclesiastical practices of the time, indulgences were touted as graceful offers to the faithful—in this case, extensions of the merits of the saints in heaven (who had done more than enough good works to achieve lasting security) to those who did not quite merit this final respite. Consequently, the faithful sought indulgences in order to dispel any anxiety that either their loved ones might be trapped in purgatory or that they themselves might soon suffer there.

Luther shared with many Catholic humanists of his time a revulsion at the worldly benefits indulgences afforded some church leaders and secular princes. However, it was his perception of the practice's failure to provide what it promised that troubled him most. An Augustinian monk and professor at the University of Wittenberg in 1517, Luther was distressed to learn that indulgences were being dispensed in the neighboring city of Brandenburg by the Dominican friar Johannes Tetzel, who lured many anxious penitents there as he had been forbidden to peddle his wares in Wittenberg. When they returned from Brandenburg, those terrified penitents relayed to Luther in the confessional the sum and substance of Tetzel's ultimately disturbing message: "As soon as the coin in the coffer rings / the soul from purgatory springs."[5]

Not only to counter Tetzel's practice in Brandenburg, but also to forestall the appearance of imitators within the walls of Wittenberg itself, Luther posted ninety-five theses on the castle door for debate on October 31, 1517. After he did, a reformation ensued, in part[6] because Luther's concern in these theses was not simply with the activities of one particularly garish hawker of indulgences, nor with the selling of indulgences themselves. Rather, Luther was troubled by the theology assumed in the practice. In a later elaboration on those theses, Luther countered that theology and the various practices it produced: "We are taught that the law is fulfilled not by our works but by the grace of God who pities us in Christ and that it shall be fulfilled not through works but through faith, not by anything we offer God, but by all we receive from Christ and partake of in him."[7] That is to say, one does not perform prescribed penitential acts or do good works in order to achieve this consoling relationship, but accepts the right relationship God freely bestows.

In his subsequent theological writings, Luther developed the consoling implications of his understanding of justification by directing the faithful away from speculation on God's awesome attributes and toward the trust that God freely bestows on the faithful. The subject of theology is never simply God but always God's relationship with humanity: "God for us" *(Deus pro nobis)*. This teaching contains a dialectic. On the one hand, God's righteousness is "alien" to ours: "alien righteousness . . . is the righteousness of another, instilled from without."[8] On the other hand, God does not hold fast to God's righteousness but, through the life and death of Jesus Christ, bestows it on those who trust in it: "Through faith in Christ, therefore, Christ's righteousness becomes our righteousness and all that he has becomes ours; rather, he himself becomes ours."[9] Through Christ, the righteousness of God becomes the property of humanity, and the sin of humanity becomes the property of God. Luther called this swap of properties the "happy exchange."[10]

Only two years after he posted the Ninety-five Theses, Luther employed his reformed understanding of the divine-human relationship in three pastoral treatises. His first work, "A Meditation on Christ's Passion" (1519), was a best-seller, attracting an even wider audience than his already popular polemical works.[11] Here Luther proposed that one does not attain consolation for the troubled conscience by imitating the sufferings of Christ, but rather that God brings consolation to those who trust that Christ overcame suffering and death on their behalf. Luther directed persons away from trying to prove their worth through various kinds of heroic suffering and toward the promise of the end of their suffering contained in God's work in Christ.

In August of 1519, Luther composed a treatise for the Saxon elector Frederick the Wise, who had fallen gravely ill upon returning from a court function elsewhere in Germany. Though he originally intended this work as a comfort solely for his ailing prince, Luther and others repeatedly published his "Fourteen Consolations" for public edification. At this time, a common practice for consolation involved the contemplation of altar screen images of fourteen saints, each of whom represented protection for a group of particularly needy people, such as scholars, or shielded believers from a particular ailment such as tuberculosis. In his revision of this devotional, Luther offered the reader a mental or "literary screen" of images with the first section representing seven evils and the second section seven blessings. Through the very shape of his devotional, therefore, Luther indicated that God offers consolation in both blessings and evils.[12]

In a subsequent pastoral treatise, "Sermon on Preparing to Die," Luther reformed a common genre of the late Middle Ages—manuals on the art of dying—according to his understanding of justification.

These manuals had directed the dying to do what they could to place themselves in a right relationship with their maker at the very moment of death. In his reform of this practice, Luther directed the dying away from reviewing past sins and searching for signs of God's future favor, and directed them instead toward trusting the present promise of consolation: "So then, gaze at the heavenly picture of Christ, who descended into hell [1 Pet. 3:19] for your sake. . . . In that picture your hell is defeated and your election is made sure."[13] The sacraments of the church are not so much means to security in the face of death, but rather consoling gifts for the terrified conscience at that "extreme" time: "The sacraments, that is, the external words of God as spoken by a priest, are a truly great comfort and at the same time a visible sign of divine intent. . . . He who thus insists and relies on the sacraments will find that his election and predestination will turn out well without his worry and effort."[14] To be sure, Luther maintained aspects of the late medieval manuals by calling on the faithful to set their assets in order, to forgive their enemies, and to receive the sacraments, but Luther recast these practices in light of the assurance of the grace that God grants through them.[15]

To summarize, matters concerning the cure of souls and terrified consciences did propel Luther's early writings and remarks about justification.[16] Moreover, as the early Lutheran tradition developed— that is to say, as remarks and teachings on justification became somewhat more settled among the Lutherans in the form of doctrines—concerns about these matters did not diminish. Rather, they increased.

Justification and Consolation in the Lutheran Confessions. In 1530, the Holy Roman Emperor Charles V called an assembly of Roman Catholics and Lutherans within his realm to Augsburg for the express purpose of preventing further schism. Accordingly, the Lutherans presented their beliefs in a series of articles that have become known as the Augsburg Confession. The article on justification is often referred to as the heart of the confession.

> Furthermore, it is taught that we cannot obtain forgiveness of sin and righteousness before God through our own merit,

work, or satisfactions, but that we receive forgiveness of sin and
become righteous before God out of grace for Christ's sake
through faith when we believe that Christ has suffered for us
and that for his sake our sin is forgiven and righteousness and
eternal life are given to us. For God will regard and reckon this
faith as righteousness, as St. Paul says in Romans 3[:21-26] and
4[:5].[17]

The article's claim that such righteousness is "reckoned to us" echoes
Luther's teaching that this right relationship with God is not something we obtain but something God grants.

In response to Catholic criticism of the Augsburg Confession, the
evangelical theologian Philip Melanchthon wrote a lengthy treatise,
the Apology of the Augsburg Confession, which later was included in
the Book of Concord. In his commentary on the fourth article,
Melanchthon elaborated on the consoling purpose of the doctrine of
justification. As he did so, he frequently bemoaned his counterparts'
propensity to engage in what he called "idle speculation" when discussing humanity's relationship with God.[18] These theologians, he
contended, had constructed a fantasy world in which humanity is
capable of producing love, fear, and trust in God in the midst of its
many woes. To be sure, God commands such things: "It [the Law]
also requires other works that are placed far beyond the reach of reason, such as, truly to fear God, truly to love God, truly to call upon
God, truly to be convinced that he hears us, and to expect help from
God in death and all afflictions."[19] But the claims of his opponents
that one can summon forth faith in, or affection for, God do not cor-
respond to reality: "They do not realize what they are saying."[20] For
sure, Melanchthon maintained that such trust in God when we suffer is possible: "This faith, which arises and consoles us in the midst
of those fears, receives the forgiveness of sins, justifies us, and makes
alive. For this consolation is a new and spiritual life."[21] However,
Melanchthon expounded on Article 4, and indirectly on Luther, by
maintaining that such faith is not the product of human will, but is
itself a gift of God to humanity.[22]

In the Smalcald Articles (1537) in the Book of Concord, Luther
proposed that the Lutheran teaching on justification constituted the
core of the Christian faith: "Nothing in this article can be conceded

or given up, even if heaven and earth or whatever is transitory passed away. . . . On this article stands all that we teach and practice."[23] Robert Jenson suggests its significance for contemporary Lutheranism: "This dogma is not a particular proposed content of the church's proclamation, along with other contents. It is rather a meta-linguistic stipulation of what *kind* of talking, whatever contents, can properly be proclamation and word of the church."[24] Later commentators have contrasted the Catholic teaching in Trent that "God and people are thought of as working together," with that in the Lutheran confessions whereby salvation is completely the work of God, apart from our willing or working for it.[25]

While Luther and the authors of the Augsburg Confession proposed that God consoles unconditionally, their proposals did not put the matter to rest for all time, or for even a short time. After the formulation of the Augsburg Confession, Lutherans directed much of their attention toward their differences with one another, including what became known as the synergistic controversy. Ironically, this dispute was spawned by Melanchthon who, in his 1535 *Loci Communes,* argued that the human will cooperated with the Holy Spirit and the Word to effect conversion. In his 1548 edition of the *Loci Communes,* he maintained that a cause of a person's salvation lies within that person. Following 1548, arguments erupted among the Lutherans about whether the human will works with ("synergizes") God. And while the Formula of Concord attempted to settle the matter, it did not do so in all Lutheran theology or lived religion.

Having detailed some of the key features of the theology of justification and that theology's implications for the consolation of those who suffer, I would like to look at a second important theme of the early Lutheran tradition: the theology of the cross. The theology of the cross is not completely separable from the theology of justification, but focuses more closely on the relationship between the will of God, the suffering of God, and the suffering of humanity.

The Theology of the Cross and Human Suffering

Luther's posting of ninety-five theses in the fall of 1517 stirred up more discord—in Saxony and beyond—than he anticipated, and far more than Pope Leo in Rome desired. Hoping to restore harmony,

Luther's own religious superior and *Seelsorger,* Johannes Staupitz, invited him to address the chapter meeting of their Augustinian order in Heidelberg during the spring and summer of 1518, on what Staupitz believed to be inherently noncontroversial topics: sin, free will, and grace.[26] However, in a manner that would subsequently characterize all his work, Luther seized the opportunity to examine the theological roots of his pastoral concerns. Luther contended that it is useless—even dangerous—to speculate on the glorious attributes of God, and rather derisively labeled those who did so as "theologians of glory." Theologians of the cross look for God's making Godself visible on an earthly instrument of execution. The God revealed on the cross shows a side of Godself at odds with humanity's expectation of how God ought to comport Godself. Instead of remaining in the realm of the invisible, God shows Godself on what seems far removed from divinity—suffering on a wooden cross.[27]

Anfechtung *and Suffering.* While Luther only on occasion referred directly to the suffering of God after the Heidelberg Disputation, he did write extensively throughout his life about the suffering of the Christian. He believed that often connected to physical and social suffering is the experience of spiritual suffering called *Anfechtung.*[28] The term has a sense not captured in its usual English translations as either "temptation" or "trial." The root experience of *Anfechtung* is one of being attacked. Often Luther described the devil, horns and all, as the source of such attacks: "He [the devil] hates you and looks for opportunities to trouble you."[29] However, Luther was not a Manichaean. That is to say, he did not believe that the devil is on the loose with no reins attached, but that God somehow is behind all that the devil manifests. A host of other demons—despair, doubt, and melancholia—often accompany this particular temptation. While any experience of physical and social suffering can produce tribulation, the experience of direct assault by God is its most troublesome form. Luther detailed his own encounter with it: "I myself 'knew a man' [2 Cor. 12:2] who claimed that he had often suffered these punishments. . . . At such a time God seems terribly angry, and with him the whole creation. At such a time there is no flight, no comfort, within or without, but all things accuse. . . . All that remains is the stark-naked desire for help and a terrible groaning, but it does not know where to turn for help."[30]

If God is the source of spiritual attacks, one might wonder whether God were not after all the devil undisguised. In fact, Luther himself did so wonder—not idly, but in the throes of his own *Anfechtung*.[31] Though assaults from God may occur without our provoking them, they do so invariably if, like Job, we ask God why we suffer: "When such trials of 'Why' come, beware that you do not answer and allow these attacks to get control. Rather, close your eyes and kill reason and take refuge with the Word. Do not let the 'Why' get into your heart. The devil is too powerful; you cannot cope with the situation."[32]

Luther distinguished between what he called the "hidden God" *(Deus absconditus)* and the "revealed God" *(Deus revelatus)* to explain why one should not traffic with the "Why" of God. The revealed God is the God who sends consolation for suffering. The hidden God is the God we encounter when we seek to know God's will for suffering. "We have to argue in one way about God or the will of God as preached, revealed, offered, and worshiped, and in another way about God as he is not preached, not revealed, not offered, not worshiped. . . . To the extent, therefore, that God hides himself and wills to be unknown to us, it is no business of ours."[33]

In the throes of various tempests, we may seek safe harbor by aiming for an understanding of God's will for our suffering, but if we do so, we will crash into the wrath of the God hidden beneath the surface of that suffering. A contemporary Lutheran theologian believes that a particularly frightening feature of God's wrath resides in not so much its hot anger as its cold indifference.

> So even though inescapably present [when hidden or not preached as being on the side of humanity], God is terrifyingly absent in this presence. God is, as the tradition (especially Martin Luther) put it, "hidden" *(absconditus)*. The Latin has a more active flavor to it than the English, as when someone absconds with the "goods" and leaves behind only an absence, an emptiness, a nothingness. . . . Not preached, God is the absconder,

the one who will not be seen and leaves behind only an emptiness, a blank space. In that sense, God is not merely "hidden" (that is, more or less passively unseeable or unknowable), but the one who actively hides from us, always "gives us the slip."[34]

Luther's strong advice not to concern oneself with the hidden will of God, but only with God's revealed will to console humanity through Christ, has led some to characterize his theology as one of "single predestination" and thereby contrast it with Calvinist teachings of double predestination, that God elects some for damnation and others for salvation.[35] Still, not long after Luther's death, some Lutherans held what others judged a more Calvinist version of the doctrine. To forestall any dispute on this matter—and to settle ongoing arguments such as the synergistic controversy—some, but not all, Lutherans agreed to the Formula of Concord (1580), the final work in the Book of Concord, whose very formulation was the occasion for the publication of the book itself. The authors of Article 11 on election first attempted to distinguish their faith from that of the Reformed by advising against speculation on the will of God apart from God's revealed will for salvation, and then indicated the consoling intent of this teaching. "This doctrine also gives us wonderful comfort in crosses and trials, that in his counsel before time began God determined and decreed that he would stand by us in every trouble, grant us patience, give us comfort, create hope, and provide a way out of all things so that we may be saved."[36]

For the early Lutherans, therefore, the doctrine of election was a pastoral tool. Luther himself repeatedly used this tool to attend to those who worried whether God was on their side in this life and the next.[37] However, even with the forceful pronouncements of the Formula of Concord and Luther's repeated use of single-predestinarian language in his explicitly pastoral writings, the matter of predestination was not settled for all Lutherans for all time.[38] The ongoing tension about predestination in the Lutheran tradition may reflect a similar tension not only among the early Lutherans but also within the mind of Luther himself.[39] For all his good news that God is on the side of humanity, Luther persists in referring to a God who "gives us the slip" when we need that God the most. Furthermore, as we shall see next, he presents us with a God who sends us suffering as a means of consoling us.

God's Work of Suffering and Consolation. Just as one might wonder if the God who absconds were, in fact, the devil, so one might wonder if the hidden God who brings such tribulation and the revealed God who brings consolation were not two different Gods. As a theologian of the cross, Luther advised against speculating on the nature of *Deus absconditus* and *Deus revelatus,* and focused instead on what was visible—the different character of their "works." The hidden God brings an alien work *(opus alienum)* to God's beneficent nature by bringing suffering to humanity. The revealed God brings a work in keeping with God's nature *(opus proprium)* by bringing consolation. While Luther believed that these two works of God were distinguishable he also believed that they were related. Specifically, he taught that God uses *opus alienum* in order to effect *opus proprium* by driving the believer to faith in the God who promises the end of suffering.[40]

Accordingly, throughout his career Luther taught a doctrine at which many today take offense: that God may send suffering in order to send redemption. For example, early in the Reformation, Luther employed the categories of the Heidelberg Disputation to claim that God may use our suffering to make us saints. "A theologian of the cross (that is, one who speaks of the crucified and hidden God), teaches that punishments, crosses, and death are the most precious treasury of all and the most sacred relics which the Lord of this theology himself has consecrated and blessed."[41] Near the middle of his life, he claimed that the sufferer "must thank God diligently for deeming him worthy of such a visitation. . . . Therefore, we should willingly endure the hand of God in this and in all suffering. Do not be worried; indeed, such a trial is the very best sign of God's grace and love for man."[42]

Toward the end of his career, in his *Commentary on Genesis,* Luther claimed that suffering had served to strengthen the faith of the patriarchs and had done so for Christians throughout history. Tribulations are God's means of driving persons away from reliance on their own power to save themselves and toward reliance on God's power to save them.[43] He went so far as to call the suffering that God sends a kind of "game," like that played by a father who teases his child by hiding a desired object in order to make the child fonder of the father for eventually bestowing that object.[44] This game is the alien work of God by which God brings about God's proper work of consolation.[45] The story of Joseph is paradigmatic of the experience of such alternating tribulation and consolation. Joseph's many adversities—being torn from his homeland, sold into slavery, and suffering under false judgment—are the means by which God produces faith and good things for himself and his family. However, in the midst of the game God plays with Joseph—and with us now—there is no consolation: "The game is very unpleasant to us and bitter."[46]

One may conclude, therefore, that Luther taught throughout his life that God may send suffering to produce faith in God's goodness. However, one may not conclude that he ever taught that such suffering is itself a good. Rather, he proposed that suffering comes to a good end when one trusts that it is joined to Christ who overcame suffering in the resurrection.[47] For example, in his writings after 1520, Luther pointedly broke with a common teaching of the time that one must seek out suffering in order to merit the grace of God: "Many want to take heaven by storm and would like to enter at once. Therefore they impose a cross on themselves at their own discretion. After all, reason always wants to extol only its own works. God does not want this."[48] Luther labeled as "monkish" what he perceived as an Anabaptist practice to court danger in order to gain the glory of God: "Christ does not say: Plunge yourselves in danger in a foolhardy manner; forsake your wife and your family. Rather: If it comes to pass that tyrants persecute you and want to banish you . . . then the time for boldness has come."[49] Obedience to the word of God may lead to suffering at the hand of opponents of this word, but one must never seek it out: "Since there is a bridge across the Elbe, it behooves us not to wade through the river, lest we drown."[50]

In his "Commentary on the Sermon on the Mount," Luther again distinguished between the suffering that God sends and that which the self-righteous seek. The former "should be the kind of suffering which we have not chosen ourselves, as the fanatics choose their own suffering. It should be the kind of suffering which, if it were possible, we would gladly be rid of, suffering visited upon us by the devil or the world."[51] While Luther employed the theology of the cross to teach that God sends suffering in order to bring consolation, he used that same theology to teach that self-imposed suffering has no merit: "Behold, that is the way of the cross; You cannot find it, but it must lead you like a blind man. . . . You must not follow the work you choose, not the suffering which you devise, but that which comes to you against your choice, thoughts, and desires."[52] Contemplating God-incarnate, we see that God's will is not for our suffering but for our well-being: "No matter what misfortune befalls us, pestilence, war, famine, poverty, persecution, melancholy thoughts which deject us and make the heart pound and flounder—we must know and conclude that this does not come from Christ."[53]

In his theology of the cross, therefore, Luther did not exalt suffering but taught that the grace of God might be found in its midst.[54] Nor did he try to justify God's ways to anyone, for to do so would have involved attending to invisible things. Some later interpreters of Luther's theology of the cross have turned to that theology precisely to move away from speculation about suffering and to move toward action to overcome suffering.[55] A number of feminist theologians have attempted to reappropriate Luther's theology of the cross in a way that helps, not hurts, both women and men. For example, Elizabeth Moltmann-Wendel counters oppressive renditions of Luther's theology of the cross with one based both on Luther himself and the needs of women.[56] Referencing a variety of feminist epistemologies, Mary Solberg finds sympathies between their concern for the particular, the least, and the marginalized with the epistemology assumed and articulated in Luther's theology of the cross.[57] Deanna Thompson contends that, just as Luther theologized "occasionally"—that is, by "speaking to various human needs in a timely fashion"—so, even as she writes, the occasion has arrived to reform his theology in light of feminist theological concerns.[58] In so doing she engages Gerrish's understanding of the hiddenness of God found both in God hidden and God revealed.

According to Thompson, Gerrish calls the first position "Hiddenness I,"

> the hiddenness found in Luther's *theologia crucis,* the God hidden *within* the revelation of Christ. . . . Hiddenness II (where God hides *behind* the revelation), on the other hand, implies a God beyond the God we perceive in Christ. . . . Gerrish understands Luther's Hiddenness II as a pastoral response to the question of predestination. . . . The unsettling reality of Hiddenness II ultimately pushed Luther toward Hiddenness I, the God hidden *within* the revelation of Christ. Only the hidden God glimpsed by faith in the human, earthly incarnation of Christ can move faith to trust in the gospel. Without Hiddenness I, the Christian would remain in a permanent state of *Anfechtung*. With Hiddenness I, however, we can see God as a merciful, forgiving God, a visible image that orients human life to its present, earthly existence.[59]

Clearly, talk about God's hiddenness is complicated, and, as Luther indicated, a somewhat risky business. Even in the midst of that complexity, however, I have tried to demonstrate, in apparent contradistinction to Gerrish and Thompson, that even *within* Luther's theology of the cross (Hiddenness I), there is certainly talk about God's mercy but also talk (as there is in Hiddenness II) of God sending suffering in order to send mercy.[60] We are also left with another question, which I will address in the following chapters: How do persons informed in the early Lutheran tradition negotiate tensions between God hidden and God revealed when they suffer and seek consolation?

The doctrine of justification and the theology of the cross point sufferers, then and now, away from a preoccupation or bedevilment with unanswerable questions, invisible things. Do these theologies do more than eschew such speculation but also direct believers *toward* things that console? The next section will show that the tradition does propose a number of very visible, or at least sensible, means by which persons may receive consolation from God and, as a reflex of such consolation, battle suffering in the world.

Means and Practices of Consolation

Article 4 of the Augsburg Confession proposes that God through Christ freely bestows saving solace on those who trust that God does so. Article 5 describes God's particular means of consolation:

> To obtain such faith God instituted the office of preaching, giving the gospel and the sacraments. Through these . . . he gives the Holy Spirit, who produces faith, where and when he wills, in those who hear the Gospel. . . . Condemned are the Anabaptists and others who teach that we obtain the Holy Spirit without the external word of the gospel through our own preparation, thoughts, and works.[61]

Just as the word "external" is key for understanding the means of justification, it is also key to understanding the means of consolation. The consolation of the Holy Spirit is not something one may confer on oneself but something God confers on the faithful through the material means of the Word and Sacrament. In fact, God consoles precisely through the message that one cannot provide for oneself: "Such a person [one who suffers] must by no means rely on himself, nor must he be guided by his own feelings. Rather he must lay hold of the words offered to him in God's name, cling to them, place his trust in them, and direct all the thoughts and feelings of his heart to them."[62] God through the Holy Spirit alone consoles, but God bestows that Spirit only through very finite and sensible means.

Scripture and the Word of God

Luther repeatedly taught that the consolation of God comes through the word of God.

> Therefore, do not let any terror overwhelm and subdue you. . . . Take comfort in this, that you have a God, that you know Him, and that you can rely on His presence and aid, as He has guaranteed to you in His Word. There he has promised that He will surely never fail you even though everything opposes you, but that He will stand at your side, protect and rescue you while you suffer all for His sake.[63]

Luther believed the proclamation of the word of God, whether in a sermon or by one Christian's communication with another, to be the living voice of the gospel. Consequently, in many—though not all, as we shall see—of his letters of consolation and his numerous treatises on suffering, Luther quoted Scripture liberally. His epitome of spiritual counsel for those who suffer, "Comfort When Facing Grave Temptations," is replete with references to the Bible. Luther often referred to the biblical narratives of the "matters" of those who found consolation from God in their suffering. "These matters often recur in these stories, and so they must be often repeated; it is a serious and difficult matter. They are not just empty words. . . . Nor is there anyone who has perfectly exhausted this wisdom in such a way that he has no further need of practice or instruction. For we must always learn and grow, and, in truth, this wisdom must be learned from the Word."[64]

Just as faith in the word of God is not something we are able to produce but something God produces in us, so prayer also is not our work but something God works in us. Though we may be troubled by great difficulties without and an awareness of sin within, we are enjoined to pray: "You should not look at your unworthiness; you should look at God's command [to pray] and not debate whether you are worthy or not."[65]

Just as Luther was concerned less with the nature of God than with the nature of God's relationship with humanity, so he was concerned less with the nature of the Bible's authority than with its power to produce, among other things, consolation. Similarly, the Lutheran confessions do not contain extensive arguments, like those in some Calvinist confessions, about the nature of the divine authority of Scripture.[66] In keeping with the teaching that we should seek only the God who is for us, Luther taught that one should best read and hear the Bible, along with its many commands, as a gift for salvation. That the word of God is first and foremost for us is also made manifest in the sacraments.

Consolation through the Sacraments

Article 5 of the Augsburg Confession taught that the Holy Spirit comes not only through the preached word but also through the sacraments. Therefore, in this tradition, consolation is produced by the sacraments, not by anything we bring to them. This is most manifest in the Lutheran teaching that infants should be baptized: "We do not put the main emphasis on whether the person baptized believes or not. . . . Baptism does not become invalid if it is not properly received or used, as I have said, for it is not bound to our faith but to the Word."[67]

Accordingly, Christians may rely in the midst of any trial on the unconditional promise of God granted by their baptism.[68] Baptism helps Christians face daily struggles.[69] In the midst of any difficulty, "Baptism is certain, and the promise and absolution are reliable . . . for I have God, who is taking care of me, and about this I am in no doubt at all, even though all things seem to be against me."[70] Because of baptism, "to be sure, they can take away this life or property, wife and children, likewise good health; but I will hope in God forever."[71] Baptism bestows the unconditional promise of a right relationship with God: "Therefore, one should hold fast to this comfort, that what God has once declared, this He does not change. . . . You should know that this is His unchangeable Word, and you should not permit yourselves to be drawn away from it."[72] In the midst of any difficulty, one may receive consolation by recalling, "I have been baptized."[73]

While Luther directed most of his diatribe about Baptism against the Anabaptist reformers, he directed much, though not all, of his diatribe about the Sacrament of the Altar against the Catholic church.[74] In place of the doctrine that humanity, first graced by God, cooperates with God in producing grace in the Lord's Supper, Luther taught that the grace conferred by that meal is unequivocally God's doing. Just as he warned against speculating on the nature of God, Luther also warned against "subtle sophistry," explanations of how bread and wine become the body and blood of Christ.[75] Rather than concerning oneself with the relationship of the elements of the Mass to the person of Christ, one should concern oneself with their saving benefits.[76]

The Sacrament of the Altar helps dispel all *Anfechtungen:* "If you are burdened and feel your weakness, go joyfully to the sacrament and let yourself be refreshed, comforted, and strengthened."[77] This sacrament is of little benefit to those bereft of "misfortune, anxiety, or who otherwise do not sense their adversity. For it is given only to those who need strength and comfort."[78] Through the sacrament, Christians are made members of the body of Christ and are never alone in their suffering.[79] The sin and suffering of one Christian are the "property" of all.[80] Just as baptism is an indelible sign to which one may turn for consolation, the Sacrament of the Altar promises that both Christ and all other Christians share our suffering.[81]

Through Scripture, one is consoled by the promise of God as related by and through the company of fellow saints. Through the Sacraments, one is joined with other needy believers. In the priesthood of all believers, what Word and Sacrament confer through religious ritual is conferred by both ritual and nonritual means.

Consolation through the Priesthood of All Believers

At one point, Melanchthon maintained that penance might be retained as a sacrament, "though not as an activity of the believer, but as a work brought about in the believer by the Word of God."[82] Luther broadened the goal of penitential ministry to include the priestly intercession, guidance, and consolation of any one Christian for another.[83]

Consolation through the priesthood of all believers is not a means of grace separate from that given by Word and Sacrament. Having been comforted by the Lord's Supper, one should then minister to others, said Luther.

> When you have partaken of this sacrament . . . you must in turn share the misfortunes of the fellowship. . . . Here your heart must go out in love and learn that this is a sacrament of love. As love and support are given you, you must in turn render love and support to Christ in his needy ones. You must feel with sorrow all the dishonor done to Christ in his holy Word, all the misery of Christendom, all the unjust suffering of the innocent with which the world is everywhere filled to overflowing. You must fight, work, pray, and, if you cannot do more, have heartfelt sympathy. See, as you uphold all of them, so they all in turn uphold you; and all things are in common, both good and evil. Then all things become easy, and the evil spirit cannot stand up against this fellowship.[84]

Biblical narratives of the saints are sources of consolation for those who now suffer.[85] Just as the Word and Sacrament come from God but are handed from person to person, so the infinite God is found in the finite mediations of the priestly ministry of mutual consolation. Referencing 1 Cor. 1:3-4, Luther wrote that "[the Apostle] teaches us by his own example that we are to comfort those who are in trouble, but in such wise that the comfort be not of men, but of God."[86]

The praxis of this priesthood is revealed in Luther's many letters of spiritual counsel that he wrote to persons suffering a variety of ills. For example, Luther advised an ailing colleague to be of "good courage" because "you are not alone when you are occasionally afflicted, for 'the same afflictions are accomplished in your brethren that are in the world.'"[87] Consoling a father whose son had apparently fallen to his death while repairing a roof, Luther assured him that God's wrath was not the cause of this death. Rather, he said, God loves both this man and his son, though how God loves them is hidden from everyone's view.[88] Luther also comforted persons who apparently suffered from melancholy or depression, including Jonas von Stockhausen, a ruminative nobleman who was considering suicide. "My dear friend, it is high time that you cease relying on and pursuing your own thoughts. Listen to other people who are not subject to this temptation. . . . *Thus God will strengthen you and comfort you by means of our words*" (emphasis added).[89]

The word of God for von Stockhausen, mediated through the words of Luther and others, was that God wills his well-being. Similarly, Luther advised Matthias Weller, a former organist apparently suffering from depression, to attend to the consoling interventions of others, because God cares for Weller directly through these interventions: "For God has commanded men to comfort their brethren, and it is God's will that *the afflicted should receive such consolation as God's very own*" (emphasis added).[90] Depressive ruminations come from free-floating spirits such as the devil, whereas embodied human care is the means by which God reveals Godself.

> If you are convinced that such thoughts come from the devil, you have already gained the victory. But since you are still weak in your faith, listen to us, who by God's grace know it, and lean

on our staff until you learn to walk by yourself. And when good
people comfort you, my dear Matthias, learn to believe that
God is speaking to you through them. Pay heed to them and
have no doubt that it is most certainly God's word, coming to you
according to God's command through men, that comforts you
(emphasis added).[91]

To console Barbara Lisskirchen, who fretted over whether God
had any favor for her, Luther first reminded her that her own brother
had overcome similar worries. He then asked this same brother to
counsel her because "he knows very well what happened to him
before in a similar situation."[92] The kinship, the common suffering,
and the communication between this brother and sister are the very
means by which God may bring God's consolation to the latter.

Nor was Luther himself spared kinship suffering and therefore the
need to be consoled. He and his wife, Katherine, lost two of their six
children—their first daughter, Elizabeth, when she was eight months
old and their second daughter, Magdelene, when she was fourteen
years old. After Magdelene's death, Luther wrote to his friend Justus
Jonas of his and Katherine's grief. "The countenance, the words, the
gestures of our daughter . . . remain firmly fixed in the old heart so
that the death of Christ (in comparison to which what are all other
deaths?) is unable to drive out sorrow from our innermost depths, as
it ought to do. You therefore give thanks to God in our stead!"[93] In
their grief, Martin and Katherine could not on their own bring themselves, in Melanchthon's words, "truly to fear God, truly to love God,
truly to call upon God, truly to be convinced that he hears us, and to
expect help from God in death and all afflictions."[94] Instead of producing their own consolation at that moment, they sought it in the
priesthood of their companions in Christ.

In summary, Luther taught that God reveals Godself through
very human means: through Word and Sacrament (whose authority
he believed to be divine but which were gathered together by persons and then handed on to other persons), and through various
embodied forms of ministry including preaching and pastoral care.
In teaching that God consoles through word, sacrament, and the
company of believers, Luther was teaching what many before and

during his time taught. However, in teaching that God does God's business through ordinary human communication, Luther did break new ground.[95] He also rendered what is ordinary and quite human—practices that are not bound to Word and Sacrament—to be means of consolation.

Practices of Consolation through and for the World

In keeping with a part of the medieval tradition, Luther warned in his Large Catechism and elsewhere that one should not seek final refuge in earthly goods. To do so is to commit idolatry, which "does not consist merely of erecting an image and praying to it but is primarily a matter of the heart, which fixes its gaze upon other things [than God] and seeks help and consolation from creatures, saints, or devils."[96] The solace afforded by earthly goods is different from that granted by God's Word and Sacrament. The latter is often hidden, whereas "the flesh would rather have evident, temporal consolation and help, and be above anxiety and need."[97]

However, Luther also taught in the Large Catechism and elsewhere that God brings a kind of consolation through creation because God is the maker of both heaven and earth: "We should not spurn even this way of receiving such things through God's creatures."[98] In his "Commentary on Psalm 118:1," Luther further detailed these indicators of God's providential care.

> Every time he eats or drinks, sees, hears, smells, walks, stands; every time he uses his limbs, his body, his possessions, or any creature, he should recall that if God did not give him all this for his use and preserve it for him despite the devil, he would not have it. He should be aroused and trained to thank God for His daily goodness with a joyful heart and cheerful faith. . . . This verse also serves to comfort us in our misfortunes.[99]

Even though we may suffer various evils, God still showers us with abundant blessings: "We also are to look at our misfortunes in no other way than that with them God gives us a light by which we may see and understand His goodness and kindness in countless other ways. Then we conclude that such small misfortunes are barely a drop of water on a big fire or a little spark in the ocean."[100]

Luther advised that we make use of the good things of creation, including the desire for sex[101] and the love of music.[102] When he corresponded with Barbara Lisskirchen's melancholic brother, he suggested that moderately bold sinning might help him battle his ailment.

> Whenever the devil pesters you with these thoughts, at once seek out the company of men, drink more, joke and jest or engage in some other form of merriment. Sometimes it is necessary to drink a little more, play, jest, or even commit some sin in defiance and contempt of the devil in order not to give him an opportunity to make us scrupulous about trifles. We shall be overcome if we worry too much about falling into some sin.[103]

Luther also wrote to Weller's wife, Katherine, that in caring for her husband, she might use many earthly pleasures to console him.

Out of his belief that God is the maker of things both heavenly and earthly, Luther advised combining both religious and what we today call "secular" means of care.[104] In his schema, there is no need to label created goods as Christian because they have inherent value, and, when used well, may serve good ends.[105] To be sure, without our asking, God showers us with many blessings. At the same time, God uses our service to the neighbor as God's way of showing up and helping out.

> What else is all our work to God—whether in the fields, in the garden, in the city, in the house, in war, or in government—but just such a child's performance, by which He wants to give His gifts in the fields, at home and everywhere else? These are the masks of God, behind which He wants to remain concealed and do all things. . . . We have the saying: "God gives every good thing, but not just by waving a wand." God gives all good gifts; but you must lend a hand and take the bull by the horns, that is you must work and thus give God good cause and a mask.[106]

In temporal matters, it is God's law, accessible to human reason, that is authoritative: "Christians are not needed for secular authority. Thus it is not necessary for the emperor to be a saint. It is not necessary for him to be a Christian to rule. It is sufficient for the emperor to possess reason."[107] While reason cannot fathom the mind of God, it is a God-given tool for managing earthly affairs.[108] Accordingly, Luther often employed reason, not revelation, in his spiritual counsel. For example, when he pleaded with civil authorities for a reduced penalty for "a fisherman who had wittingly or unwittingly invaded waters reserved for the use of the prince,"[109] he did not quote Scripture, but instead used common parlance and simple logic to argue that harsh punishment of this individual would benefit no one. On another occasion he bargained in a straightforward fashion with the Wittenberg town council to match his private philanthropy with their public funds to assist a starving theology student.[110]

While Lutheranism has had its fair share of quietists, Luther himself did not advocate a world-avoiding form of faith. Accordingly, his thought was efficacious in reforming care for the poor, especially for the increasing numbers of urban poor. Some in the late-medieval church had heralded charity as a means by which those with surplus capital could secure their own salvation by diverting a portion to those who had none. In return, the poor had an obligation to receive these gifts so that the beneficent rich might pass through the eye of the needle. According to this schema, poverty was a divinely ordained condition not to be eradicated but to be carefully cultivated: "God has ordered that there be rich and poor so that the rich may be served by the poor and the poor may be taken care of by the rich."[111] To be sure, the medieval church cared for the poor in many, tender ways, especially through its religious orders, but "as the Middle Ages grew in complexity . . . the medieval church and its theology increasingly became less effective in and even a hindrance to the poor's welfare."[112]

The Lutheran response to this arrangement was that, having been justified by faith, the rich and poor did not need to remain separate and unequal to be saved.[113] For the faithful, service in the world is not precluded by the right hand of God, by the kingdom of faith, but made possible by it. In his treatise "The Blessed Sacrament of the Holy and True Body of Christ, and the Brotherhoods" (1519), Luther taught that the Sacrament of the Altar unites one who suffers with all who suffer; he also taught that all should care for anyone who suffers. Charging that the late-medieval brotherhoods were turned in on themselves—more concerned with doing meritorious charitable deeds than with actually helping those in need to overcome their need—he called for good works produced by the priesthood of all believers: "Would it not be unnatural behavior, if a fire is raging through the town, for someone to stand back quietly and let it burn more and more wherever it would, only because he does not have the power of mayor? . . . Is not every burgher here obliged to sound the alarm and call the others?"[114] Christian citizens and all in civil authority are commanded to work for the common good.

It is clear that a confident and helpful worldliness was the desired goal of the early Lutheran tradition, as it construed the ability to challenge social forces that bring suffering to be a reflex of the consolation of God. However, it is less clear whether Lutherans have achieved this goal in lived religion or whether—as is sometimes charged—they have lacked a vocabulary for addressing systemic sources of suffering.

In Conclusion

We began this chapter by asking what distinctive meanings are brought to the notion of consolation by the early Lutheran tradition. Those meanings may be summarized this way: First, the tradition proposes that humanity has no essence and that it has only a disconsolate existence apart from a right relationship with God. Second, it teaches that God does not bestow this consoling relationship directly on any of us, but offers it to all of us only through the ministrations of other Christians. The meaning of these proposals may be elucidated by several works on the pastoral theology of the early Lutheran tradition.

In a recent writing, Gerhard Ebeling contends that, at both the beginning and end of his career, Luther taught that consolation comes from God and from God alone.[115] To be sure, Luther built on humanist traditions that call for the suffering to become cultivated at finding consolation, but subverts that tradition by claiming that such cultivation [Bildung] is not a human enterprise but God's business.[116] Reflecting on the pastoral significance of Luther's writings on consolation, Martin Treu notes that, for Luther, God alone is the source of consolation,[117] and that therefore we have been freed from the burden of being producers of consolation both for ourselves and others.[118] Both Ebeling and Treu, therefore, discern what I call a "consolation by God alone" leitmotif in Luther.

Ebeling and Treu are not alone in doing so. In concert with them, Christian Möller sees Luther's distinction between consolation from God and consolation from humanity as a "red thread" (the same metaphor employed by von Harnack, Lindberg, and Tanner) that appears throughout Luther.[119] Still Möller detects, near this red thread, something else in Luther's theology of consolation that Ebeling and Treu also discern but do not highlight. Möller calls this something else "another emphasis."

To exemplify Luther's writings that reveal this other emphasis, Möller selects the letter, cited earlier, to the suicidal Jonas von Stockhausen. "My dear friend, it is high time that you cease relying on and pursuing your own thoughts. Listen to other people who are not subject to this temptation. . . . *Thus God will strengthen and comfort you by means of our words* (emphasis added)."[120] For Luther, Möller contends, the incarnation overcomes the chasm between consolation from God and consolation from humanity. That is, "God binds his Word to the human word and lets his voice be heard in, with, and under the human voice."[121] This incautious conjoining of things divine and human, epitomized in the claim that "the finite can bear the infinite," disturbed not only some Roman Catholics during the time of the early Lutheran tradition but also a few of the Calvinist faithful. It disturbed some Christians then, and may still do so now, because it expresses so clearly the uniquely Lutheran understanding of justification by faith—that God gives to the faithful all that God is, and that God does so only through the ministrations of the faithful.

The doctrine of justification is not the only source for this "other thread" according to which the consolation of God is mediated through humanity. Building on Luther's theology of the cross, Gerhard Forde contends that theology alone cannot aid our tribulation and actually may add to it by appending more abstractions to the pain of not understanding why it occurs: "Theology, no matter how sweetly done, does not cure tribulation."[122] Neither the theology of justification nor the theology of the cross, but only proclamation through word, sacrament, and the priesthood of believers, may bring consolation.

Out of his theology of the cross, Luther frequently taught that the Hidden God and the devil appear to be one and the same. The devil is the disembodied spirit *par excellence,* who offers correspondingly disembodied (that is, spiritual), and therefore disconsoling, words. To elaborate on this point in Luther's theology, Forde tells the following story.

> Suppose you were to get a note in your mail box, and the note contained the words, "I love you," but there was no name attached to the note. You might be excited at first. But what if the notes kept coming, regularly and often, and yet none of them had any name attached, but only the words, "I love you." After a while, the notes and the words themselves would be a source of concern, for you would ask, "Who is this that loves me?" The discomforting answer would be this: "'No-body' loves me. 'No-body' is saying 'I love you.' There is 'no-body' attached to these words."[123]

In this schema, the Hidden God and the devil are one in being "no-body," in each having no embodied way of wishing or making us well when we suffer. In this schema, only that which comes to us through the ministrations of others can move us away from the Hidden God above us and the devil below us to consolation in the world around us. This consolation always comes to the sufferer through other persons; Scripture, the sacraments, and the priesthood of all believers are all various embodied means through which God offers it.

To be sure, the early Lutheran tradition insists, and is somewhat distinguished by its insistence, that the consolation of God is never immediate but always mediated. However, does it not also teach that there is yet another means, not humanly mediated, by which consolation comes? In a sense, the answer is yes. As noted, Luther contends that we may receive the consolation of God through creation. But in another, more significant sense, the answer is no. For in Luther's schema, we have no immediate encounter with creation but come to creation—or rather, creation comes to us—only through the aid and instruction of other persons.

Having reviewed the concept of consolation in the early Lutheran tradition, we may now turn to the present day. How have some contemporary Lutherans who have suffered and sought consolation been informed by this tradition? That is to say, what may we see of the tradition's red threads, or other threads, in their beliefs and practices? And how have some Lutherans reformed the tradition by their very beliefs and practices? In later chapters, we shall explore these and other related questions in light of the reported experiences of seven such Lutherans. In the next chapter, I shall introduce these Lutherans and a method for asking these questions about their tradition and practices.

3.
Significant Negative Events in Seven Lives

⇛•⇚

A major impetus for this book has come from the challenging studies on religion and suffering primarily conducted not by theologians, but by social scientists under the rubric of "religious coping." Though these inquiries into religious coping do not provide—and may never be able to provide—conclusive answers to the questions they pose, I find them valuable exactly because they force us to ask those very important questions. My own research led me to investigate the ways in which tradition informs, and is reformed by, the religious coping beliefs and practice of its members. Therefore, in a previous work, I examined the "kind of religious coping" practiced by some Lutherans in a variety of difficult situations.[1]

In this book, I use data obtained from my interviews with seven "co-researchers" to look more closely at the relationship between their experience and their tradition. This chapter begins with a discussion of my methods, then presents the case history of each co-researcher, including a brief biographical sketch, a summary of the "significant negative event," and consequent search for consolation. In closing, I comment on some unique aspects of my method of analysis and raise questions about the normativity of tradition in lived religion that will guide the subsequent analysis.[2]

Introduction to This Empirical Study

Method of This Study

Kenneth Pargament, who is primarily a quantitative researcher, notes the benefits of interviews in research such as mine.[3]

> Interviews make particularly good sense when it comes to top-
> ics as sensitive as religion and coping. There is an old Talmudic
> saying: "The deeper the sorrow, the less the voice." Under-
> standing how people come to grips with the most painful times
> of their lives requires some ability to connect to people, draw
> them out as far as they are willing to go, and listen to what may
> be some very quiet voices in a sensitive and compassionate way.
> Through the interview, we can form this connection, brief and
> limited as it may be, one which helps us understand a bit more
> about religious experience in critical points of life.[4]

Qualitative techniques such as interviewing also are employed in practical theological research. For example, in his *Fundamental Practical Theology*, Don Browning states, "To be genuinely practical, the book will center around three rather extensive case studies of congregations." Employing "value active interview techniques," he sought to challenge and to be challenged by the subjects of his study.[5]

Inherent in all qualitative research is the difficulty in generalizing what one learns from the researched sample to others in the same population. Accordingly, it is not apparent how the findings of my study of seven Lutherans represent the many millions of other Lutherans inside and outside the United States. At the same time, I believe that the richness of the following in-depth analysis of these individuals' praxes compensates for this disadvantage. That is to say in the language of the social sciences, what this research may lack in its immediate applicability to other persons and settings, it will compensate for in *bandwidth*—addressing a large number of theoretical and empirical questions.[6] My study is not meant to be conclusive but suggestive—the first step in an ongoing practical theological study in the relationship between tradition and lived religion not only among Lutherans, but also among members of other religious traditions.

Background of the Co-Researchers

The co-researchers are seven adults, aged thirty years or more, who met the following conditions:

- They had experienced some significant negative event within the past seven years.
- They reported that the degree and intensity of that event's impact had lessened for at least one year.
- They are active members of a congregation of the Evangelical Lutheran Church in America.
- They were willing to be questioned and interviewed on the relationship between their faith and seeking consolation for that negative event.

The second requirement was meant to reduce the risk that the research itself might exacerbate their suffering, and to increase the likelihood of their having, to paraphrase Kierkegaard, greater objectivity about the subjectivity of their suffering. The third requirement was to help ensure that they called themselves Lutheran out of an ongoing appropriation of their tradition. The definition of active membership varies slightly for every Lutheran congregation, but it usually indicates that one has officially joined that congregation, worships there with some regularity if possible, and participates in some form of congregational stewardship. The co-researchers signed an informed-consent form that listed, among other things, the possible benefit of their taking satisfaction by participating in a study that might further an understanding of the religious practices of Lutherans.

While two of the co-researchers were reared in the Lutheran Church–Missouri Synod, I required that all currently be members of the Evangelical Lutheran Church in America. I did so because I judged that most members of other U.S. Lutheran church bodies (e.g., Lutheran Church–Missouri Synod, Wisconsin Evangelical Lutheran Synod, Finnish Apostolic Lutheran Church) have a distinct enough belief and piety that, had I included them, cross-denominational comparisons would have been necessary, but, with such a small sample, impossible. I interviewed both clergy and laypersons because religious professionals typically are consulted in pilot studies such as this, while laypersons are often information-rich subjects in quantitative and qualitative studies.[7] I chose four male subjects (two clergy and two laypersons) and three female subjects (one clergy and two laypersons) to note any gender similarities or differences.

These seven were not chosen randomly from the North American Lutheran population—all are members of congregations referred to this study by other Lutheran pastors. As a result, this sample was loaded with those who identify closely with their tradition. Nevertheless, while these Lutherans may not necessarily be typical of other men or women, clergy or lay, in their denomination, they may represent persons who claim a strong denominational identity and have been informed by the religious tradition of their denomination.

While some studies focus on how individuals handle a particular kind of stress, others focus on a certain dimension of their experience—such as their religious tradition—across a broad range of stressors. As a pilot study for further research, I interviewed persons who had experienced a "significant negative event," the definition of which I adapted from Pargament's work: "A loss (through death, divorce, job loss); a chronic or acute illness, or the chronic or acute illness of a loved one; a major inter-personal dispute; a major financial or professional disruption; experience of major calamity or trauma or the experience of a major calamity or trauma of a loved one."[8]

Both to facilitate conversation and to cover some of the same topics with each co-researcher, I utilized the Semi-Structured Interview Schedule for Lutheran Coping and Consolation as the primary investigative tool.[9] I formulated my questions based on my research into consolation in the early Lutheran tradition and by consulting with several Lutheran pastors and theologians. The questions covered a number of areas including the co-researchers' associations with the term "consolation," whether they found certain religious practices (e.g., prayers, worship, hymns) helpful or unhelpful, whether they received support from persons inside and outside of their congregations, their beliefs and activities directly associated with their suffering, and finally, their reflections on the relationship between their Lutheran identity and their experience of consolation—or lack thereof.

I also employed another method common in qualitative research—triangulation, or the verification of findings from other sources.

Before each interview, therefore, I administered two instruments frequently employed in such research, the Religious Coping Activities Scale (RCA) and the Religious Coping Styles Scale (RCS). These ask subjects to rate their endorsement of a number of items on a Likert scale (usually ranging from zero to either four or five) covering topics very similar to those in the survey. At various points in the interview, I questioned co-researchers about their rating responses. I also invited them to comment on the scales' items and questionnaires themselves. This inquiry proved lively and fruitful.

In analyzing the transcripts of the interviews, I searched both for common themes and for unique themes in each of their accounts. In my final analysis, I focused on the major research question of this study: the relationship between the co-researchers' lived religious experience and the normative teachings of their tradition.

A Variety of Significant Negative Events

In the following sections, I have distilled some of the central themes in the co-researchers' responses to the questions contained in the Semi-Structured Interview Schedule for Lutheran Coping and Consolation and to the items of the various scales they completed. I reserve my analysis of their responses for the following chapters. As noted earlier, I have altered relatively insignificant but possibly telltale biographical details in order to protect their confidentiality.

Allison: "The church is the people."
Allison is a thirty-nine-year-old widow who attended a vocational training school and is employed as a middle manager in a major regional industry. She lives in a medium-sized city in the lower Midwest and is a member of a growing congregation on the outskirts of that city. She has three children: Larry, nineteen; Mitchell, fifteen; and John, ten. Her husband, William, who had worked as an independent mechanic for most of his life, was killed three years before this interview by a "freak mechanical accident" at a workplace where he was moonlighting.

Early in the interview Allison shared what she thought was "important" in coping with this sudden and painful loss. "I was brought up Lutheran and Missouri Synod–Lutheran, and I guess I was always told to never ask, 'Why me?' And so I tried very hard not to ask that question, 'Why did I have to go through these things alone?' But I think we have such a marvelous support group, a circle of friends that we were a part of, that they just made it as easy as possible."

I then commented, "I asked about religion and your coping, and you immediately referred to people. How would you explain to someone what the support of people has to do with your religious faith?" Allison responded, "I think the church is the people. At least at [her congregation], the church is the people, the church isn't the pastor. The church isn't really a specific thing from the Bible. I think the church is the people—that's what makes it the church. And they were a very important part, and still are today, in helping us get through this."

Allison gave numerous examples of how she relied on the people of her church through this period. She wept as she related the following story:

> I had a friend who would stop by on her lunch hours. I took a short, three-week leave of absence after the accident. And what I thought I wanted was to be by myself and sort things out because I didn't figure I was very much fun. And I wouldn't answer the doorbell and I wouldn't answer the phone, and she would come over for lunch every day, and just stay at my door until I answered because she thought I needed someone, and I really did.

In the months following William's death, her congregation offered material support: "Members from our church have done everything from haul rock in under my deck for me. A neighbor and church friend from down the street have helped when my furnace has gone out." The church also provided emotional support as well: "Larry and his confirmation mentor have become very, very close friends. One will take them out hunting or fishing or, you know, do the male bonding things that the boys need to have."

Despite this support, Allison avoided some church activities immediately after William's death. "Mainly because Sunday mornings—we were very active and William worked six days a week—

but Sunday mornings, he was always in church by my side. And so, I pretty much eliminated whatever in church reminded me of him or caused me pain. Also, I didn't want to embarrass myself." Gradually, however, she returned to many—but not all—congregational activities.

While Allison found comfort in the care of her congregation, she also looked for assurance in "verses that I've heard from childhood. 'For by grace you're saved through faith.' We knew that William was saved because he believed and God so loved the world that He gave His only begotten Son." She also sought guidance from other scriptural sources. "Everything happens for a reason and there are verses in the Bible that the Lord won't give you more than you can handle. And so He obviously thought that I could handle this, and so I just did my best to resume my normal life and support the boys and just, you know, keep the faith."

Nevertheless, she was troubled by this faith claim and its corollary—that God had willed her husband's death.

> I guess God's will was to take him from this earth because he would not have enjoyed being in the world not being able to function as he did prior to the accident. And as far as God's will for us and how we can handle it, I think for the most part, I've become a stronger person, but not immediately. After William's death, my furnace went out, my garage-door opener broke, my son got in his first [minor] car accident, and, though now it seems trivial, at the time it was very real and I questioned myself and I questioned the Lord, "How much more will I have to handle?"

Charles: "Faith is simply a part of you. Consolation was there before you began."

Charles is a sixty-nine-year-old retired pastor of the Evangelical Lutheran Church in America. He is married and has one adult child. As noted earlier, Charles was raised in the Lutheran Church–Missouri Synod; he traces his lineage to several renowned orthodox theologians of the 1600s. Charles shared that "after a lifetime of good health," he endured a number of life-threatening cancers and heart ailments that required multiple surgeries and treatments. Talking about his cascade of sicknesses, he claimed that modern medicine had healed him by paradoxical means. "There's something kind of ludicrous about the whole thing when one looks at it. Well, first of all, what they do to you. What it means to be cut up and slashed open. I got scars from my chin to my pubic bone. And what a ridiculous thing to go through when you think about it—that they make you well by tearing you up."

Charles also spoke at length about what he usually hesitates to tell those who are not sick.

> The whole process of acute care is humiliating. You become a patient, which means a "sufferer." And they always say, "Be proactive." There's very little room to be proactive in modern medicine. You're on a conveyor belt and you go through it. You have to pee when they tell you to so that they can take a sample of how it looks, you have to shit when they tell you to get your bowels cleared out. And then you have to lie down when they tell you. You're under orders all the time and you can do nothing. So it's total loss of control. Total loss of autonomy. Total loss of identity.

At the same time, he is appreciative of "the good I got from modern medicine."

> The whole hospital staff is trying to help you, but they're all under pressures and limitations or budget and everything else . . . I always prayed for them. I told the doctor I was praying for him. He said, "You're praying for me?" I said, "Yeah. Because I sympathize with you having to take care of all these sick people." Everybody wants attention. Everybody considers themselves the center of the universe. Why the hell should I live more than the next guy? All of this is part of the faith experience. This being alive is not an easy task even though the young dudes don't know this.

Following his apparent recovery, he also has become involved in support groups for persons who have similar diseases. Asked to explain his involvement, he responded: "I owe, I owe."

As noted earlier, Charles looks for "natural" explanations of his illness. "Cancer or heart problems which are part of our lifestyle in this country and our civilization are no one's fault. We Westerners put that on ourselves. The Japanese don't have it, same way Indians don't have it. It's a product of this kind of capitalism and stress culture. How can you blame God for that? You walk into a fire and you get burned." Yet in the midst of his suffering, Charles found comfort in his faith. "Faith tells you that it's all right what you're experiencing. It is all right. It is all right. And, that doesn't mean it's pleasant. And, there is no relief where you say, 'Oh, I was worried that it's not all right, but now I know it is all right.' And, see, consolation was there before you began."

He also found comfort in recalling that his faith was part of a tradition: "The church hands you a Bible and the church hands you its liturgy, and the church hands you its devotional store, and people found it meaningful, and you handle that and you let yourself be handled by it and it works." In particular, certain hymns in "the old Missouri Synod hymnal" comforted Charles: "What they all had is what the Moravians call *Gelassenheit*. This means not a resignation. It's a kind of a way of saying, letting go, letting God. . . . No, no, it's not Stoicism."

Julia: "It was a sanctuary for me."

Julia is a fifty-three-year-old divorced pastor. She and her former husband have two adult children. Julia was reared in a small town in the Midwest and for over twenty years served as the church secretary to her home congregation. Ordained two years ago, she is currently serving a small suburban congregation. She reported her "significant negative event" as her "divorce after thirty-five years of marriage. It began seven years ago with a series of events between my husband and me which clearly could not be resolved. We employed the therapist we had used to facilitate our telling the children and their spouses—a difficult meeting."

When asked about sources of consolation during and after her divorce, Julia responded,

> The consolation that was effective came from my therapist [who is] a pastor. We are both Christian and we had really struggled with whether or not we were breaking a sacred

promise until the therapist said, "It's already broken. The question is not 'What am I going to do with this whole covenant?' but 'What am I going to do with this broken covenant?'" Which was helpful for us.

She also explained that prayer helped her manage the stress of her commitments at both home and seminary: "And I pray, 'God, I'm in a quandary. Discernment is not working. And I need and I will wait for answers from you.'"

Julia reported that she suffered from and was professionally treated for clinical depression. During that period, she suffered further from the experience of being in a kind of "darkness." "I think someone said, 'Don't forget that given an opportunity, God can work good out of chaos. That's how creation happened.' I thought, 'Oh, this is chaos, this is the dark. Light will come.' Now I can't tell you that every day that I believed that, because the darkness is pretty dark. But it did come."

Julia identified certain teachings in the Lutheran tradition as helpful during this time.

> I think "justified by faith" was important because when your husband asks you for a divorce—or maybe vice versa—one of the first things I felt was failure: "What if it was my fault? I'm guilty." Then I remembered [a seminary professor] saying, "Guilt? You're forgiven. Don't let guilt drag you down and keep you from being part of this kingdom." And knowing that forgiveness was there and ready and having once gone for private confession and knowing the power of that service, I thought, "If I need that, it's there."

Even though the teachings of the tradition provided Julia some solace, attending her home congregation was difficult during her divorce. "The thing that did impact me was when I went back to the church where we had always worshiped as a family for twenty-five years and we always sat in the same pew. And [now] I sat on the other side of the church with other people, to break the pain." She found comfort worshiping elsewhere.

> I started attending [a congregation near her seminary], which is a multicultural church. Although they used the same liturgical

book, because it was so multicultural, so many things were brought into the service—African American, Hispanic, music, language—I was blessed by that difference. And I was accepted there just for me as a single person. And that was a gift. Because if you've never been single, and you've never lived alone, you don't know what that is.

The comfort that scripture and hymnody brought her was mediated through this congregation: "The context was more important. I don't remember hearing scripture differently. I don't remember any hymn that evoked any particular meaning. In church, we were just all in church. So I had time to sit in a sanctuary and kind of work through how I felt." In response to this comment, I remarked, "When you said 'sanctuary'. . . I had to stop for a second and say to myself, was she talking about that part of the church building or was she talking about her experience of the church?" Julia responded, "I was talking about the building. But it was a sanctuary for me. And it's where I was ordained. Because the [church synod] couldn't pull off an ordination before I started my call, and so I was ordained there along with Nicole from Australia and Paul from Namibia. It was some evening."

Ruth: "'Lord, to whom shall I go?'"

Ruth, whom we met in the introduction, is a thirty-nine-year-old "Afro-Saxon" daughter of an African-American Baptist father and German Lutheran mother. She spent most of her life in a major East-Coast city, where she completed her undergraduate education. A recent graduate of a business school in a major city on the West Coast, she is currently a vice president at the headquarters of a large corporation there. She has two children: Jerome, eight, and Elizabeth, two. As noted earlier, her "marriage had been quite abusive. As a result of my husband's persistent pattern of abuse, I was unable to pass a professional exam despite having a degree from a good university." Summing up how she found "help in my troubles," Ruth said, "It's me being able to be patient while God figures stuff out. And to sort of stay out of God's way and not be in more control than what I feel is important. And so I just need to do the pieces that I can seem to do. So, I need to go to work, to pay my bills. I need to leave other parts of them alone." Her "assurance" in the providence of God gave her strength to face many problems associated with her divorce.

However, in the midst of this assurance, Ruth reports that she also feared that God was "punishing" her through the divorce court proceedings. "And I cried and I said, 'Lord, can you give me some faith?'" Further intensifying her suffering, Ruth believes that her racially mixed identity often makes it hard for her to find an accepting community. "I'm used to people going to a certain extent with me and then just sort of saying, 'Oh, you don't know what that is. You're black; you can't have that feeling that I have because I'm a white person—we're different.' Or, 'I'm black and you can't know my pain because your skin is too white.' You can't know what I go through every day."

In the midst of her isolation, Ruth claims that she finds her comfort in "the Lord." "What I discovered was that maybe the whole process of divorce and being separated from everyone that I had ever been close to, and having young children depending on me while I was going through that, brought me to the understanding of that really ancient prayer, 'Lord, to whom shall I go?' Of course, I can go to God. That's where I can go. I can stay in prayer and be peaceful." Ruth several times referred to particular sources of comfort.

> At some point about ten years ago, I just picked up the Bible and the *Lutheran Book of Worship*, and the lectionary of daily readings; I did that for three or four years. And so I kind of got a "passage familiarity" with the Bible and it became my text. You know, that narrative became my life in a really important way. Because that narrative charged me up. It means something. It reveals itself to me. And it's as alive for me as another person.

In the midst of these doubts, she reported, she repeatedly rediscovered that God was on her side in the person of Jesus and in the sacrament of her baptism. "I'm safe in my bed and knowing that there's Jesus—that's why I'm here, that's why I'm not being judged right now. I would have to come before God and account for what I said or what I did. But I have this baptism, I have this Christ. And just trying to remember that is important, because, you know, I want God to reveal Himself to me."

Michael: "There are signs, messages that you have to be aware of."

Michael is fifty-eight years old, divorced and remarried, and resides in the suburb of a major metropolis in the mid-Atlantic region. A member of a large and moderately affluent congregation near that suburb, Michael has worked as a specialty salesperson for most of his life. Born in New England and raised there in a congregation with a conservative Baptist heritage, he reported that he became a Lutheran ten years ago when he remarried. "The only two Protestant religions I really understand are Baptist, where I had been until I became a Lutheran, and Lutheran. And I would say that I'm a Lutheran number one because my [current] wife is a Lutheran and I enjoyed being with her more than where I came from."

In the face of Michael's impending surgery, he searched for and found signs from God.

> The name of a doctor, Dr. Smith, kept coming up. [A congregation member] who had an emergency surgery for his heart went to General Hospital and Dr. Smith did his operation. It seems like I would pick up an article in the paper and I'd see Dr. Smith's name. This name kept coming and coming. I called my doctor and asked him what his thoughts were. And he said, "There's a very good surgeon up at General Hospital named Dr. Smith." Everywhere I turned, I kept hearing about him. And I just feel I was getting messages from God—that He was sort of sending his angels to me saying this is the guy to go to. I was led to him.

Michael reported that in most major difficulties, he tries to discern the will of God in such a manner: "It is kind of subconscious. God doesn't come down like you read the Bible where the angel comes down and speaks to you. That doesn't happen today. But I believe there are signs, messages that you have to be aware of." Michael reported that he found comfort in scripture during and after his surgery. "The Twenty-third Psalm has always been a real favorite of mine. It's one of the first Psalms that I learned going to Sunday school, and that gave me a tremendous amount of comfort. And I kept repeating it at any time that I felt nervous about anything before the operation and after the operation." However, this psalm primarily brought comfort to Michael because he saw "signs" of its importance.

> Right after the operation, I was at a church council meeting and somebody couldn't read scripture on a certain day that was theirs and they said, "Would you mind switching with me?" and they handed me the reading, and it was the Twenty-third Psalm. Shortly after, one of my sisters died in New Hampshire. We flew up to the funeral and they gave out little bookmarks with her picture on one side. Turn it over and there's the Twenty-third Psalm. I'm quite a football fan. And I read a lot of articles about [a particular player] and they said that before he goes into the ball game, he always reads the Twenty-third Psalm.

Michael also found the social support that he received from members of his congregation significant for his recovery. "A number of people came to visit. In fact, a couple that I never really knew. I mean they're in church and they sit on one side of the pew, and I was aware of them, but not totally. So the Sunday after my surgery, they came and brought the altar flowers to me. And at that point, I felt a very, very warm feeling towards them."

Also important in Michael's "healing" was another religious tradition. "I just think I believe in the Christian Scientist way. Their outlook is you got to have that positive attitude. You got to know that you're going to be getting better. You got to know that there's a hidden power and it's going to take care of you. I really firmly believe that." But Michael also voiced his questions about his illness and the will of God. "Why did it happen to me and not somebody else? I mean, here's another guy who smokes four packs of cigarettes a day and he doesn't live a real clean life. And you try to keep an upright kind of living and so forth. That does cross your mind, and I don't know if there's any answer to it, really."

However, Michael does look for divine recompense for such seeming injustice. "I think if my life ends on earth, I'm going to have a better life later on. Maybe some of these other people, maybe their life won't be so good then. There'll be a reckoning along the way. Right hand and left hand."

Oscar: "Justification by faith means that God will take care of us at these difficult times."

Oscar is an eighty-six-year-old who lives in a suburb of a metropolis in the upper Midwest. He is a member of a very small congregation near the inner city of that metropolis. A bachelor Norwegian-American businessman, he served stateside as a staff sergeant in World War II, graduated from high school following the war, and then was a "very successful" salesperson for a major food distributor. He and his only sibling, Sheldon—also a bachelor—shared the same household throughout their adult lives. Sheldon was diagnosed with inoperable cancer eight months before his death and spent most of that time at home with relatively "little pain." Oscar was his primary caregiver during that period and claims that now, three years after Sheldon's death, he still grieves for his brother. "My brother was a wonderful person. He and I lived together for our entire lives. His loss is very, very difficult because we had just the finest of relationships, and I would say thanks to him more so than to me—I'm kind of a feisty person. But we got along just wonderfully well."

He reported feeling "great care" from members of his congregation, of which his brother and their parents had been lifelong members. He emphasized that he received needed support from his pastor just before Sheldon died.

> We have a lot to do on our house and I'm a little embarrassed by it. And it's just carelessness on my part and so forth. And so I'd been truthfully kind of hesitant to have the pastor come as often as he would have liked, I tell you. Early during that period, not knowing how long it was going to be, Pastor Olson on numerous occasions was wanting to set up a time to come visit, and I guess I was wrong on my part, but I put it off. But then the pastor on his own, he decided to come and he witnessed with Sheldon and me, and later toward the end was there—I'm just grateful that he took that initiative and did come.

Oscar spontaneously related the "help" he finds in a particular Lutheran teaching. "Justification by faith means that God will take care of us at these difficult times. It's so strongly instilled in us that we don't get down to specifics. Really, I don't even know how to express it. It's in you and you believe in it. And this is from childhood on up. You just never get away from that."

Even with this belief, however, Oscar still experiences the pain of his loss. "The closeness that we enjoyed together—I just miss that terribly. And of course, I guess time heals, but I'll never get over it 100 percent." He claimed that he found "comfort" for this loss in a particular part of the liturgy: "I am able to say that the Lord's Supper is more meaningful to me now. And when I take the Lord's Supper, I do think of my brother being with me." While Oscar spoke at length about how central this congregation is to him and has been to his entire family, he also referred in detail to how helpful it was to his own vocation. "I think my bringing up in this faith has helped me to get the kind of respect necessary to be successful in my sales endeavors. I don't mean to be boastful, but my life's work was with the biggest accounts in the United States, and to gain their confidence and respect—knowing when I knocked on their door, the door was open to meet with me—that was important. And I think it had a lot to do with my bringing up as a Lutheran."

Describing this congregation as "very small now" and needing new members, Oscar reported that since his brother's death, he is even more attentive to the needs of his church. "But I think this, that any member of this church, I think they realize and they know—and I'm saying this boastfully, so you'll have to excuse me—that I'm available to help if I possibly can."

Robert: "God was saying to me, 'You blew it here, you know,' even if that's not part of my theology."

Robert is a fifty-six-year-old married pastor with two grown daughters; he is currently serving a medium-sized congregation outside of a metropolitan area. Robert has spearheaded important fund-raising campaigns in various congregations and served on the financial boards of several important public concerns. Robert reported that he had recently experienced two significant negative events that he often compares and contrasts.

About a decade ago, Robert co-signed a loan for a young acquaintance who had purchased a small business. This person neglected the business and finally skipped town, leaving Robert to assume an overwhelming financial debt: "I had to cope with working full-time in running an over-the-counter enterprise and also being a full-time minister." For five years, Robert suffered the stress of overseeing this operation—firing employees who used illegal drugs, responding to both state authorities who threatened to close down the business and to the I.R.S., which threatened to seize all his personal assets—before he was able to repay the many outstanding loans and sell the business. Throughout his "ordeal," Robert wondered if his suffering was a "test." "I wondered if God was disciplining me for not listening to others and for trying to take on too much. Part of the discipline was God saying, 'Okay, you're going to learn through the school of hard knocks.'"

Robert claimed that even though he does not teach or preach that God punishes in such a manner, he nevertheless wondered at the time if God were not doing so. "I had thoughts that God was really saying to me, 'You blew it here, you know' even if that's not part of my theology. I hear people saying, 'What did I do wrong that I got sick and everything else?' And I'm always telling them, 'God doesn't work that way. You didn't do something wrong.' But I have to admit when I was in the financial part of it, I did look at it that way." He specifically wondered if God warned him through the challenges of family and friends. "I do believe that God certainly does work through other people. And I think I should have listened to others because the clear picture I was getting from anybody and everybody who knew I was going to do this—people at the church, my wife, my family, and everybody else—was that I should not do this. And I was bullheaded. And I think I was wrong." Robert summarizes the "burden" he experienced this way: "It was kind of just me and God at the time going through that part."

Robert contrasts this isolation and "concern with God" during his "financial disaster" with his experiences in coping with and subsequent recovery from metastatic cancer that was diagnosed and treated just after that disaster. "My immediate family and the community were there to support me and lift me up and reaffirm God's presence through all of that. Through them God was present. So I never had the feeling that I am a Job here and God is saying, 'We'll test Robert on this one and throw some cancer down and see how he handles it.'"

Thus while he experienced no comfort from prayer during his period of financial struggle, he did during his illness. Robert noted that even with this comfort, he often petitioned God: "There's things that I wanted. I'm not saying that I all of a sudden said, 'Well, it doesn't matter whether I'm there at my daughter's wedding.' I was saying, 'God, if at all possible, I want to be there.'" He also reported that taking communion in the hospital before his surgeries was especially important.

> I don't want to say I took communion and that because of that my high blood pressure went down to sixty. I asked for communion before the operation, and I felt an assurance and a calmness, though I don't know whether it was detectable in my blood pressure. And to be honest, I'm not saying that I was confident that the cancer would be gone. But I thought that whatever happened, it would be okay and that my family would be okay and that I would be okay.

Robert concluded that the major contrast between his coping with financial difficulties and his coping with illness was that he did the former alone and the latter with others.

> Here I am a pastor, here I am a member of a church my whole life, but I—for the first time—I sensed the community literally picking me up: my spirits, my health, everything. That I was not going through this alone. I didn't always feel that [during his financial problem]. There were times I doubted that I was going to get out of it. Maybe because I put blame on myself and tried to handle it more on my own than I did rely on others.

In Summary

Further Remarks about the Method of Analysis: "We never see . . . the innermost core."

In 1987 Pargament and his colleagues developed a scale to measure whether persons are "indiscriminately pro-religious," an orientation defined as "the tendency to respond positively to religious material regardless of its plausibility."[10] In other words, these persons are prone to put their best religious feet forward. Pargament's scale (the IPOR) contains twenty-eight true/false items. Persons who endorse more than a pre-determined number of implausible answers, (e.g., "Tensions do not exist among members of this church," "This church has programs to meet the needs of all the members," "I am always inspired by sermon topics," "I never disobey the teachings of my faith") are considered indiscriminately pro-religious and, consequently, their scores on other measures of religious beliefs and practices are not taken into account.

Since Pargament's scale is typically not employed in studies such as mine, I did not use it. Even so, by questioning the co-researchers about whether they experienced any difficulties with their beliefs or practices during hard times, I believe that I tapped a dimension similar to that measured in the IPOR. For example, I read to each of them the following item from the Lutheran Coping and Consolation Semi-Structured Interview:

> Some people say that their faith did not help them deal with the emotions and feelings that result from a negative event. [Interviewer may prompt if necessary: Sometimes people tell themselves, "I am not really so sure that God cares about me," or "Maybe the pastor was not telling the truth and my sins are so bad that I will never be right again."] Did you experience that your faith was not helpful in dealing with the emotions and feelings that resulted from this negative event? If so, how so?

All the co-researchers reported troubling beliefs or difficulties in their religious practices—all, that is, except for Oscar. Therefore only Oscar demonstrated significant features of indiscriminate pro-religiousness. Yet, as we shall see, even Oscar, manifestly the most pro-religious of the seven, expressed beliefs that many other Lutherans might judge to be beyond the pale of Lutheranism.

My method of analyzing the beliefs and practices of these co-researchers is patterned after that of several European practical theological studies of lived religion.[11] This method permits the researcher greater latitude to speculate about the "latent meanings" of the co-researchers' reports than is characteristic of most empirical-qualitative research—certainly more than I engaged in during my previous qualitative study of religious coping. In such inquiry, the researcher listens for the interplay between the co-researchers' expressions and their possibly hidden meanings of those words. Without overriding the subjects' agency, the researcher may propose that there are forces, even structures of thought, at work in their lived religion that are manifestly at odds with their words.

Consequently there is another way in which my method of analysis differs from much qualitative research: it does not seek confirmation from the co-researchers of my interpretations of their beliefs and practices. My reasons for not doing so are very similar to those that Regina Sommer lays out in her research of contemporary Christian, socialist women. Having asked whether not seeking confirmation from her co-researchers is contrary to the principles of the feminist scholarship out of which she works—"Are these women not thereby made into objects of research if they do not participate in the process of interpretation?"—Sommer concludes that, were she to have done so, she would have overstepped her task as a researcher and instead have become a "quasi-therapist."[12] In keeping with Sommer's method, my analysis of the beliefs and practices of consolation in the lived religion of these Lutherans will be more suggestive than it will be conclusive. That is to say, I will offer what I regard to be plausible interpretations of their reports without suggesting that my interpretations are necessarily accurate or the only possible ones. The method of my analysis constrains me from doing more, but so also do the assumptions of the theological anthropology out of which I work: "The Christian life can never be fully identified with the empirical life that we lead. The Christian life is an object of faith and, as such, it is hidden. What we see is never the real thing; only God and faith see this innermost core."[13] Working with these assumptions, I am able to be both bold in my interpretations as well as admittedly often uncertain of their accuracy.

Problematics with Tradition

Working with the limits and possibilities afforded by my method of analysis, I shall explore these questions in the following chapters:

Through their suffering how have these seven Lutherans become a part of the Lutheran tradition? That is, how have they shaped that tradition through their beliefs and practices? And how has the "red thread" of the early Lutheran tradition shown itself—or not—in their beliefs and practices?

Of course, these questions assume that there is something called the Lutheran tradition that may manifest itself in one's experiences and of which one may become a part. As noted in the introduction, this assumption—that there is a something called the Lutheran tradition or other entities called religious traditions—is contested. In *Theories of Culture,* Kathryn Tanner builds on her understanding of the new agenda of cultural studies to provide a new agenda for theology around a number of hot topics, including tradition. Talk about tradition, she believes, arises from theologians' anxiety in the face of the diversity of beliefs and practices in Christian life.[14] Tanner criticizes the "red thread" metaphor of tradition and points to "three problematic assumptions" at work in similar understandings of tradition.

The first occurs when tradition is "viewed as a natural preexisting reality" and continuities in practices are seen as existing by virtue of this reality. Such a notion is akin to the notion that culture is grounded in some unspoken but quite real "consensus" among its members, thereby ordering all their beliefs and practices. To those who hold this notion, Tanner offers this stunningly simple retort: "But from a post-modern point of view, this is all backwards."[15] That is, the many beliefs and practices by members of any one tradition always remain many and cannot be subsumed by any one tradition. Consequently one may argue for or dispute the particular ordering of various experiences by any tradition.

The second problematic assumption is "that the various results of transmission maintain their identity by approximating what is transmitted." Even in a more "organic" understanding of tradition, only those beliefs and practices may blossom forth that were somehow seminally present in the past. Also at play is the metaphor of tradition as a substance that perdures through space and time. To the contrary, Tanner contends that tradition "is always a selection from the wide array of material that could not be so designated by virtue of their transmission from before and elsewhere."[16] In this giving and receiving, new things may be added that cannot be predicted from or predicated on the past.

The third problematic assumption is procedural: "The different results of transmission are neatly lined up without differences of time and place and are thereby insulated from significant challenge by one another."[17] But Tanner argues that, in fact, members of traditions do not behave this way. As traditional materials are applied in a situation, they often use them in various, and often, conflicting ways.

What does this three-pronged criticism mean for the view I am taking of these seven Lutherans through the prism of tradition? Following the sequence of Tanner's problematics, it means the following: First, it signifies that this prism is only one of many. One might analyze the subjects' histories, for example, according to their educational backgrounds, income levels, or political attitudes. Who can say which is more real, which has priority, which orders what? Neither we nor even the seven themselves can say with certainty. Second, it means we must inquire what, if anything, appears in their beliefs and practices that is new to the tradition. No matter to what degree any one of them identifies himself or herself with the early Lutheran tradition, not one of them lives in the world of that tradition. Third, it means while the subjects share some of the same cultural material—texts, scripture, sacraments, informal practices—they may employ that material in differing and conflicting ways. That is, we must look to see if they "tradition" the tradition differently.

Tanner summarizes her concerns about tradition not on the basis of postmodern philosophy but, it seems to me, out her convictions as a Barthian theologian. The shape of what is Christian is determined by God's providence, she contends, not by the finite and fallible deposits of human practice. In other words, she is troubled that tradition can be and often is idolatrous. The unity of the many Christian beliefs and practices is not in what is handed to us but in God's as-yet indeterminate future.

Tanner's analysis of these three problematics raises questions similar to that posed in chapter one: Does the use of tradition to analyze lived religion avoid or obscure criticism of the notion of tradition? Or does it add a new perspective to this criticism by showing both the power of tradition and the multiplicity of lived religious experience? I will attend to these questions indirectly in the next two chapters and more directly in the concluding chapter, which considers whether finite and fallible practices may both idolatrously obscure God and at the same time be the means by which God brings consolation.

4.
Consolation in Lived Religion: Beliefs

In this chapter, from the perspective of the early Lutheran tradition, we will examine the beliefs of the seven Lutheran co-researchers, while the following chapter focuses on their practices. Of course, my distinction between beliefs and practices in this or any religious tradition is, in the language of the medieval scholastics, more a mental than a real distinction. All beliefs have implications for practice and are themselves kinds of practices. All practices, if not belief-informed, are belief-producing.[1] Still, the distinction is helpful, especially since it is common in theology and in pastoral theology in particular. Furthermore, for reasons I shall discuss in the conclusion of the next chapter, making this distinction at the outset of the analysis will assist in assessing its outcome.

What does analyzing lived religion through the lens of that religion's tradition reveal? What does it obscure? The next two chapters provide the material with which to address these questions in the concluding chapter.

Justification

A Doctrine and a Meta-Linguistic Principle? "It's in you, and you believe in it."

Reflecting on the death of his brother Sheldon and his subsequent grief, Oscar also spoke of many things that he and Sheldon had experienced while living under the same roof and worshiping in the same church. He also briefly reminisced about his service in the military, work achievements, and his decades of hard but happy stewardship in his home congregation. Returning to his brother's death at the end of our conversation, Oscar attempted to specify how he received "some ease" for this loss. Without prompting, he referred to a key teaching in the early Lutheran tradition: "Justification by faith means God will take care of us at these difficult times. It's so strongly instilled in us that we don't get down to specifics. I don't really know how to express it. It's in you and you believe in it." What did Oscar profess as he came to the end of his reflections about his career, his church, his brother, his life? He professed that he was certain—even in the midst of his diffidence—that God cares unconditionally for the faithful like himself. Even after many decades of religious practice, faith that justifies is more something at work in him than something that he himself produces. Even Oscar's diffidence seems to testify that this caring God is someone over whom he believes that he has no power, but of whose power for his well-being he is quite convinced.

As noted in chapter two, Jenson understands the early Lutheran tradition's teaching about justification to be not so much a doctrine as a "meta-linguistic principle" that shapes certain kinds of speaking to convey the gospel-promise for humanity's unconditional well-being. A number of other co-researchers reported experiences indicating that they too may have been informed by this principle. Thus, while Ruth at first could not enumerate the activities that brought her solace during her abuse and divorce, she went on to describe that solace not so much as something she attained by those activities, but as something given to her by them—as if by a caring parent "who puts a Band-Aid" on her injury, thereby letting her know "inside" that she is "okay." Like Oscar, she found it difficult to describe this experience: "It was much, much harder to put into words. It was much more a feeling, much more just a sense of comfort about the circumstances, and I could give you examples, but it would kind of fall short." Later Ruth detailed another source of her suffering—her shame as an African American single mother: "Reading the newspaper, listening to the news of the radio, hearing other people, I feel like a stereotype. I'm just at the bottom of the heap. I don't have what it takes to get out of bed in the morning." She then became more specific about the source of her comfort for this and other difficulties: "But I've decided to run my life through a different set of filters. I turn to scripture, remember a sermon." Later, she further specified what assures her of her worth: "I have this baptism, I have this Christ."

Other co-researchers were also more specific in detailing the beliefs congruent with the Lutheran tradition that consoled them. In addition to the support of family and friends, Allison found support for her grief in a scripture frequently cited by Lutherans. "'For by grace you're saved through faith,'" she quoted. "We knew that William was saved because he believed and God so loved the world that He gave His only begotten Son. So He died for him so that William could have eternal life." In a similar reflection on his own difficulties, Robert commented, "I do look at our primary doctrine, justification by faith, to mean that my works are not important, but that my justification really does come from what God has already done for me."

In Lutheranism, as in many Christian traditions, sin is understood as the broken relationship between humanity and God. Seemingly unlike certain Christian traditions, Lutheranism teaches that humanity is sinful, but through grace is completely forgiven. Several co-researchers expressed an awareness of sin and justification congruent with this teaching. Allison commented, "I'm taught that I should forgive and that there is no greater sin—no greater or lesser sin. One is not worse than the other."

Julia claimed that sinfulness showed itself in her divorce: "We live in a broken world and we're humans. Given divinity, this wouldn't happen. But it shows how far our relationship with God has been broken." Nevertheless, Julia believes that she is fully set right with God by God, and related this belief to her claim that "justification by faith" means that she should "not let guilt drag [her] down." Having rated the item "I tried to be less sinful" on the Religious Coping Activities Scale with a score indicating that she never made the attempt, Julia elaborated on her rating with some humor, and some bite in that humor: "I don't perceive myself as terribly sinful. I don't believe there's a scale of sin. But since it [the Likert instrument] was numbered one, two, three, four—what do you know? [four-second pause]—sin is scaled."

Responding to this same item on the RCAS, Charles wryly remarked, "I never try to be more sinful. So therefore I don't try to be less sinful. I just try to be God-pleasing. I know I'm a sinner my whole life, but I don't do many wicked things, at least not consciously. And, to do less of them, I don't know even what it would be. I didn't do anything bad all day except get mad at the guy next door. But that's about it."

In summary, most of the co-researchers indicated that the doctrine of justification, or belief possibly informed by it was key to their consolation. Did any of them offer an account in which this understanding of justification appears even more clearly, and relates even more directly to the early Lutheran tradition? And did any give an account that seems significantly *less* related to the tradition?

Inside ("Faith is not separable from the believer") and Outside ("You've got to have that positive attitude") the Tradition

It seems to me that in some of the remarks of Charles, the ailing pastor of orthodox ilk, there is an account that reflects on—that strives to reflect—the early Lutheran tradition. Of his Lutheran orthodoxy, Charles wryly remarked, "I carry a copy of the Augsburg Confession in my breast pocket so that, if I'm in an accident, they'll know who to call." However, as he considered the connection between his religious beliefs and his coping with many sicknesses and surgeries, Charles spoke earnestly: "Faith is simply a part of you. Consolation was there before you began." Later in our conversation, he elaborated on these statements.

> For once-born personalities, which I think most Lutherans are, if they have been apprised of the tradition like I was, it's hardly something you think about—to invoke. The idea in popular magazines and articles on "how my faith helped me through" always sound artificial to me—they sound, in a way, contrived. They don't speak to me. Faith is not separable from the believer.

Faith and the believer are one person. There's never a point at which suddenly I realized the fact that I'm okay when I was sick. That's more like a twice-born experience. I think schooling people in the idea that I'm going to give you a faith that you can really use as a tool is an erroneous concept. It's not the way of the faith-formed personality.

What does Charles claim? First, he claims that during his illness, he did not will consoling faith. Nor, in contrast to the practices of "twice-borners," did his consolation involve repenting of past evils in order to overcome current troubles. Rather, Charles carefully argued that he was consoled prior to, perhaps even apart from, his own willing and repenting. As he reflected on his own experience, and as he pondered the Lutheran tradition—and it seems he cannot do one without doing the other—Charles described consolation as something that God already has provided. In doing so, he gave not only a fairly complete summary of that tradition, but also a sense of how he believes that four-hundred-year-old tradition has "traditioned" him. Moreover, in speaking for himself, he seemed to articulate most of the beliefs of the other co-researchers throughout their suffering.[2]

However, Charles did not represent Michael, who spoke neither out of nor for the Lutheran tradition. Indeed, my conversation with Michael included the following exchange.

> **Leonard:** As you think about how you handled your surgery, and as you think about what you understand about Lutheranism, are there any things about how you handled that event that seem to you to have something to do with being a member of the Lutheran tradition?
> **Michael:** No.

When Michael later elaborated on this response by saying that he was a member of the tradition primarily because of having married a Lutheran, he also reported a variety of beliefs and practices that bear a family resemblance to those found in other religious traditions. He identified one of those traditions as he described God's healing as contingent on his own positive—"Christian Science"—attitude: "You've got to know that you're going to be getting better." Here Michael's understanding and application of Christian Science is somewhat "traditional." While apologists for, and even critical historians of, Christian Science argue that this religious path should not be reduced to a facile form of positive thinking, none of them dispute its origins in the mind of Phineas P. Quimby of New England, who taught that "disease itself is primarily a mental phenomenon."[3]

What other traditions influence Michael's ways of experiencing consolation? One he claims as part of his rearing: his theologically conservative Baptist denomination, which has its roots in New England Puritanism. Michael displays a religious belief system and a number of related practices very similar to those of his heritage. Specifically, Michael's search for assurance is reminiscent of the lived religion of Puritans who searched the world for signs of God's purpose.[4] Like them, Michael's world is full of "signs and messages that you have to be aware of" to discern God's purposes in the world. In a manner also similar to later American evangelical piety, Michael scans this world for indicators of God's intentions for him and for what actions he should then take. Perhaps further echoing his Baptist upbringing, Michael repeatedly condemned those who use tobacco— especially those who seem to have suffered none of its ill effects: "I mean I have a co-worker who smokes like a chimney. So why did I suffer, who never smoked in his life, and hasn't done these things they talk about?" While not all Baptists have condemned the use of tobacco, some in northern states have preached that the road to hell is strewn with the leaves of this particular plant.[5]

To be sure, Michael does not make these exact claims about smokers, but in making similar claims, he makes another possibly tradition-informed belief. As noted earlier, Michael consoles himself with the belief that righteous persons will be rewarded in heaven while the less righteous—such as smokers—may not be: "Some of these other people, maybe their life won't be so good then. There'll be a reckoning along the way. Right hand and left hand." Michael's belief in an eschatological tally is clearly derived from the Matthean saying of Jesus that in the final times, sheep will be located on the right and goats on the left. While this prophecy is the common property of all Christians, it has been stressed by some—but by no means all—American Baptists, as reflected in the final clause of their arguably most famous statement of faith, the 1833 New Hampshire Confession.

> [We believe] that the end of this world is approaching: that at the last day, Christ will descend from heaven, and raise the dead from the grave to final retribution; that a solemn separation will then take place; that the wicked will be adjudged to endless punishment, and the righteous to endless joy; and that this judgment will fix the final state of men in heaven or hell, on principles of righteousness.[6]

For sure, Michael's beliefs and practices surrounding his sickness and surgery are not carbon copies of the beliefs and practices of either Christian Science or more theologically conservative Baptist traditions. It is a central premise of this book that no one's beliefs and practices are carbon copies of any tradition. Yet if it is also true that "no one . . . comes to be a human being alone,"[7] then in light of this brief historical overview and given Michael's own reports and self-assessment, it seems reasonable to judge that these other traditions influenced how he coped with his illness. Furthermore, given that both the early Lutheran tradition and its revisions generally dissuade the faithful from doing what Michael claims he does—willing their own well-being—and given his reflection that "no," the Lutheran tradition did not influence his beliefs, one may ask what, if anything, connects Michael, who met all four criteria for being a co-researcher, to Lutheranism. I will return to this question in the conclusion of the book.

If Charles typifies the norms of Lutheranism in both its tradition and in the beliefs of five other co-researchers, then is Michael the odd man out—the one of seven outside of the boundaries of the Lutheran belief system? Clearly, Michael understands his current Lutheran identity as accidental—he married a Lutheran. On the other hand, Charles, with his unbroken Lutheran lineage, believes that he not only speaks for but actually represents this four-hundred-year-old tradition. Furthermore, Charles attempts to set a boundary between Lutheranism and certain other traditions by extolling his "once-born" way of being in the world, contrasting it with that of "twice-borners." "I think once-borners have a different kind of way of going through this. Having to use your faith is more a born-again Christian type of employment than it is what I think the Lutheran baptismal identity is." But does the boundary that Charles attempts to fix, in fact, hold up? Or is it permeable? Or, to use another metaphor, are there indications of other threads woven into the fabric of Charles's faith-life and those of the other co-researchers? A closer look reveals many such indications.

Permeable Boundaries, Other Threads: "No, no, it's not Stoicism."
Throughout our conversation, Charles focused on the importance of *Gelassenheit* in his consolation. "Both the music [of church hymns] as well as the words have a very, very powerful effect. And among those hymns that we used to have in the old Missouri Synod hymnal was a section called 'Cross and Comfort.' What they all had is what the Moravians call *Gelassenheit*. This means not a resignation—it's a kind of a way of saying, letting go, letting God."

What does Charles mean by this term *Gelassenheit?* It is usually translated in words like Charles's: as the state of mind/heart of "letting be" or "letting go" in the face of adversity. *Resignatio ad infernum et mortuum*—resignation even in the face of hell and death—was how Tauler described and recommended it.[8] How does Charles's use of this schema in the face of suffering fit with his other beliefs?

To answer this question, it is helpful to briefly review those beliefs. As noted, Charles distinguished his beliefs from those of "twiceborners." He may be referring to a number of Christians whose names signify rebirth: Anabaptists such as Thomas Munzer during the Reformation, and present-day Mennonites and other related denominations. As noted earlier, during the Reformation, these Christians came under heavy fire from Lutherans for purportedly making salvation a matter of the will—just as Charles attacks twiceborners now for "using faith as a tool." Charles may also refer to those Lutherans whose beliefs and practices have been judged with some severity by the orthodox to be similar to the more traditionally twiceborn: Lutheran pietists since the 1700s and the Lutheran charismatics of the 1970s.[9] Furthermore, he employs a distinction passed on by William James between two types of religious personalities: once-borners, who have adjusted to and are happy amid the adversities of the world, versus twice-borners, who are not.[10] Given his knowledge of church history, concern for contemporary Lutheran matters, and interest in lived religion, Charles appears to be quite cleverly referencing all of the above.

Yet while Charles distinguishes his beliefs from those of the twice-born, he very much speaks their language when he refers to *Gelassenheit* and therefore—either intentionally or in spite of himself—holds beliefs that cannot be divorced from theirs. *Gelassenheit* is an approach to suffering very dear to these twice-born folk, as revealed in Klassen's study into the traditions and practices of caring in the Anabaptist tradition. "The chief characteristic of well-being [for the Anabaptists] was *gelassenheit,* the ancient mystical, non-resistant surrender to the will of God, the abandonment of all self-will, all struggling for security, and all attempts to save one's soul and body. True *gelassenheit* promised cessation of inner conflict and disharmony over all the 'ills that flesh is heir to,' including physical ailments."[11]

It is conceivable that, in Charles's mind, *Gelassenheit* somehow has a place in the heart of the Reformation teaching on justification. Especially in his 1519–1521 "Operationes in Psalmos," Luther tried to use Tauler's mystical term not as an attitude produced by human will but as an activity spontaneously produced in the believer by the promise of God's love. However, the degree to which Luther succeeded in doing so is questionable, especially since the term became a favorite among those whom Luther and his followers derisively labeled as enthusiasts. Luther's early usage may have been vestigial of ideas he thought he had left behind.[12]

Charles moves with ease across the centuries that separate his lived religious experience from the early Lutheran tradition and Lutheran orthodoxy. Accordingly, it is also very likely that Charles has in mind—it is hard to imagine that he does not—the use of this term by the leading figure of the theological movement with which Charles most closely identifies, Johann Gerhard (1582–1637).[13] At a point in his writings, Gerhard adapted portions of Tauler's mystical approach, including *resignatio,* in a way that he thought fit within Luther's later theology and most especially within the Augsburg Confession and the Formula of Concord.[14] However, after much effort, he concluded that it would not fit—that this approach was ineluctably linked to synergism, which, as noted earlier, proposes that the human will cooperates with the grace of God. For Gerhard and the later orthodox Lutherans, even *Gelassenheit,* or adopting an attitude of resignation before hell itself, turned out to be a kind of willing by just another name.[15] Rather, *Gelassenheit* found a more permanent abode in later years, among Pietists whom the orthodox regarded as their arch opponents. In arguing for the necessity of spiritual rebirth through *Gelassenheit,* they judged that the Pietists had so conditioned the unconditionality of justification by faith as to have negated it.[16]

Gelassenheit, then, whatever the intent of those who use the term, often seems to go against the grain of the gospel as defined by the early Lutheran tradition. It is surprising, therefore, that Charles would focus on such an approach when he suffered, given his orthodox Lutheran orientation. It is also surprising that he used a concept that lies not only outside Lutheranism, but also outside Christianity—in Stoicism.

Charles addressed this as he further reflected on what *Gelassenheit* meant for him in the face of his multiple medical problems.

> And I would say that *Gelassenheit* almost sounds like Stoicism. And I think Stoicism falls short because Stoicism seems like metaphysical sour grapes where people say, "Well, these things aren't all that hot, and life itself isn't all that hot, so what can I expect?" But *Gelassenheit* means "No, I'm just going to give myself over to a larger reality. I don't pretend to understand and I don't want to understand. I don't have to understand. There's no fight and things are all right." *Gelassenheit* is not resignation exactly, because that seems to be Stoic—that you do not really care that something bad happened to you and you just sort of struggle through it and take it.

And yet it was precisely as *resignatio* that *Gelassenheit* was translated into Latin in Gerhard's day, and it is as "resignation" that it is usually translated into English today. Furthermore, what Charles describes as his own experience of *Gelassenheit* sounds similar to that commended by classical Stoicism—without the sour grapes, if they were ever part of it.[17] Nor is Charles's voicing of a somewhat Stoic attitude surprising, since his suffering involved the disappointment of becoming repeatedly ill at the very point of retirement, and then "being under [medical] orders all the time . . . [suffering] total loss of control. Total loss of autonomy. Total loss of identity." Furthermore, what Charles describes is at the heart of Gerhard's theology, for the classical Stoics, among others, were an important source for Charles's orthodox forebear.[18] Gerhard exercised a kind of *Gelassenheit* by finally abandoning his struggle to direct this material to Christian ends. However, Charles seemed not to be resigned but to be struggling on as he, without being queried on the matter, protested vigorously—perhaps too much—"No, no, it's not Stoicism."

Are Charles's intellectual struggles, in effect, defenses from his own suffering, themselves Stoic thought-exercises to ward off the passion and pain of his illness? Riding "the conveyor belt" of modern medicine, not knowing whether he would be dead or alive at the end of the ride, Charles clung to that which offered respect and security. Is this arcana with which Charles then and we now concern ourselves? If so, it is not only lively arcana, but a matter of spiritual life and death for Charles. It indicates that, despite himself, Charles may hold to a way of experiencing consolation that has many elements of what he regards as twice-born religion.[19] It indicates that even the most orthodox of the seven—the one who consciously attempts to norm his beliefs and practices according to the early Lutheran tradition—holds some beliefs at variance with that tradition. It indicates that the one who seems most *within* the tradition may share a fair amount with the one most manifestly outside of it—Michael. It suggests that it is worth seriously considering Tanner's claim about all religious beliefs and practices: "The drawing of sharp boundaries never seems to settle anything."[20] In the concluding chapter, we shall consider Tanner's claim more closely. In order to do so, it is helpful now to consider her claim's applicability to the accounts of some of the other co-researchers.

Other Ways of Being Lutheran and Being Justified: "Do I defer ignorantly? No, I defer thoughtfully."

In her account of seeking consolation during her abuse, divorce, and the aftermath that was frightening for both herself and her children, Ruth frequently and pointedly referred to a number of specifically Lutheran sources: her "love" of Luther's Small Catechism, her "fear and love" of God, which she relates to passages from that catechism, her rich experiences with the Lutheran liturgy, and her regular reading of the *Lutheran Book of Worship*. Similarly, her experience of justification—being consoled by God, who through external means, like a mother's kiss and care for her child, provides assurance—fits well within the Lutheran tradition. Finally, Ruth's seeking consolation by recalling the words, "I have this baptism, I have this Christ" almost replicates Luther's own method and words for fending off despair.

But just how specifically Lutheran is Ruth's consoling recollection? A closer look suggests that she is informed not only by the Lutheran tradition, but also by certain approaches that some African American Christians take in the face of difficulties. These approaches have been described by a number of black social scientists who have criticized religious coping research that seems to devalue them. Interestingly, though perhaps not surprisingly, Ruth makes a number of these very same criticisms.

What are the salient points of this research? In "Religious Orientation as a Coping Resource among Black Americans," Cunningham "investigates black religiosity, observing the roles of prayer, the black church, minister and other religious activities that are included in a survival ideology."[21] Cunningham does not attempt to measure the merits of religion as a coping resource among black Americans, but rather simply to describe how it functions. For black Americans, many biblical beliefs "prepare one to accept crisis as part of life, guarantee one's ability to cope with any situation successfully and finally guarantee an inexhaustible, ever-present, continuously available access to supernatural resources."[22] Cunningham's study suggests that some African Americans cope with stress and suffering not in spite of but because of their belief in God's control throughout stress and suffering.

In their article "The Relationship of God Control and Internal Locus of Control to Intrinsic Religious Motivation, Coping and Purpose in Life," Jackson and Coursey directly address the issue of God's providence and human agency. They do so first by countering "a common secular perspective . . . that believing God is an active agent in one's life requires relinquishing a sense of personal or internal control."[23] That is to say, they differ with social scientists who assume that the more one ascribes control to God over the affairs of this world, the less power one feels to change those matters. Jackson and Coursey counter this "psychological perspective" with a hypothesis based on an aspect of the African American religious experience: "There is no intrinsic theological or rational necessity for a negative relationship to exist between God control and [human] locus of control."[24] The authors conducted an empirical study among African Americans that they believe confirmed their hypothesis: "While this may be contrary to some popular notions about relying on God to solve one's problems . . . the formulation that effective coping is achieved via personal control *through* God . . . is suggested by the data in this study."[25] In other words, Jackson and Coursey propose that many whites' perspectives on how people cope with suffering may not describe the experiences of some African Americans.

Like Jackson and Coursey, Ruth counters a similar "secular" perspective. Again, Ruth reveals that, like the subjects of Jackson and Coursey's research, she experiences no correlation between ascribing power to God and avoiding problems on earth. On the Religious Coping Activities Scale she had endorsed two items with the highest rating: "I let God solve my problems for me" and "I prayed or read the Bible to keep my mind off my problems." When I invited her to elaborate on the reasons for her ratings, she responded, "I think sometimes I see a secular bias in thinking that activities like praying and reading the Bible are avoidance, keep people from doing what needs to be done."

Ruth commented, with some force and feeling, on the very name of the sub-scale on which these items were listed: "Religious Avoidance." "I have trouble with the term 'religious avoidance.' You know, it sounds like in other words, 'Oh, so you run off and hide in your

closet and read your Bible while the rest of us are out taking on the
world and reading the *Financial Times.*'"

Ruth believes that the more power she attributes to God, the more
empowerment she experiences. She elaborated on that belief by commenting on another label—"Religious Deferral"—of a sub-scale of
the Religious Coping Styles Scale: "Do I defer ignorantly? No. I defer
thoughtfully." Describing herself as an "impatient person," a trait
that "works well in my business," she explained, "You know I want an
outcome, but sometimes I have to sit back and kind of thank God
that I don't have to figure this or that out—God's going to figure it
out. And so I just need to do the pieces that I can seem to do. So, I
need to go to work, to pay my bills. But then, I need to leave other
parts of my life in His hands."

In *Soul Theology: The Heart of American Black Culture,* Cooper-
Lewter and Mitchell analyze the role of what they call some of the
"core beliefs" in that tradition: "In Africa and Afro-America, the most
treasured and trusted word about our life here on earth is that God is
in charge."[26] Certainly, Ruth's case history reveals that her most treasured and trusted belief throughout her suffering was something
quite similar, if not the same: "I'm going to sit back and kind of thank
God that I don't have to figure this out and that God's going to figure
it out."

To be sure, Ruth's style of religious coping is not the only one exercised by urban, African American single mothers, or in the lived religion of the many millions of other blacks in America.[27] The African
American Christian tradition is not a monolith, but a mosaic of
many different ways of living with God.[28] Ruth displays a way of religious coping that is not typical of all African Americans, but appears
to be characteristic of some.

The fact that Ruth displays features of coping and being consoled
that are common to both Lutheranism and to some African Americans certainly accords with her self-description as an "Afro-Saxon."
Not only are African American Lutherans one piece of the African
American Christian mosaic, they also are a piece of the mosaic of
contemporary Lutheranism. Therefore, as members of the Lutheran
church, some African Americans may display distinctive ways—but

by no means ways contrary to those of nonblack Lutherans—of seeking consolation, thereby reconstituting the "core beliefs" of the Lutheran tradition. In doing so, they do not simply add themselves to this tradition, but give it a shape that was not seminally present in its past.

Outward Signs of God's Favor? "[I was] successful in my sales endeavors. . . . It had a lot to do with my bringing up as a Lutheran."

As Oscar reminisced about his life and that of his deceased brother, he also reflected on growing up as Lutheran: "We were taught the catechism and we learned it, and what was meant by the Commandments and so forth. I don't think it's right to say, but I think that kind of training hopefully made us somewhat better persons, more forgiving persons."

Oscar detailed how this training strengthened him through the tribulations he experienced as a noncommissioned officer during World War II: "I worked with the lieutenant in charge to do as much as I could for the enlisted men during that difficult time. I knew just how to say to him, 'Sir, do you think it would be a good idea if we tried it this way?' And I just tried to be helpful." Oscar paused as he related this, then commented, "I don't know whether this makes a difference." In response, I said, "Well, you're saying that it's made a difference to you." He replied, "No question, and it stayed with me all my life!" Then Oscar spoke about his sales career: "You have to gain the respect of your customers. I think my bringing up in this faith has helped me in my business life to get the kind of respect necessary to be successful in my sales endeavors." Referring to his good relational skills, and his consequent ability to garner important accounts, he concluded, "I think it had a lot to do with my bringing up as a Lutheran. But maybe that has nothing to do with what we're talking about here." Again I answered, "Well, what's important is that it's important to you."

As I made this last—possibly pastoral—response, I was also weighing the significance of what Oscar was sharing for my investigation. Does the consolation of God show itself in external signs in the manner that Oscar described? Without elaborating on this complex issue, it is fair to say that some Christian traditions, more than others, propose that the consolation of God has outward features and predictable consequences. Typically Lutherans have taught that the consolation of God has few, if any, such features and consequences, as exemplified in the remark by von Loewenich cited earlier, "The Christian life can never be fully identified with the empirical life that we lead. The Christian life is an object of faith and, as such, it is hidden. What we see is never the real thing; only God and faith see this innermost core."[29]

Where does such a rendering of normative Lutheran teaching locate Oscar's claims? Does the Lutheran theology of the cross obviate the achievement of both spiritual righteousness and worldly forms of well-being as manifestations of the grace of God? Does the normative theology of this tradition rule out claims like Oscar's, which, despite his stated intentions, do in fact contain a bit of a boast?

Yes and no. The "yes," as expressed by von Loewenich above, is clear. This sentiment is also evident in many of the remarks of the co-researchers, especially the clergy. For example, Julia asserted that "following Christ means preaching political sermons and guaranteed suffering." Charles lashed out at "victory theologies," and, eschewing success through religion, opted instead for a "crucified God who is hard to sell." Robert was very careful to claim that receiving communion before his surgery did not necessarily *cause* his high blood pressure to drop—even though it appeared to be related.

The "no" is less obvious in both Lutheran tradition and practice, but it may be found in the tradition, surprisingly, in Luther himself. For example, in his *Commentary on Genesis* Luther observes that, while Joseph sojourned in Egypt, he suffered many indignities—including an unjust jailing. Yet, Luther contends, Joseph was consoled in the midst of this particular difficulty—not once, but twice: "And this was his first consolation, when his conscience within was gladdened, made peaceful, and healed, and his life and his well-being were restored."[30] This "first consolation," directed toward the inner person of Joseph, did, however, affect his subsequent success and well-being in the world.

> The other comfort is external. The Lord gave him grace or favor
> and it is favor that is felt. . . . Accordingly, while others who

were being kept in the same prison were groaning, wailing, and raging, Joseph alone was resolute in heart. He taught and comforted the rest, although he was in the same danger. Yet he did not conduct himself otherwise than as if he were completely free and altogether certain of his liberation.[31]

As Luther further notes, Joseph's shrewd conduct and worldly wisdom benefited not only himself, but ultimately was also the means by which God saved his family from famine. In some ways Joseph displayed something of the confident worldliness that Luther understood to be the reflex of consolation. And in some ways, it seems that Oscar does also.

Are sales success and productive negotiations with military superiors the kind of fruits that Luther had in mind as "external comforts"? It is hard to avoid asking this question, but it is difficult to answer because it assumes—somewhat more than I do—that the thought-world of Luther can be directly applied to beliefs and practices now. Nevertheless, the dominant opinion of theologians who interpret Luther and the early Lutheran tradition clearly rules out anything that looks like victory theology—that is, any belief that one may win in the world via one's right relationship with God. However, it is possible that Luther then, and Lutherans like Oscar now, may hold beliefs that are hard to locate within Lutheranism, but that are equally hard to banish completely from it.

A closer look at Ruth's story has indicated how one may be very much a part of both the Lutheran tradition and another broader Christian tradition. Oscar's account indicates that one may espouse beliefs that are very much at odds with this tradition and yet are still a part of it. Another look at Robert's interview indicates that even the key doctrine of the early Lutheran tradition may produce beliefs at odds with that very doctrine.

Justified but Predominantly Sinful: "And bad feelings rather than positive came out of it. . . . It was kind of just me and God at the time going through that part."

While Robert reported that he was frequently surprised by grace during his illness, he claimed—with much sighing and rapid speech—that throughout his financial hardship he was plagued by fears that

God was showing displeasure over Robert's foolishness in bringing about that hardship in the first place. As noted earlier, Robert claimed the key doctrine of Lutheranism as something he himself professes: "My justification really does come from my faith in God." However, after he made this profession, he paused, and then added a disjunctive claim: "But I could not shake that [tribulation] during the process of the whole thing." In other words, Robert revealed that he does not believe his faith helped him through this particular crisis. Moreover, he believes that in some ways his theological understanding only accentuated the suffering the crisis brought him. Thus, unlike the pastors Julia and Charles who report that because they profess they are justified by faith, they therefore experience little worry about their sin, Robert professes the same faith but still feels unforgiven and trapped inside of his sin. Robert is aware that he is experiencing what is well within the bounds of his tradition's teaching about justification and yet somehow in opposition to it.

> There is a sense in what we Lutherans say about sin, that sin is something that we can't ourselves get out of. For me, it was a feeling that I couldn't extricate myself from. You know, that I needed something greater than myself to get out of that. I kind of just kept pushing myself, and the depression, worry, and doubt got worse by doing that. And bad feelings rather than positive came out of it.

Robert connects his unremitting sense of sinfulness with the belief that God was disciplining him: "'You're going to learn through the school of hard knocks.' Even if that's not my theology." To paraphrase an earlier citation of Gerhard Forde, Robert's theology may have been sweet, but his lived religion was sour.

Robert describes his experience of depression, worry, and doubt as "trapped in sin . . . just me and God at the time going through that part. . . . God was disciplining me." Robert's suffering bears many of the marks of what the early Lutheran tradition called *Anfechtung*: *Anfechtung* as that from which the faithful pray to God to deliver them; *Anfechtung* as the immediate result of a game God may play with the faithful anyway; *Anfechtung* as that which strains—sometimes breaks—the trust of the faithful. And while *Anfechtung* is always for the good, it is never experienced as a good. This tension is buried within the doctrine of justification. It is a tension explicated in the theology of the cross. And, as we shall see next, it is a tension apparently made manifest in the lived religion of some co-researchers.

Theology of the Cross

In her article "Do Theories of Atonement Foster Abuse?" Leanne Van Dyk considers some of the same issues examined by Deanna Thompson and Elizabeth Moltmann-Wendell about the potential harmful effects of atonement theologies for women and arrives at similar conclusions:

> In spite of the seriousness of the accusation that atonement theology fosters abuse, I do not believe it is a charge that holds. First of all, it is my observation that some feminist theologians have frequently neglected a simple, although crucial, logical distinction. Admitting that Christian theology in general and atonement theology in particular have at times, even at many times, been used abusively does not lead to the inevitable conclusion that Christian theology in general and atonement theology in particular are always abusive or necessarily abusive.[32]

Van Dyk suggests that, to a degree, the question of the abusive quality of atonement theology for men as well as women calls not only for theoretical discussion but also for empirical inquiry. That is to say, she calls for investigations of the theology of atonement and into the lived religion of those who have appropriated that theology. By looking at how the co-researchers may have appropriated the theology of the cross in the midst of their suffering, I will investigate similar concerns.

"God is frightening."

In the midst of her abusive marriage, throughout her anxious hovering at the edge of poverty during her divorce, and in her subsequent struggle to secure a livelihood for herself and her children, Ruth believed that God sent her each of these forms of suffering. Furthermore, she specifically connects her own suffering with Jesus' suffering and death on the cross. Having agreed "not at all" with the RCAS item "I didn't need to suffer because Jesus suffered for me," she expressed what she meant by that rating. "Maybe it seemed like it was a little bit of a cop-out to say that 'I didn't need the suffering' that made me rate it the way I did. You know, somehow it seemed to signal to me that I could just skip the suffering or 'Jesus did that and I don't really need it.' I think that some of how God is revealed to us isn't without suffering."

However, this last thought was not a source of consolation for Ruth—at that time or in retrospect. Instead, she directly connects the suffering she believes God sent her with her conflicted "fear and love" of both her husband and God, which "can make you nuts. . . . You can't get right with that." Ruth further connects her fear of God to her fear of the wrath of God. For example, she describes how her own reading of the Book of Jeremiah aroused this fear.

> God is really beating down Israel, the Babylonians having come in and God having raised up Nebuchadnezzar and really kind of struggling with that horrible, horrible tension. All these horrible things—sieges and plagues and young men fainting in the streets. While you're reading Jeremiah, it's terrifying, it's overwhelming. It's like I could be judged for what I did today. I could be judged for what I said to people. I know that I can't run away from Him; I do have to face Him, but doing it is frightening. God is frightening.

Accordingly, Ruth understood her custody fight for her son as a punishment from God.

> It's like God said, "All right, you want an answer to your prayer. I'm going to strip all these things away now. I'm going to take away your sense of security, take away your husband, take away these friends and put you at odds with your mother, and going to make you be—you know, many miles from home and kind of isolated."

Commenting on the same item on the RCAS, Allison claimed that it "did not apply" to her after her husband's tragic death since "I still felt like I was suffering." Allison had heard others say that if she had faith she would not suffer, but "that was just not the way it was." Like Ruth, she believes that God sent her suffering, and like Ruth, she does not seem to find comfort in that belief. Furthermore, her tribulation appears to be connected with wondering why God would do so. Thus being told that "the Lord won't give you more than you can handle. . . . He obviously thought that I could handle this" not only brought her no respite, but made her suffer more: "But at the time it was very real and I questioned myself and I questioned the Lord, 'How much more will I have to handle?'" Like Robert during his economic hardship, Allison's suffering was intensified by her awareness of the faith-life she had previously experienced. "I guess I felt guilty because being raised in the church I thought I shouldn't have the feelings that I was feeling. And so I wondered if my faith was as strong as what it should be because I just didn't know if I could handle what was happening."

Reflecting on his financial woes, Robert also found that the saying "God would not give him more than he could handle" only increased his suffering.

> I just always find that saying to be cold. When somebody's going through something that seems to be overwhelming, for example, the business problems I was having, you don't see the solution in a saying like that. Instead you ask, "Do I not have enough faith and so I don't see the answer? Am I that far from God or is He that far from me? What is the concept that you're trying to get across to me here?" You're thinking, "Man, I don't know if I can make it through this," and somebody says, "Well, you know, God will never give you more than you can bear." That's not how it feels, though.

Despite his seminary-informed theology of suffering, Robert wondered during his financial difficulties if God were not punishing him.

> I really did examine my life and said, "What all went wrong? There must be some things that I've done or didn't do that this is related to." Even though I think that's poor theology. Because I yelled at somebody today or didn't read my Bible or whatever—I coveted my next-door neighbor's new car—God doesn't say, "Okay, you're going to have economic disaster this week and cancer next week." But during the economic disaster, that's exactly what I wondered, if God had done just that.

Reflecting on the desolate periods of Joseph's captivity—and with a mind to the tribulations of Christians anywhere—Luther simply commented, "The game is very unpleasant to us and bitter."[33] In the midst of this game, the faithful do not perceive any game plan. Furthermore, Luther does not suggest that they would be consoled even if they did. Rather, in the midst of such unpleasantness, bitterness, suffering, and doubt, there is no consolation. Is the desolation experienced by Allison, Ruth, and Robert tradition-specific or even tradition-induced? Of course, it is hard—indeed, arguably categorically impossible—to answer this question. However, it is certain that these three Lutherans believe that their tradition contributed to their experience of this particular kind of suffering. Furthermore, it is certain that their understanding of Lutheranism is not idiosyncratic. This tradition teaches that persons like Ruth may face the wrath of God if they do not keep the commandments. Clearly it warns that those like Robert who feel trapped in sin cannot remove themselves from the trap, and, furthermore, that if they try to, they will only wedge themselves deeper into it. And clearly the tradition teaches that God has a "why" for suffering like Allison's, but that her—and our—natural inclination to pursue such "whys" will wreck the soul.

An understanding of the early Lutheran tradition helps one locate the beliefs of Ruth, Robert, and Allison within what Thompson and Gerrish have called Hiddenness I—questions about the good will of God for us in times of trouble. However, as noted earlier, in that same tradition there is talk of another hiddenness: that God is hiddenly present with those who suffer and thereby offers consolation. This teaching also shows itself in some of the remarks of the co-researchers.

"God's will is not for suffering." "God . . . is not someone jerking me around this way and that."

Having suffered with, and been treated for, clinically diagnosed depression in the aftermath of her divorce, Julia expressed a kind of theology of the cross in claiming that she believed that God could bring light to her darkness, bring some creation out of her experience of chaos. However, she carefully qualified how she believed God was involved in that suffering. "Christ's suffering in life and on the cross is related to a gift of grace from God. It has nothing to do, in my mind, with the suffering that would happen to a human being because of our relationships or illness or whatever." Julia distinguished her experience of God's presence in such suffering from the kind of suffering one might experience from following Christ.

> If I'm walking the way of Christ, that's guaranteed suffering. Someone said to me here [in the congregation], "We don't want you to preach any political sermons." And I said, "Well, then, how can I preach? I'm preaching Jesus Christ and Christ crucified—that's the most political thing you can do." But was I caused to suffer through a divorce because Jesus suffered on the cross? I don't equate those two things. I don't equate taking up a cross to what happens by being alive and human. When I sprain my ankle, I'm not suffering with Jesus. Jesus is with me, with my sprained ankle and—darn it anyway—but I don't see those two sufferings as the same.

Reflecting on her divorce, Julia claimed that she makes no correlations between her suffering and the will of God.

> God's will is not for the divorce. God's will is not for suffering. The divorce was not the will of God—although I can't know the will of God. God wants wholeness for God's people, and had Frank and I been able to achieve that, that would have been the optimum way to live. But we couldn't. We loused it up early on. To go on living together and not giving either of us an opportunity for the fullness of life—I don't think would have been the right thing either. It shows how far our relationship with God is broken, I believe.

Even given this broken relationship and the reality of sin, Julia did not "feel particularly sinful." Looking for some "good that can come" from her experience, Julia believes that her divorce has helped her counsel those about to marry: "You can rarely prevent a couple from making it to the altar, because by the time they come to your office, they already have the reception hall. But you can help them understand what's happening when they talk to each other, or don't talk to each other."

Charles expressed convictions similar to Julia's. He could not "finger" this God—he can never clearly discern God's revelation in the world. To search for God "means you're not going to find God, because God is found in the cross." Charles further linked this notion of God's paradoxical presence to the Lutheran tradition: "We Lutherans always talk about 'in, with, and under.' We're trying to say that God's working is kind of mysterious and a lot of times oblique and indirect." As he pondered his experience of illness, he perceived that God came to him indirectly and surprisingly through a clearly non-Christian book on spirituality, about which he has no "spooky ideas."

For Charles, the cross provides not a program for how to face suffering, but assurance from God: "I think that Lutherans have the best faith for rough times. We live in a fallen world as fallen creatures. . . . We sort of expect that things are not going to be rosy: People can be mean and things can be bad. People always said this is Lutheran pessimism or Lutheran realism." However, Charles believes that this is the anthropological correlate of the theology of the "crucified God who is hard to sell." Like Julia, Charles believes that the will of God has nothing to do with his own negative event or that of anyone else. Therefore, he directly challenged the theology of the Hidden God: "I didn't focus on God's actions when I was sick. God is more the environment in which I live rather than someone who is playing tricks on me or jerking me around this way or the other." To be sure, Charles believes that God is involved in all things, but he added, "My measure of faith is to say I'll let God figure these things out and I'll ask Him when I get there."

When I asked Oscar if he believed there was a relationship between his brother's death and the will of God, he responded, "No, I don't think about things like that." Like the other co-researchers, Michael cannot make sense of the will of God in relationship to his heart ailment. However, he cannot make complete sense of it through natural explanations either. "Now I know a guy who's a chain smoker. I mean, he's like a chimney all day. He's seventy-two years old. . . . He goes out and plays golf all day. You don't wish anything on him, but he should be dead if you—all the medical things you read. So why me, who never smoked in his life and hasn't done these things they talk about?" Unlike the other co-researchers, Michael reported that he finds some consolation in believing that those who are less moral than he will face God's "reckoning" in the life to come.

Consoling Beliefs

The theology of the cross and suffering in the Lutheran tradition is complex, nuanced, and varied. It teaches—or more accurately, warns—that God works in an alien manner by sending suffering. It also teaches—or proclaims—that God cares for those who suffer and dissuades them from dwelling on God's alien work. The reports of these seven Lutherans reveal similarly complex, nuanced, and varied understandings of the relationship between God and human suffering. Neither those who make correlations between their negative events and the will of God, nor those who deny the possibility of such correlations, express beliefs outside the norm of their tradition. Furthermore, most of them expressed their beliefs with a sense of personal urgency and earnestness, focusing on them for significant portions of their interviews. In their lived religion, the will of God, their suffering, and all suffering, was a lived reality.

Only Oscar claimed that he did not struggle with tribulation. Only Charles protested that, during his illness, he was not afflicted with anything remotely like *Anfechtung:* "It was a bad experience. And it confronted me with death. But it didn't say to me that there ain't no God, or that God hates me, or God is not alive." However, after he made this protest, Charles paused and then reflected that, in other difficult times, he has come close to tribulation: "I've been tempted many, many times to unbelief. But, I've always withstood the temptation." He follows this reflection with one that echoes the teachings of the early Lutheran tradition: "I withstood that temptation because the God I believe in is so impervious to the attacks of reason."

May anything further be said of those who directly linked their negative events to the will of God? Given the concerns of Van Dyk, Ray, and Thompson about the possible effects of atonement theologies on women, I find it interesting and perhaps significant that two of the three co-researchers who most directly made these links were Ruth and Allison, the two laywomen in my study. Furthermore, they clearly attributed these beliefs to teachings in the early Lutheran tradition. Did Ruth and Allison appropriate these teachings about suffering in a way that brought them more suffering? They themselves believe that they did. Believing that God had a reason for the death of her husband, Allison suffered even more because of that belief. Believing that God metes out suffering on those who do not do God's will, Ruth similarly suffered something much like *Anfechtung*. For both these women, as for many men and women in the Lutheran tradition, it seems that the God of wrath hovers eerily above the God of grace. Even Charles, whose theology rules out the workings of such a God, nevertheless has come close to encountering the specter of that God.

Does worry about a condemnation by this hidden God ever dissipate for these co-researchers? Is there a resolution between their beliefs in the God who condemns and the God who saves? In the realm of beliefs, such a resolution does not appear to occur for all of them. However, as we shall see in the next chapter, their religious practices reduced this tension for some of these co-researchers, and may be the means by which others arrived at the beliefs that spared them tribulation. That is to say, for most of these co-researchers consolation occurred through their experience of the goodness of God mediated by various practices. Through their doing so, we shall see how the distinction between their beliefs and their practices—as described in this chapter and the next—collapses.

5.
Consolation in Lived Religion: Practices

❧•❦

This chapter continues my investigation of consolation in Lutheran lived religion by focusing on the various practices of which the co-researchers were either the subject or the object. For most of them, the quality of their beliefs was closely related to those practices, and to the kinds of relationships they have, or do not have, with other persons. This close relationship of beliefs to practices and interpersonal relations is very congruent with the summary of consolation I put forth at the close of chapter two.

> The tradition proposes that humanity has no essence and that it has only a disconsolate existence apart from a right relationship with God. It also teaches that God does not bestow this consoling relationship directly on any of us but offers it to all of us only through the ministrations of other Christians.

In this chapter, I shall note that not only regarding the analysis above but also regarding a variety of related topics—the use of scripture, the use of reason, and the goodness of creation—the co-researchers reported practices remarkably congruent with the Lutheran tradition. Yet I shall note a departure from that tradition in their seeming inability to find in it resources to combat social sources of their suffering.

Bedeviled by God: "It was kind of me and God ... going through that part."

At the close of the last chapter, we noted how three of the co-researchers—Ruth, Robert, and Allison—experienced tribulation, not consolation. Ruth after her abandonment and divorce, Robert during his financial difficulties, and Allison in her grief each experienced something like tribulation, each doubting their right relationship with God. For example, as Ruth worried about "being judged today for what I said and did," and Robert, during the depression that accompanied his financial troubles, felt "worse, not better, as I tried to pull myself out of those feelings," they were each aware of something like their sinful existence. Ironically, Robert reported that during that financial hardship it was precisely because his relationship with God was immediate (that is to say, not mediated by the witness of other believers) that it did not comfort but bedeviled him: "It was kind of just me and God at the time, you know, going through that part." Similarly, in the darkest periods of her grief and loneliness following her husband's death, Allison asked God how long she would have to handle alone all of her mounting spiritual and material concerns. In the midst of her marital discord and afterwards, Ruth was distanced from all who had been close to her—family, friends, and God. In sum, it seems that to the degree they experienced themselves to be separated from others, Ruth, Robert, and Allison experienced tribulation from God.

These co-researchers also experienced tribulation when they believed that God had for no understandable reason caused, and yet remained above and beyond, their suffering. That is to say, in the language of the early Lutheran tradition, when these co-researchers concerned themselves with the Hidden God—that is, to the degree that they made lonely attributions about a disembodied God (keeping in mind Forde's description of the Hidden God as "no-body")—they experienced tribulation. For example, not only Allison but also Robert had heard the saying that God would not cause them more suffering than they could bear, but that belief only seemed to make the suffering of both more unbearable.

How then did these persons receive consolation? It appears that they were consoled by being connected through various interpersonal means to the promise of their unconditional right relationship with God. For example, in contrast to his self-imposed isolation from others and consequent lack of consolation from God during his "financial disaster," Robert related that, during his illness, "immediately, the community was there . . . through them God was present." He then explicitly described the form of *Anfechtung* that "not going through it without others" spared him: "I didn't seem to come up with that response of saying, 'Why me, God? Why are you doing this to me?'" Similarly, Allison reported that she suffered when she asked, "Why did I have to go through these things alone?"[1] Without hesitation, Allison then described the ways in which her congregation was the embodied means of easing the torment of such questioning: "I think the church is the people—that's what makes it the church. And they were a very important part, and still are today, in helping us get through this."

Through the ministry of others, therefore, it appears that both Robert and Allison were directed from the absconding God *(Deus absconditus)* toward the gracious God *(Deus revelatus)* who was made manifest through that ministry. Likewise, Ruth believed that through her baptism, a humanly transmitted means of grace, "God . . . reveal[ed] Himself to me." Ruth also turned to scripture as a source of consolation: "One of the ways that I can turn and have faith, is to read the Bible. Because that narrative charged me up. It means something. It reveals itself to me. And it's as alive for me as another person." God's revelation and scripture's aliveness (which is like that of one person communicating to another) were commingled in her consolation.

In many ways the experiences of these three co-researchers reflects the premise of the early Lutheran tradition that, while God alone is the source of consolation, it is mediated in ministry. Solace through other persons was not received only by Allison, Robert, and Ruth— the three who reported experiences most like *Anfechtung* when they were left face to face with God. For most of the seven, it was the humanly transmitted means of consolation—scripture, the priesthood of all believers, and apparently to a lesser degree, the sacraments—that brought them consolation.

The Means of Consolation: Scripture and Sacraments

Scripture: "Someone else has given them to you."
The Lutheran tradition teaches that there are specific means—scripture, prayer, and the sacraments—through which one may receive consolation. The co-researchers gave accounts of how they did so. Ruth turned to the readings in the daily lectionary of the *Lutheran Book of Worship:* "I kind of got a passage familiarity of the Bible and it became my text." Later in our conversation, she elaborated on what she meant by "passage familiarity."

> I would look at a situation in a Bible story and I would think, "What's the challenge of faith, and to faith, here? What's going to work out with the players in this situation? There's someone who's being deceptive here, and someone who's being deceived. Here's a person who has faith, here's a person who has no faith—they're all in this situation together and what's the outcome?" And then I'd look for an historical piece from the Old Testament and I'd ask, "How did that play out?" And what the Bible narrative said to me was this: "If you have faith, you can walk into this unspeakable situation with your ex-husband and come out alive on the other side."

Scripture was alive for Ruth, like persons who, in sharing their stories, become part of one's own story. Through that aliveness scripture communicated to her that she would live. Additionally, Ruth claimed that the Lutheran liturgy brought her comfort.

> I have a favorite Bach cantata. And shortly after my husband abandoned me, I ended up back at [a large metropolitan congregation]. And just sort of out of the clear blue, they did that cantata. And I couldn't control myself. I was sitting in church just weeping openly. And the same thing with very, very moving sermons. The pastor would have a particular take on something that had been quite troubling for me up to that point. And I'd hear it and say, "Oh, I get it."

However, Ruth quickly noted that she could not easily identify how these religious means brought her comfort: "So, it's like something gets revealed. And I don't know [if] it's something that's secret. It's like you can't really talk about it." Again, she connected the power of scripture to comfort with the power of a person—a caring mother—who provides solace: "Somehow you feel . . . okay."

Just as Ruth used the image of a caring parent to describe the means of consolation she experienced through scripture, Robert and Allison located much of the Bible's consolation in its being a text passed on to them by those closest to them. Allison meditated on "just common verses that we've known because we've been brought up in the church from the time we were very young." Like the other co-researchers, she read scripture not for any particular information but because she was looking for comfort. "I would take it to bed. I had difficulty sleeping, and so I was hoping that it would cause me to become tired, so I was going to start at Genesis and just read all the way through the Bible. So I just used it as a pastime. It was nothing that I would have to think particularly hard about, just reading that would relax me."

The Lutheran tradition teaches that the means of consolation are external to the one consoled. In a number of practices that he pointedly related to this tradition, Charles was comforted by reading scripture and scripture-based hymns during his medical treatment. Moreover, he emphasized that he had no sense that these were means he employed but saw them rather as "gifts" handed to him by the Lutheran tradition. "Hymn 333 of the *Lutheran Book of Worship:* 'Oh Lord, Take Thou My Hand and Lead Me.' I read that. I really believe in the recitation of hymns. And the reading of scripture is a tremendous asset because it's coming through something else—someone else's given them to you." These are part of the "devotional store" that Charles described as something that one may both "handle" and let oneself be "handled by."

After her divorce, Julia was comforted not so much by the message of particular hymns or verses from scripture, but by the experience of hearing them in her new congregation: "The context was more important." Oscar expressed a sentiment similar to Ruth's in claiming that he "cannot put into words" how the Lutheran liturgy had brought him comfort for his brother's death, except to say that it "is a part of us" and has brought him closer to his congregation.

In chapter two I argued that, while the Lutheran tradition teaches that God's word is bound to the Bible, it demonstrates the primacy of scripture not so much by doctrine about scripture as by its frequent appearance in theology and practice. In a similar manner, all the co-researchers liberally cited scripture to describe how it shaped their beliefs and practices. Of the seven, Charles referred to the most passages including the Twenty-third Psalm, the Lukan saying about the Tower of Siloam, and suffering as described in 1 Peter and the Book of Hebrews. While Julia could not name any scripture read aloud during worship that consoled her during her divorce, scripture itself played an important role in the "consolation" she received from her priest-psychiatrist: "We talked about a lot of things in terms of faith and the Bible." The story of Job provided a narrative by which Robert measured his own financial difficulties and illness. He also turned to a number of Psalms, especially the twenty-third, because he knew it by heart. "And I found myself reciting it to myself as something that gave comfort and support . . . because it was familiar. I mean it was something that kind of had been with me as part of my faith life, the whole time."

Like Allison, Robert, and Charles, Michael turned to the scripture—particularly the Twenty-third Psalm—for comfort: "He's the shepherd and we are the sheep. He fights off the enemies and he feeds us. So when I was wounded, it told me that God is going to nurse my wounds and bring me back to health. He's the veterinarian. He's the doctor." However, unlike those co-researchers, Michael looked for "signs and messages" of the psalm's import in its frequent use by a variety of persons and appearance in a variety of places: by a professional athlete he admired ("Before he goes into a game, he reads the Twenty-third Psalm") and when he went to visit the surgeon whom he finally choose to care for him ("There it was again, this time in the doctor's office, the Twenty-third Psalm").

Just as prayer in the early Lutheran tradition was believed to be that which God brings forth from the believer, a prayerful searching of scripture for consolation characterizes most of the co-researchers' reading of the Bible. However, a number of the co-researchers did comment specifically on the significance of their praying during their personal crises. For Julia, God's consolation through prayer is often hidden: "I don't recognize that the answers come, but things fall into place." Yet she discloses that meditative prayer helped her face hard days at seminary.

I was depressed and thought, "I can't crawl out of bed and go to class this morning." And I don't miss classes. So I closed my eyes and Jesus was standing there and His arms were out and I said, "If you could just carry me today, I think I can do what it is you have called me to do." The feeling was that I was lifting myself into His arms. And He would carry me. That was and continues to be very helpful, and I also use it for other people. I feel as though I can pray and put them in the arms of Christ.

In her isolation, Julia employed the image of one person—Jesus—lifting and holding another person—herself.

In summary, it seems that most of the co-researchers approached scripture and scripturally informed practices—prayer, liturgy, and hymn singing—in a manner congruent with, and by their own accounts, informed by, a central precept of the early Lutheran tradition: They experienced consolation through interpersonal means. Is there further evidence of the early Lutheran tradition informing their experience by the other means of grace—the sacraments?

The Sacraments: "Something tangible."

Collectively, it appears that the co-researchers appropriated the tradition's teachings about the sacraments in their practice to some degree, albeit not a great one. For example, to quell her worries about the judgment of God, Ruth recalled her baptism and linked it to the baptism of Christ. In his account of being consoled before he sought consolation, Charles distinguished "Lutheran baptismal identity" from that of "twice-born" Christians who, in his belief, claim an experience of God's Spirit as an indicator of their regeneration. However, Charles never directly referred to his own baptism as a source of consolation. Only Ruth made a direct reference to this sacrament.

Similarly, only two co-researchers clearly claimed that communion (another, if not the only other, sacrament of the tradition) was a source of consolation. Robert recalls that receiving the sacrament before surgery brought him comfort: "Communion was a very strong positive sign of God's presence. It gave me something tangible, something I could hold on to, when I was facing something like having [a major organ] taken out." As he prepared for a part of his body to be removed, Robert saw a sign of God's present care for him in his receiving something "tangible." Furthermore, it is noteworthy and possibly significant that that something is also referred to as a "body" in his tradition.[2] Similarly, in his grief for his departed brother, Oscar reported, "I am able to say that the Lord's Supper is more meaningful to me now. And when I take the Lord's Supper, I do think of my brother being with me." The other co-researcher who referred to this sacrament, Charles, qualified how it was a means of consolation: "Well, the communion itself is helpful, but the pastor's touch—as far as a blessing is concerned—was very important."

In summary, some of the co-researchers reported that either their reception of communion or recollection of having been baptized was a significant dimension of their experience of consolation. But only Robert, Ruth, and Oscar mentioned the sacraments directly. Charles did so obliquely, while Julia referred to the arguably third sacrament of penance. Michael and Allison, however, made no reference to any sacraments.

How might one account for this finding? The Lutheran clergy, the tradition's religious professionals, made no more claims about the significance of the sacraments than the laypersons. For while one minister clearly claimed that the sacraments brought consolation, so did two laypersons. Perhaps a more helpful way to account for this finding is to conjecture that, despite Luther's teaching that the Word and Sacrament are inseparable means of grace, some Lutherans do separate them and, in doing so, believe that their reception of the former suffices. It is also possible that many of these co-researchers came of age at a time when communion was a less frequent practice.

However, another way to account for it is to note that perhaps the sacraments did in fact mediate consolation to each of these Lutherans, since all of them, except Allison and Michael, claimed at least some benefit from them. Nor, from the perspective offered by the early Lutheran tradition, may one say with certainty that Allison and Michael did *not* receive consolation through the sacraments, for that tradition teaches that consolation may be hidden not only from the eyes of those observing one who has been consoled, but even from the awareness of the one consoled. Only an "ultra-Pietist" brand of Lutheranism would contend that one receives consolation from the sacraments only if one can recognize that one has received it.

In summary, it appears that Scripture, and to some degree the sacraments, mediated consolation to the co-researchers. Additionally, in a manner very consistent with the tradition, it appears that it was the interpersonal mediation of scripture and sacrament that was important in, if not central to, their experience of consolation. This mediation is suggested in Charles's remark that when he received communion, the most important part of the ritual was his pastor's tactile bestowal of a blessing. Further, immediately following this remark about human touch, Charles referred to the scriptural tradition as something one may handle and by which one may be handled. Consider also Ruth's summary remarks about scripture's power to console through its portrayal of persons who faced similar tribulations: She linked the power of these Bible stories to "charge her up" to their "being as alive for me as another person."

These accounts by the co-researchers also are in accord with the Lutheran tradition. As noted earlier, the authors of the early Lutheran tradition did not separate the consolation granted by Word and Sacrament from that granted by the priesthood of all believers. Nor, as we shall see, did most of these co-researchers.

The Priesthood of All Believers: "That warmth."

Among the co-researchers, only Robert explicitly referred to the priesthood of all believers as a source of consolation. "The sense of community [when he was sick] was extremely important and I understand that in the context of the communion of all believers. I think the caring for me by others—I knew them to be the priesthood of all believers. They were the priests to me and were in many ways my pastor."

However, this construct, named or not, appears to have informed most of the co-researchers' views. Certainly, it is implied in Allison's faith-statement that the material and spiritual support of members of her "church [who] are the people" was the means by which she overcame her preoccupation with the "why" of God's will. Oscar reported that after his brother's death, he had been "more mindful" of the small congregation that "formed my character" and was "important" to his brother. He then added—admittedly somewhat boastfully—that in return, "I'm ready to help if I possibly can."

In a similar manner, Julia mentioned having received consolation from a practice directly associated with the priesthood of all believers—the Office of the Keys: "Having once gone for private confession and knowing the power of that service, I thought if I need that, it's there." Throughout her interview, Julia focused on the importance of her congregational life during her divorce and subsequent depression. Throughout these isolating difficulties, that congregation was "a sanctuary" for her that guided her through that time and was the place where her new vocation—and new life—began.

Michael repeatedly referred to the assistance of his pastor and his current congregation as helpful not only during his coronary bypass surgery but throughout his ten-year membership:

> I don't think it's Lutherans over Baptists or anything like that. But this is a very, very warm congregation and I attribute a lot of that to Pastor Smith. He conveys that feeling, that warmth. I mean, that helped me tremendously. And then when I went back, the people were there for me—stacks of cards and gifts and visits and phone calls from people that I really didn't know that well. But the whole congregation was very, very supportive.

Like Michael, Oscar received support from members of his congregation who assured him that he had done everything possible for his ailing brother. While much of Robert's tribulation during his financial difficulties was his concomitant isolation from family, friends, and church, much of the consolation he experienced during his illness came from his close connection to these same people.

As noted in the previous chapter, three of the co-researchers had moments not of consolation, but of tribulation. In this chapter, I have described how consolation came to not only those three but also to most of the others, through practices they experienced as embodying the grace of God. They experienced grace from God alone, but this grace came to them through their relationships with other Christians. Simply stated: This seems to be the "other emphasis" of the Lutheran tradition showing itself in their lived religion.[3]

In the early Lutheran tradition, this other emphasis showed itself not only in the priesthood of all believers, but in how those believers received and employed the goods of creation. Both Luther and the various other authors of the Book of Concord taught that while the faithful are passive in relationship to God, they are concomitantly empowered to use those goods. Furthermore, believers are enjoined to honor as God-given their impulse to preserve their own lives. How do the practices of these co-researchers compare with these teachings?

Responses to Consolation

Living in Creation: "I mean, there's the human side."
The early Lutheran tradition clearly teaches that, when used well, the goods of creation, including the human body, may be directed to good ends: "We should not spurn even this way of receiving such things through God's creatures."[4]

A number of co-researchers witnessed to a valuing of creation and their own createdness. In the midst of his reflections on Lutheran doctrine, Charles also reflected on his need for bodily comfort: "Doctors, those big son-of-a-guns, they take so much money, they're so busy, they don't have time for you—they don't touch you or pat you on the shoulder. My [medical specialist] did, though, the last time I talked to him. He put his hand on my shoulder and said, 'Everything is going to be okay.' I almost fell over. Touch is important."

Immediately following her husband's death, Allison coped by keeping busy, thereby exercising what she experienced as a prudent flight because she could not fight. "The boys each played sports two nights a week, and I was involved in watching them play ball. And then I played ball once a week on Friday nights, and then we still continued to watch the team that Paul had been on for several years. I tried to stay busy in order to stay on track, and to keep my mind occupied." Later she tried to reduce her stress by daily walks around her neighborhood and by a wooded stream. She also reported, "Our entire family truly enjoyed the healing power of music, whether it be hymns or contemporary songs." Following his open-heart surgery, Michael took long walks not only for the exercise but for the relaxation. He also enjoyed light reading: "I read mysteries. I didn't sit there with my Bible and study the whole Bible every day." In sum, the co-researchers communicated that they experienced a respect for their embodied, created existence and for seeking means of consolation through that human existence.

The Use of Reason: "I learn from those mistakes."

Did the co-researchers give any evidence of the use of reason, which the tradition construes as a God-given tool for coping? May one, in accord with the teaching of the early Lutheran tradition, be passive in relationship to God but active in solving problems in the world? As noted earlier, even though Ruth believed that God enabled her to face the difficulties resulting from her abuse, abandonment, divorce, and subsequent single parenthood, she still maintained agency in those matters. For example, while praying, "Lord, to whom shall I go?" Ruth was assured that God would act on her behalf, that assurance does not lead her to be inactive.

> I can stay in prayer and be peaceful. I can trust that, you know, even though there's $24 in the bank at the end of the month, there will be $724 and I can pay the rent. And it's not as though I can have it magically happen, but that if I pay attention, then the opportunities will present themselves. I go to my great job and I have final deadlines and I stretch out my hand and fifty-dollar bills fall in them. That's what I do. But I don't kid myself about where that comes from. That's not my marvelous effort. That's not my genius.

Ruth reported that, with God's help, she chose activities that would help her through her crisis.

> So, it's not that I try to solve it, you know, out in the world and then God comes along and straightens it out. It's sort of like He's just there with me. I make mistakes; he works them out. I learn from those mistakes. I come at the same situation again another time and I know, okay, I remember what we went through last time. . . . I thought about a lot of solutions, but God provided the ones that worked.

In a manner similar to Ruth, each of the other co-researchers (with the possible exception of Michael) chronicled their many conscious choices and actions when faced with their negative events. That is to say, seeking consolation did not prevent them from taking what they judged to be reasonable actions to overcome their problems. However, all seven reported they were empowered to take action because they trusted that God cared for them prior to, and, in some cases, apart from their choosing and acting. In summary, these seven Lutherans indicated no difficulty in being both passive in their relationships with God and active in relationships with others and the world.[5]

The Secular: "Even the secular can be sacred." "What it means to be human . . . even in seminary, you don't learn much about that." The Lutheran tradition teaches that secular care may be the means by which God provides for the faithful. In keeping with the tradition, a number of co-researchers carefully sought assistance from psychotherapy and self-help groups without any religious orientation. With a son "acting out his grief" for his father, Allison turned to and found help in family counseling.

> The counseling was helpful because they recognized at least for Mitchell something that they referred to as "angel on the outside, devil at home." We went from being best friends to practically arch enemies. But the counseling helped us to at least identify what was a normal fourteen-year-old teenager going through growing pains and what was his dealing with the loss of his dad. It was comforting for to me to know that there would be an end in fighting, that we would get over this.

Allison's belief that God caused her suffering did not rule out her attempting to alleviate it. Thus she reported that in order to care for herself and her children, she "didn't sit around waiting" for God's direct intervention but took action by seeking counseling for all of them.

Faced with the "broken covenant" of her marriage and her subsequent clinical depression, Julia found guidance from a priest-psychiatrist. She emphasized that the "psychology" of her therapy was particularly helpful.

> We are not taught anywhere in our standard education what it is to be a human being: how minds work, how people hurt and help each other verbally. That's what therapy does. It teaches

you that. And even in seminary, you don't learn that much about that. You're never in a class long enough and therapy does not get a high place in pastoral care in seminary. In therapy we learn about how people get along. . . . So, for me, for the divorce and for the children, it was invaluable.

Reflecting on our exchange about his many medical treatments, Charles remarked, "I never—hardly ever—talked about this stuff outside a support group or in a conversation like this one where you're asking me about it. You can't, you can't describe [it] to people." Wishing that he had had more support from persons to whom he could have described his sufferings, Charles has become a leader in various patient support groups similar to his own. He explained this activity: "I think that the Golden Rule is 'Do unto others as you would have them do unto you.' And I said, 'I owe, I owe.' I got well because of the tremendous resources in modern medicine which I think are a gift of God, and so I owed back to humanity to do something for others who have the same fix that I do."

In sum, a number of the co-researchers found help in various nonreligious forms of care. In Charles's words, "With the gospel, even the secular can become sacred." Here, too, the co-researchers appear to have acted in congruence with tradition: Empowered by the priesthood of all believers, they reported being empowered to face problems in the world.

This account could be the end of the story of the co-researchers' practices as they sought consolation, but it is not. We have not yet addressed another significant factor—the way in which various social forces contributed to their negative events and affected their religious practices. A survey of these social forces reveals that they are just as embodied and just as powerful as those interpersonal forces found in the priesthood of all believers. Furthermore, an even closer look at these accounts will reveal that these forces actually work against these interpersonal means of care and consequent ability to deal with the problems in the world. To be sure, as noted earlier, the early Lutheran tradition proposed that battle with such systemic sources of suffering is a reflex of consolation. But questions still remain. First, has the tradition provided a vocabulary adequate to both name and confront those sources so that those who suffered from them may receive better care? And second, has the tradition provided adequate resources so that those who battle systemic sources of suffering may do so in league with others? In the remainder of this chapter, we will consider these questions.

Social Factors in Consolation and Tribulation

Divorce: "She left the church building." "And I left that church."
While the congregation near her seminary offered much support during her divorce, Julia shared that her relationship with her home congregation, of which she was a "first daughter" and from which she had received support for her candidacy for ordination, became awkward. "I had been so active in that congregation. I was a trusted person. I think there might have been a sense of betrayal because I didn't tell them—for a long time, they just didn't know. There was no way to stand up and announce, 'By the way, I don't want you to be shocked, but we're getting divorced, you know.' And so they had to find out through the grapevine. And now it seems like it was a deception." Julia believed that the previous pastoral leadership of this congregation contributed to her reluctance to step forward. She recalled an incident fifteen years prior to her own divorce.

> **Julia:** One of the pastors in an adult Sunday school class used the passage from Paul that says divorce is wrong. Period. It shouldn't happen and could not be permitted in the church. And he was really insensitive to what might have happened to anybody in that group of people over their life. In fact, someone in the class had just gotten a divorce. And after he did that, she left the church with her daughter. [Pause] She couldn't stay, so she left.
> **Leonard:** Left the building?
> **Julia:** She left the church building—walked right out of the class—and then later transferred from the church.

Of all the co-researchers, those who were divorced described the most persistent and apparently painful lack of support from the priesthood of all believers. After her divorce, Ruth reported, her isolation increased. Asked whether he sensed any lack of support from his Lutheran congregation during his illness, Michael said that he had felt very supported by them, but then referred to something else on his mind—his relationship with the Baptist congregation of which he had been a lifetime member when he divorced fifteen years ago.

> During my divorce, I really felt there was nobody in my church for support. My pastor didn't support me, members of the congregation who I thought were friends, the guys on the board of deacons, didn't. I mean one guy is calling—I'm not even out of the house yet—and he's calling my wife and offering his services. And I left that church. I don't want to say I left my religion or I left my belief in God. But I just felt that church was not the answer. I felt that they let me down. Here, in this congregation where I am now, I have found a new family. But I don't think it's Lutherans over Baptists or anything like that on this issue.

Julia's and Ruth's accounts offer support for Michael's hypothesis. The problems associated with divorce for couples, their families, and even their congregations is well known, although I believe it is curiously under-researched in pastoral theology. Therefore, it may be that those who divorce often experience the particular suffering of lacking support from their congregations. There are certainly indications of this elsewhere. In Jane Rutledge's *Coping with Intimacy: A Problem for Single Adult Mormons,* many of her subjects were divorced persons who experienced their religious community as a social milieu that did not provide means for them to cope but was a force with which they had to cope.[6] And in accord with Michael, I hypothesize that non-Mormons may not fare better than Mormons on this issue.

"She left the church building." "And I left that church." Both Julia and Michael tell of persons who felt driven to leave their congregations by powerful social forces within and around those congregations. However, the divorced co-researchers were not the only ones whose consolation was obstructed by social forces.

An Ailing Health Care System: "They're under pressures, too. . . . Why the hell should I live more than the next guy?"

Charles claimed that there are often unpleasant, but unavoidable, aspects of suffering with and being treated for illnesses like his. These aspects are hard to talk about and hard for those who have not suffered in a similar manner to understand. "It's an embarrassing thing to have to lie yourself on a gurney, and a nurse comes in and grabs a hold of your penis, holds it straight up in the air, shoves something in it so they can mark you up for radiation, and then the guy takes a picture of how it's all working out. I mean, it doesn't hurt but it's weird."

However, Charles believes that his illness may not have resulted from the normal vicissitudes of human living but rather may have unique social origins. That is, Charles has been told, and believes it to be true, that people in other cultures do not experience illnesses like his as frequently as do people in his own culture: "My doctor said to me, 'You're a Westerner.' I said, 'Bingo.' . . . We live in this kind of capitalism and stress culture. How can you blame God for that?" Charles does not blame God but instead his own participation in this particular economic and social structure: "You walk into a fire and you get burned."

Moreover, Charles contends that there are social forces that not only produce sicknesses like his, but also interfere with their treatment.

> **Charles:** [During one procedure] the medical staff were running around all over the hospital getting people to keep my blood pressure from dropping through the floor. [Pause] But I knew that was going to happen.
> **Leonard:** You knew it was going to happen?
> **Charles:** Yeah, I had something like that happen to me during a previous medical procedure and I told them it often happens to me because of [particulars in his medical history] but they did it anyhow. It was in the charts and I told them, but they didn't watch for it. Even though I told them, they weren't quite prepared for it. But, you know, they make mistakes. That's why I have great compassion for doctors. They're human beings. And the whole hospital staff is trying to help you, but they're all under pressures and limitations or budget constraints and everything else.

It was precisely at this point in our conversation that Charles mentioned that he prayed for the physicians and the other staff who cared for him and other sick persons. And it was at this very point, reflecting on the medical professionals' burden, that he remarked with some force, "Why the hell should I live?"

Given the sum of Charles's remarks, one may reasonably conjecture a number of things about a few of its parts. It seems that Charles's prayer for the attending medical personnel may arise not only from his noble Lutheran need during his illness to not be turned in on himself, but also from his realization that the system of which they are a part is itself ill and turned in on itself. Furthermore, his musings that there is no real reason that he should live betray a kind of bitter poignancy. That is, his strongly stated *resignatio ad infernum et mortuum*—resignation to hell and death—may signify more than one orthodox Lutheran's effortful appropriation of *Gelassenheit*. Rather, his resignation may also reflect a letting go in the face of what may have come his way from being treated under "this kind of capitalism." In the face of an economic system that may contribute to the occurrence of, and often poorly treats, diseases like his, why should he live?

Charles is not alone in asking questions about life and death possibly precipitated and then poorly managed by social forces. In *Redeeming Marketplace Medicine,* Abigail Evans details how some of Charles's concerns—pressures, limitations, and budgets—are symptomatic of a sick system of health care. With all the blessings brought about through care administered according to the medical model of illness—increased life span, the eradication of many infectious diseases, cures undreamed of just decades ago—that ailing system often has difficulty caring for those who are ill.[7]

Single Motherhood: "I'm going further into debt."

Left alone after her divorce to care for three young children, Ruth approached a kind of poverty that she had never before experienced or expected. Accustomed to coping with many pressures at school and work, Ruth suddenly experienced a set of stresses that she felt she could not manage. Part of her difficulty arose from her isolation from friends and especially her family: "My mother's very German—she obeyed her husband all her life—and could not understand what was wrong with me or why I was letting my husband divorce me. Her instruction to me was: Go find him, apologize to him, and patch things up." And while she gave her congregation "high marks for trying to set me straight," they, too, became more distant.

As noted in chapter one, Pamela Couture has turned to the Wesleyan and Lutheran traditions to seek remedies for women's poverty in the United States. She further describes the face of that poverty: "Divorce, particularly no-fault divorce, impoverishes female-headed households."[8] And female-headed households of all types are more prone to poverty because of the economic burdens imposed on many women: lower wages, less job opportunity. Weighed down by these burdens, Ruth's spirit plummeted.

So did Julia's when she suffered a clinical depression following her divorce.

Women, Interpersonal Discord, and Depression: "The darkness is pretty dark."

The statistic almost speaks for itself: Twice as many women as men suffer from depression. In *Counseling Depressed Women,* Susan Dunlap interprets the numbers this way: "It is women's social position of powerlessness that accounts for a significant difference in depression rates."[9] That powerlessness has many sources and takes on many forms. A number of studies have indicated that marital difficulties such as those Julia experienced before her divorce, and the frequently unsettling changes experienced during and after divorce, are positively correlated among women with the onset of a major depressive episode.[10]

Julia reported many contributing causes to her depression, which she described this way: "This is chaos, this is the dark." Treated professionally, she was also consoled by thoughts such as these: "'Light will come.' Now I can't tell you that every day that I believed that, because the darkness is pretty dark. But it did come." Along with her professional treatment, Julia is clear that the "context" of her new congregation—located far from her former home and home congregation—brought light to her depression. Given the isolation she experienced when she visited her home congregation during her divorce, I do question whether that congregation would also have been a beacon had she stayed there.

Several years after her divorce, and several months after her ordination, Julia returned to her former home congregation and saw for herself a change she had previously heard about. "They had completely redone the whole nave, the sanctuary and the chancel area. And the church is not the church in which we worshiped. It is so changed that I can go in there. It's such a different place that I could now worship there without the baggage." Listening to Julia's description of her home congregation before the changes to its sanctuary—a congregation in which a pastor taught that those who divorce are, in the words Julia elsewhere uses, not only sinful but also not forgiven, and a congregation in which she felt it necessary to practice a kind of "deception" for their sake and hers—I wondered if she, too, might have been inclined to both leave the church building and then leave that church in order to save herself. I also wondered: If she had done so, would she—as a first daughter of that congregation—have found it difficult or impossible to join another, unless it provided her a very different kind of "sanctuary," a physical entity that mediated spiritual refuge? "It was a sanctuary for me. And I was accepted there just for me as a single person. And that was a gift. Because if you've never been single, and you've never lived alone, you don't know what that is."

A Punishing Economic System: "I was bullheaded. And I think I was wrong." "I found it difficult to forgive them and still do." Early in his financial difficulties, Robert decided that he would not keep his family, friends, and church current on the turmoil accompanying those difficulties. A rapid speaker throughout the entire interview, Robert raced as he expanded on the stress of this experience.

> "Wasn't this all happening because I was so stupid and made such irresponsible decisions?" That's what I asked myself. I mean, there were times when the stresses were enormous. I had the IRS calling—I had the state calling about monies that were back-owed. I was behind payments on the rent and so I had people calling at home, at the church office, at committee meetings, and down at the business. They were threatening that they'd lock the doors. There was an immense amount of pres-

sure that was exerted, and I tried in many ways to keep it away from [my wife] as much as possible. I'd jump for the phone when it would ring. Because I didn't want her to be worried. So I relied a lot on prayer and God's support.

But as we have seen, Robert's reliance on prayer and support from God alone only increased his stress and worry. Furthermore, given his responsibility for these difficulties, one might ask what God could have told him that would have consoled him. Was not the whole undertaking—his co-signing a loan for a young friend's scheme—simply foolish? Was not this particular crisis simply a manifestation of many personal flaws, exposing him as a pastor who was generous to a fault? An optimistic venturer blind to the risks involved in this particular venture? A hard-working pastor whose seemingly boundless energy led him to near financial ruin and poor health? A beloved pastor who suffered from the need to be loved? One may lament thus on Robert's near-downfall like the chorus in a Greek tragedy but unnecessarily, because Robert seems to have already asked himself all these hard questions and more. Or to frame this somewhat more in keeping with the early Lutheran tradition: One may pose these questions, but in doing so, one would pose the very same devilish questions Robert asked himself.

What, then, does Robert conclude about himself? First he simply said, "I was bullheaded." In other words, Robert seemed to agree with what others had told him, that he did not follow their advice but instead stubbornly went his own way. Yet, nowhere in the interview did he state flatly that he erred in doing so. Nor did he do so here, but rather immediately added this very curious remark: "And I *think* I was wrong." In other words, Robert was not completely certain that his wife and friends were right and that he was not. Even after five back- and spirit-breaking years of compensatory hard labor for his wrongdoing, he still does not sound fully convinced of his culpability. Is the fact that he only *thinks* that he was wrong itself confirmation of his initial self-assessment—that he was bullheaded—and also an indication that that assessment refers to an enduring personality trait—that he *is* bullheaded? Or to put a more charitable construction on his remarks, does he remain somewhat unconvinced in order to defend himself from the recriminations of God, others, and himself?

Perhaps the answer is yes to all the above questions. But I believe there are other possibilities, that, while highly speculative, are worth considering. Perhaps Robert only thinks he is wrong because he cannot be convinced—his convictions tell him otherwise—that to have trusted his young friend was wrong. That is, he may not be certain that to have acted in character—generously, hopefully, energetically, and lovingly—was foolish. Certainly, Robert's successful oversight of numerous financial enterprises in various pastoral calls, and his serving faithfully and well on the financial boards of a variety of public concerns, do not witness to a lack of worldly wisdom.

Therefore, perhaps the better questions to ask are these: Why should someone like Robert suffer almost irreparable damage for a single act of considered kindness? Is Robert not convinced that he was wrong because he is convinced that it is wrong that the buck stops with those who experience financial failure, regardless of their wisdom and ability in money matters?

Perhaps when he became mired in debt, Robert could have chosen to declare bankruptcy. Or perhaps that really was not much of an option for a person in his position. Reflecting on Robert's near financial collapse, I am reminded of Charles Dickens's underappreciated novel *Little Dorrit,* in which he paints the lives of those whose fortunes come and go for no apparent reason. In his telling, some people make money, some land in debtor's prison, some do both, but all are constrained by forces beyond their control. I am further reminded of one interpretation of this novel as "essentially a long rendering of imprisonment in its many forms, a forceful reminder . . . that a more or less democratic, capitalist society can nevertheless turn out to be— for almost everyone, it seems—one giant penal colony."[11] In Robert's case study, I am impressed also that, in suffering a physical illness, he sought and received much support, but that, during his financial tribulation, he shouldered his suffering alone. Is it more acceptable in our culture to be ill than to have financial problems? If so, is that because we assume that persons with financial problems are responsible for those problems, whereas those with illness are not?

In the account of another co-researcher, Allison, one may see similarly unpredictable and unjust forces at work in bringing about suffering. While she ascribed her husband's death to the unseen will of God, Allison also saw it as the result of unethical decision-making.

> I did and am still struggling with the fact that the business where he worked did not have insurance for him, and that they placed him in unsafe conditions. And even though they are very much aware that they were wrong, they have not corrected and are still operating under unsafe conditions. I found it difficult to forgive them and still do. I'm taught that I should forgive and that there is no greater sin—no greater or lesser sin, one is not worse than the other—but yet to not have learned from their mistakes. . . . I think it is wrong that they continue to operate by putting someone else in the same danger, and by risking making someone have to go through the same things that I had to. I struggle with how exactly I should deal with that.

Social Sources of Suffering: "I want to get in there and steal some documents, too. But I'm not going to do that."

How did these Lutherans deal with the social forces that contributed to their significant negative events? What action, if any, did they take? As we saw earlier, these co-researchers were actively engaged in facing the numerous problems that caused or resulted from their suffering: Comfortable with their created natures, they sought ways to respond to their bodily needs; gifted with reason, they carefully thought through a variety of ways of coping with their stresses; partially at home in the world, they used secular means to care for themselves. The question here, then, may be further summarized: Did they use these means to address the larger social forces at work in producing or maintaining their suffering?

It seems that they did, but only in a limited manner. Julia sought solace in her psychotherapy for the suffering brought about by her divorce and used insights from that experience to counsel others preparing to marry. Charles joined a self-help group in which he is able to care for others as he wishes others had done for him, and thereby he helps ease others' pain. While Allison held to a deep but troubling conviction that her husband's death was the will of God, she also believed his employers were negligent and therefore that she may hold them legally liable—that is to say, she is considering recourse in the civil realm for what she regards as a moral wrong. Whatever complicated—perhaps even conflicting—beliefs Ruth may hold about God, she believed that God has empowered her to take on powers and principalities that treat her as if she were of no account. Furthermore, she claimed that God enabled her to act righteously— to resist the temptation to steal court documents—in response to the unrighteous stealing of these documents by her former husband's lawyer. "He did something basically despicable, and I just felt like I lost a lot of respect for him and the process as a result of it. You know, I'm guilty of that same kind of impatience. And now I want to get in there and steal some documents too. But I'm not going to do that." Robert reported that he has picked up the financial pieces and moved on, continuing to serve on various public boards.

In sum, most of the co-researchers reported that while they made certain constructive responses to the social dimensions of their suffering, most of them struggled with these social forces alone, rather than doing so in league with or with the support of others. Perhaps this is related to the nature of their significant negative events: sicknesses, divorce, and grief. They might have reported more "communal striving" had they suffered a community catastrophe. Had they been persecuted because of their religious identity, they might have reported that they joined forces with other Christians to seek consolation and to combat their suffering. Yet, as indicated earlier, the suffering of many—most—of them had easily identified social origins and political consequences. Perhaps these co-researchers, like many American Lutherans, have been educated by either their Lutheran faith or American culture that, while their consolation for suffering is communally mediated, communal attempts to overcome suffering should not be sought after. There is, however, another explanation: These Lutherans may have found few resources to assist them in such a struggle. We will look more closely at this explanation in the next chapter.

Belief and Practice: A False Dichotomy

As noted at the beginning of chapter four, the distinction I made at the outset between the beliefs and practices of these seven Lutherans, while helpful in analyzing how they received consolation for their suffering, might be misleading. The reports of these co-researchers further suggest that it is a distinction that collapses upon close scrutiny. Consistently they reported that their consoling beliefs came through various practices. At the outset of this chapter I noted that for three of them—Ruth, Robert, and Allison—the degree to which they focused on ideas about God and God alone paralleled the degree to which they experienced tribulation, not consolation. While three of the others reported less *Anfechtung,* they too reported that it was their practice in a community of faith that mediated their consoling beliefs: Julia through the context of her congregation, Charles through the tradition that he handles and by which he is handled, and Oscar through the "faith that formed my character" and thereby enabled him to weather his brother's death.

With the distinction between beliefs and practices undone, a number of important concluding questions may now be asked: questions about the normativity of tradition in the lived religion of these Lutherans, questions about the relationship between consolation for suffering in this tradition and in some others, and questions about whether those things that are "clothed in nothingness"—finite, human, fallible practices—obscure or transmit the consolation of God.

6.
"Clothed in Nothingness"

⇛•⇚

This concluding chapter examines more closely the role of tradition in lived religion. It also compares the kind of consolation for suffering found in the tradition and lived religion of Lutheranism with that in two other Christian traditions. Finally, it reviews the implications for theology, pastoral care, and tradition of Luther's claim that the consolation of God is "clothed in nothingness."

Tradition and Lived Religion

In the conclusion to chapter three, I posed questions for consideration in this chapter: Does the use of tradition to analyze lived religion avoid or obscure criticism of the notion of tradition? Or does this use add a new perspective to this criticism by showing both the power of tradition and the multiplicity of lived religious experience?

One way to begin to address these questions is to ask another one. As noted in the introduction, one purpose of this book is to bring the beliefs and practices of a sample of contemporary Lutherans into dialogue with the normative teachings of their tradition. This purpose may be posed in the form of a question: What re-visioning do the lived religions of these co-researchers bring to the tradition of Lutheranism? Given the previous analysis of their beliefs and practices, they seem to bring very little re-visioning. To a remarkable and surprising degree, most of them expressed beliefs that they claim were passed on by others of that tradition, or that seemed to be influenced by the meta-linguistic principle of justification and its corollaries in the theology of the cross. Also in keeping with the Lutheran tradition, they found that their consoling beliefs were mediated by practices that connected them to other persons. Overall, it appears that they were informed by something like a metanarrative—a Lutheran metanarrative.

However, this appearance is deceptive for a number of reasons.

"I didn't become a Lutheran to become a Lutheran."

First of all, this appearance is deceptive because it does not take into account Michael's beliefs, which differ significantly from those of the other co-researchers and those proposed in much of the early Lutheran tradition itself. For example, throughout his interview, Michael voiced variations on the following theme: "You've got to have that positive attitude." Unlike the other co-researchers, and somewhat at variance with the early Lutheran tradition, he also strives to be aware of "signs and messages" in the Bible and in his milieu in order to discern God's good purposes for him. Concomitantly, he displayed more concern than the other co-researchers about people who engage in immoral practices ("I have a co-worker who smokes like a chimney") and consequently are not in right relationship with God now, and may not be in the time to come ("Maybe then, some of these people, their life won't be so good then. . . . There'll be a reckoning").

Yet do these beliefs make Michael less a Lutheran? While it appears that they do distinguish him from the other co-researchers in this small sample, they may not set him apart from many other Lutherans in the United States. Empirical studies have shown that Lutherans in the United States hold a great variety of religious beliefs.[1]

Furthermore, another look at Michael's reflections about the stress of his surgery reveals that he may uphold an important characteristic of Lutheran consolation: A significant source of his comfort has come through his relationships with other Christians. That is, even while minimizing the significance of Lutheranism, he affirmed the importance of something very much like the Lutheran doctrine of the priesthood of all believers.

When I walked into that [Lutheran] congregation, the people greeted me with a great deal of warmth. I'm not sure they greeted me with a great deal of warmth because they were Lutherans, because they were mostly Swedish, or because they were Finnish, but because they were people—genuine people—again, I think a lot of it is due to Pastor Ullmann. He conveys that warmth. You know, I didn't become a Lutheran to become a Lutheran. I came back to God and with the people who helped me and brought me there. I can remember this lady in church—very outgoing. She's the superintendent of the church school. I didn't even think she knew who I was. And she yelled out after church one day, "You're on the board of Christian education." Gee, I've only been here about six or seven times, I'm not even a member of this church here, and they want me to join. They want me. I feel wanted. I feel that I can offer something, and that's a great feeling.

Of course, the priesthood of all believers is central not only to Lutheranism but to many Christian traditions—in fact, it is beloved in much of the Baptist tradition from which Michael hails.[2] Michael's favorable response to the warmth of his new congregation suggests a possible confluence of his own religious background with the tradition he has joined.

Despite first appearances, therefore, Michael holds some beliefs that resemble those of the other co-researchers and fit well within the Lutheran life-world. However, there is another way to approach the question of whether Michael is a member of the Lutheran tradition. One may simply note that since he is a practicing member of a Lutheran congregation, Michael's status is not a matter of opinion but of fact—he is a member. Furthermore, since he joined this congregation, Michael has continued to serve on its board of Christian education, has been a determined promoter of congregational stewardship, has served on the church council for several terms, and has established a close friendship with his pastor.

Whatever Michael may profess, therefore, his actions are largely Lutheran. In the language of Pierre Bourdieu and others, he has developed a *habitus* (disposition) through his practices that links him to other Lutherans.[3] While it is true that Michael holds beliefs that differ from some in his tradition, he certainly experiences companionship with his new congregation through their joint practices. Tanner has described how social cohesiveness based on beliefs among Christians may be weak, thereby allowing their fellowship through practices to be strong: "Far from threatening the stability of a Christian way of life, the fact that Christians do not agree in their interpretation of matters of common concern is the very thing that enables solidarity among them."[4] That solidarity is achieved not through consensus but through shared commitments.

Michael claimed, "I didn't become a Lutheran to become a Lutheran." Then why did he do so? Of course, his impulse to do so had a socially conventional source—his desire to join the church of his new spouse. However, having followed this impulse, Michael appears to have stumbled onto something more: a God who first healed his past emotional wounds from divorce and then cared for his wounded body. A Baptist, and also a bit of a Christian Scientist, Michael—like Luther—prefers to call himself a Christian. In doing this, and by his practices, Michael is both very much within, even as he is outside of, the boundaries of Lutheranism.

Problematics in Tradition Revisited

As noted in chapter three, Kathryn Tanner has observed some problematics in claims that tradition has the power to unite, direct, and harmonize religious beliefs and practices. Through the lens of these problematics, gaps appear in the metanarrative of the co-researchers' accounts.

The first problematic Tanner identifies is the view that tradition is "a natural preexisting reality" and that continuities in practices exist by virtue of this reality.[5] That is, tradition is seen to be unified and to unite. However, as indicated in chapter one, consolation in the Christian tradition has not one but many sources, especially Stoic philosophy, which have produced not one but many notions of consolation. My empirical analysis has also demonstrated a variety of sources for the consoling beliefs and practices of the co-researchers— even the most apparently traditional, Charles. While Charles presented his beliefs as inseparable from the teachings of the early Lutheran tradition and Lutheran orthodoxy, some of those beliefs seem linked to concepts—Stoicism and the thought-world of late-medieval mysticism—that originate outside the tradition and are thought by some to remain outside of it.

During his illness, did Charles use these non-Lutheran sources in a Lutheran way? One could make this argument, and it is the argument that Charles himself made: "Consolation was there before you began. . . . *Gelassenheit* is giving oneself over to a larger reality. . . . No, no, it's not Stoicism." Just as Johann Steiger argues that Charles's orthodox predecessors were not "slavish" to but masters of the material provided them by Stoicism and the late-medieval tradition, so may one propose that Charles exercised a similar sovereignty over these traditions, even as he experienced a lack of control over his own health and healing?

Or did Charles, despite himself, adapt to these non-Lutheran sources? Or, as he lost agency during his illness, was he, despite himself, incorporated into them, thereby offering support to Tanner's claim about the tenuousness of Christian identity? Tanner writes, "To one's surprise one finds oneself in a new culture without having had any conscious intention of leaving one's own."[6] It is impossible to answer any of these questions with certainty—a fact that further supports Tanner's critique of the notion that tradition unifies all experience in lived religion.

Tanner identifies a second problematic assumption—that whatever in tradition is new may somehow be found in the past: "the idea that the various results of transmission maintain their identity by approximating what is transmitted."[7] Such a perspective cannot account for those beliefs and practices that are less like organic developments and more like additions from other traditions and cultures. Instances of this problematic were revealed in some of the co-researchers' accounts. For example, some of Ruth's ways of religious coping are hardly less Lutheran because of their possible roots in the broad African American religious tradition—nor are the additions she brings to Lutheranism "adulterations" of the tradition, "dross" mixed with its "pure doctrine." Rather, her ways of coping indicate that in the face of suffering, new things may become a part of a tradition that cannot be predicated on, or predicted from, that tradition.

I summarized Tanner's third point this way: While persons may share the same cultural material—texts, practices, and beliefs—they may use that material in various and sometimes conflicting ways. That is, they often "tradition" the tradition differently.

In line with Tanner's criticism, my empirical research demonstrated that these Lutherans arranged the constitutive elements of their tradition in different ways. For example, Oscar, manifestly the most "indiscriminately pro-religious" of Lutherans, unpacked his faith-claim ("Justification by faith means that God will take care of us through these difficult times") in a way that initially smacked more of Dale Carnegie than Martin Luther. And yet, as un-Lutheran as his theology of salesmanship appears, a closer examination reveals a family resemblance—albeit that of a distant cousin—to Luther's remarks about the "external comfort" God provided Joseph in Genesis. While Julia and Charles appropriated the theology of the cross with no apparent terror, Robert gave evidence that while the tension between *Deus absconditus* and *Deus revelatus* may be held together in theory, that tension may be unbearable in some instances of lived religion. Similarly, Allison's life was apparently untroubled and seamless until a terrible tragedy ripped it apart. Afterward, the God she had joyfully worshiped and adored with others hovered over her like a dark cloud and then, even more eerily, dissipated. In sum: These co-researchers experienced and employed the same traditional material in multifarious ways.

Is there, then, a clear answer to the question posed at the beginning of this section: What kind of consolation did these Lutherans experience? On the one hand, yes, there is a clear answer. In this study, those individuals who identify with Lutheranism experienced a kind of consolation (or tribulation) that is largely congruent with their tradition. Conversely, the one person who identified less with the tradition found solace through means correspondingly less consistent with that tradition.

Nevertheless, this answer does not completely capture the results of this study. For as I have noted, there are variations even among those whose beliefs and practices fall more within the norm. One may be a Lutheran for a variety of reasons and bring a corresponding variety of practices and beliefs to that tradition. These findings strengthen David D. Hall's contention that multiple narratives often inform religious lives, and that lived religion is "messier" than any received tradition.[8]

"No one comes to be a human being alone."

Is there, then, any place for using tradition as a lens to study lived religion? I contend that there is a place. In fact, I propose that my own study indicates the importance of attending to tradition in the study of lived religion, because the multiplicity and messiness of lived religion is startlingly revealed precisely through this lens. That is, by attending to lived religion under the principle of a single tradition, many divergent themes in lived religion show themselves.

At the same time, I believe my study demonstrates that common themes do persist among most of the co-researchers. Therefore, if tradition is not a cultural consensus that transforms all into one, it is an organizing principle that influences the beliefs and practices of many. If it is not a metanarrative that overrides the agency within, and the uniqueness of the lives of persons, it nevertheless seems integral to the narratives of their lived religion. My findings support Hall's conclusion about lived religion, "Regulation is ongoing in even the most fluid of movements. . . . Let me acknowledge, however, that it remains a challenging task to think historically about the normative and regulating dimensions of lived religion."[9]

Therefore, through my method, I believe that I have confounded post-structuralist sensibilities by indicating that there is something like a metanarrative of tradition informing the beliefs and practices of most of the co-researchers. At the same time, I believe that I have also confounded post-liberal sensibilities by bringing to attention a medley of incongruent traditions, voices, and experiences at work in their lives. To say it differently, my study reveals that there may be something like a red line of tradition to be found in lived religion, but that red line is invariably broken or twisted or braided with other threads.

Johann Gottfried Herder, a German Lutheran pastor and philosopher of the late 1700s, provides an account of tradition's power to provide unity, direction, and harmony in lived religion—and also its failure to provide them. While Herder is not an unproblematic thinker, his particular understanding of *Bildung* (culture, formation, education) bears on an understanding of tradition that addresses some of the problematics Tanner has noted. Marcia Bunge provides a helpful summary of this teaching by noting three "elements" in Herder's understanding. "The first element of *Bildung* [tradition] . . . underscores the limited historical nature of human beings. . . . No one, for Herder, becomes a human being alone. We are all connected with parents, teachers, and friends, with all the circumstances of our life and with our culture."[10]

Simply put, this "first element" refers to those larger constructions of reality that have become a part of us. This element includes "the faith-formed personality" to which Charles refers, the Lutheran identity that has produced both comfort and dread in Ruth, and the faith that Oscar claims "is inside you and you believe it."

However, *Bildung* consists of more than what is handed on: "The process of *Bildung* has a second principle—'organic powers.' . . . These powers apply tradition to the needs of the present situation. Without such powers, history would be an endless imitation of what has already been."[11]

Of course, Tanner finds "organic" notions of tradition problematic because they seem to imply that the past is prologue to all that follows: "Established patterns of action are not fixed but are themselves susceptible to change in the course of further Christian action. New practice is never simply repetitive . . . [but] brings with it additions, alterations, and unexpected twists to preestablished meanings."[12] However, Frederick Barnard contends that there is room in Herder's account of *Bildung* for such twists and turns: "Herder conferred upon *Bildung* evaluation as well as assimilation. He was aware that the merging of the old and new involves in its operation both affirmative and negative properties, and that change is not tantamount to a smooth advance or progress."[13] The co-researchers evidenced how one may sometimes obliquely, sometimes directly, bring new meanings to the material of tradition.

Herder's understanding of the third purpose of *Bildung* may be his most problematic and promising. In Bunge's words, "Herder also claims that *Bildung* is guided by a [third] universal purpose—humanity. . . . It expresses the notion that all human beings share a common purpose and direction and is based on the conviction that all human beings are made in the image of God. Herder often equates humanity with religion, claiming that it gives direction to human development in all its diversity."[14] In this schema, the unity of humankind does not lie in any one tradition but in the working out of various traditions. This unity is not a condition in which all are like one another or like any particular one, but one in which all are alike because each has fulfilled the development of its *Bildung*. Therefore, the unity of beliefs and practices is not found in what is handed on to us, but to be found in the future as determined by God. Yet that godly unity can only come about through the transmission of finite and fallible human beliefs and practices.

In this book, I have not attempted to mediate the ongoing debate about the value of tradition, but to simply suggest that it has a place in the study of religious experience. As I noted in the introduction, talk about tradition continues to be a hot topic among systematic and constructive theologians. As we shall see in the following section, it is also a lively concern among pastoral theologians.

A Comparison with Wesleyan and Reformed Traditions

How does the Lutheran theology of consolation compare with that of other religious traditions? In my investigation of consolation in the Lutheran tradition and lived religion, I examined the consoling implications of many of its doctrines, including that of revelation. Having surveyed contemporary pastoral writings, I have found other instances of tradition-specific research into the pastoral implications of the doctrine of revelation. For example, the pastoral theologians Pamela Couture and Nancy Gorsuch recently explored it in their own religious traditions—the former in the Wesleyan tradition and the latter in the Reformed tradition.[15] Although their presentations do not represent all of their respective traditions' pastoral theologians, let alone all their members, Couture and Gorsuch do outline some distinctive features of their traditions. And while their writings do not specifically focus on the theology of consolation, they have implications for the shape of that theology in their particular traditions, and thereby provide points of comparison with the Lutheran theology of consolation.

Couture begins by referencing the unmet needs of poor children and the ecclesial controversies surrounding same-sex unions in order to elucidate revelation from the perspective of the Wesleyan tradition. She maintains that in Wesleyanism revelation is active, better understood as a verb than a noun, and best illustrated by its effects on those who need and receive it. Operative in all the various means of revelation in this tradition—Scripture, tradition, reason, and experience—is the grace of God that precedes our reception of it. Out of this "prevenient grace, God does the revealing, and God prepares us for experiencing that revelation."[16] In response to this grace, believers are called to engage in works of piety and works of mercy—with priority given to the latter. In Couture's interpretation of Wesleyanism, experience, not rational truth, is the medium of revelation that transforms those who encounter it. Finally, revelation is communicated gracefully: "Over against the more rigid and doctrinaire theological formulations, including, but not limited to, the abstractions of much contemporary theology, contemporary theologians have preserved for the everyday ministry the theological gift of rhetoric."[17]

Gorsuch explores three views of revelation largely derived from the Reformed tradition. In the first view, she links general revelation—natural knowledge of God—and special revelation—knowledge of God manifest "in the history of Israel and in the incarnation of Jesus Christ."[18] She does so specifically through a valuing of experience or "cooperation with sense." Building on the insights of the Reformed theologian Daniel Migliore, Gorsuch claims that experience may be a medium of revelation, though she also warns, "There is a point at which a sense of cooperation moves toward 'incorporating' God into human experience, becoming not only idolatrous but a kind of collusion."[19] Gorsuch's second view of revelation involves "the collision of narratives"—the invariably jarring but always saving encounter of knowledge of one's self with knowledge of God. As an example, Gorsuch imagines how a woman who employed scripture to rationalize her demeaned existence might benefit were she to "collide" with the

God who wills freedom and well-being for all persons, including her. Gorsuch again turns to Migliore for her third concept of revelation as "inter-personal communication." Reflecting on her care for "Raymond," a man who struggled with an often disabling depression, Gorsuch "wondered . . . about connections between his story and the larger Christian story in which suffering is part of the story, but not the whole story, and certainly not its ultimate plot."[20]

What does a comparison between these authors' understanding of revelation in their traditions with that contained in the Lutheran tradition reveal about the theology of consolation in each of them?

The Wesleyan Tradition: Invisible persons, not the invisible things of God

In her work on revelation in the Wesleyan tradition, Couture claims that the prioritization of works of mercy over works of piety "allowed the Wesleyans to discover spirituality in those whom the dominant church had made invisible. Furthermore, it allowed the Wesleyans to find, reach out in care, and be responsive to those who were most vulnerable—the poor and children. Most importantly, it made invisible populations visible in the pastoral work and the theology of the Wesleyan movement."[21]

There are some striking parallels between Couture's appropriation of Wesley's concept of revelation and contemporary feminist appropriations of Luther's theology of the cross. For example, in *Compelling Knowledge: A Feminist Proposal for an Epistemology of the Cross,* Mary Solberg claims that those informed by this theology are enabled "to see what we have resisted seeing, drawn into the reality we share with those who have been invisible to us in their suffering; and called to responsive account for what we know."[22] The feminist epistemologies that inform Couture's thought also shape Solberg's and produce a similar conviction: "To the degree that relatively undistorted and ethically defensible knowing matters, the place of the least favored—at the foot of the cross, in all its contemporary forms—is a better place to start than any place of domination."[23] Both Solberg and Couture have appropriated revelation in their traditions to challenge what Elizabeth Kamarck Minnich has called "dominant meaning systems."

Couture contends that God's revelation always leads to caring practices. A similar understanding of revelation—one that may have contributed to the Wesleyan understanding—may be found among the Lutheran Pietists, including August Hermann Francke (1663–1727). Francke's theology led him to establish institutions and practices for the care of those children who were "in tremendous need because of poverty, neglect, and poor educational opportunities."[24] In response, Francke called for a number of social reforms including care for and education of poor children. From such interaction with not only poor children but with all poor persons, Francke believed that the piety and faith of the privileged would be transformed. It seems, therefore, that Couture's Wesleyan-informed claim—that through her own work with children in need, she came to "understand in a deeply experiential way the potential for work of mercy to deepen and transform the work of piety"—has features similar to the convictions of Francke and other Lutheran Pietists that one comes to know certain things about salvation through merciful acts.[25] To paraphrase the earlier citation of Martin Marty, a theologian of the cross makes discoveries not so much in theology itself but in merciful practices informed by theology.

As noted in chapter one, Francke was also an important source for literature on consolation in the Lutheran tradition, as were many subsequent Pietist thinkers. I believe that the Pietists' linkage of the consolation of God with human ministry for suffering is a religious understanding that needs to be re-examined, and perhaps reappropriated. Looking even farther back to Luther's contention that poverty should be eradicated, I look forward to developments of Luther's theology of the cross that will effect new ways of being in the world for the good of the world. I reflect on these traditional sources as I ponder the multiple social dimensions to the suffering of the seven co-researchers, for which they perceived they received little support and—perhaps for that very reason—over which they felt that they had little agency.

It seems to me that by "engag[ing] Luther's theology of the cross in a new, constructive project," Mary Solberg has developed a theology of the cross that speaks to those, like these co-researchers, who need support and empowerment.[26] Similarly, in *Broken Yet Beloved: A Pastoral Theology of the Cross,* Sharon Thornton builds on Luther's, as well as later appropriations of that theology, to voice the needs of those who are often voiceless. Arguing that "the personal is pastoral is political," Thornton raises awareness of the reality of, and causes for, unjust suffering: "Seeing the relationship between one's suffering and the social conditions that create and perpetuate it can help people find new descriptions and alternative meanings for themselves."[27] The new world made visible by this new consciousness unsettles all by bringing "to public expression a deeper reality which may at first appear even strange and foreign to the ones caught in the throes of suffering."[28] Thornton proposes a model of social action that "make[s] the relationship between personal suffering and the social conditions that cause it [to be] visible."[29]

Listening to Thornton, I hear again the voices of many of the co-researchers who seem to be grasping for a schema to frame, and a rhetoric to address, the social dimensions of their suffering.

> "They're under pressures, too. . . . Why the hell should I live?"
> "If you've never been single, and you've never lived alone, you don't know what that is."
> "Instead of giving me the extra money that I need to take care of these children, I'm going further into debt."
> "The business where he worked did not have insurance for him, and . . . they placed him in unsafe conditions."
> "I had IRS calling—I had the state calling about monies that were back-owed. There was an immense amount of pressure that was exerted and I tried in many ways to keep it away from [his spouse] as much as possible."

Hearing their voices, I yearn for models for them—they who are mostly middle class and yet are caught and oppressed by a variety of forces within the structure of their class. Where do persons like Robert hear voices criticizing economic structures that leave many like him destitute by quick upturns and downturns? Where do persons like Allison find support to oppose the grinding forces of unsafe work conditions that kill and maim many? Where might Charles hear sustained challenges to a health care system that is turned in on itself? Where do middle-class African American single mothers like Ruth find solidarity rather than sneers if they begin to lose their standing? Where is the locale in which the divorced are not scorned or scapegoated for the perceived threat they bring to the church's social and moral fabric? Listening to the co-researchers, I yearn for better frames by which pastoral theologians may address these questions and thereby assist persons who live with these questions.

As I have noted earlier, the constructive and systematic theologians in our midst are increasingly voicing such concerns. Similarly, numerous practical/pastoral theologians are looking at the systemic forces at work in producing unjust human suffering. As hopeful as I am about the intent of these works, I am still concerned that they make a difference in the praxis of religious communities and their members. More particularly, I am reminded of the interpretation, cited earlier, of the claim that truth "has to do with making real or *wirklich* what is asserted as being formally and materially true—that is, *wahr*—in action or in life as lived."[30] Accordingly, I suggest that only insofar as the understandings of systematic and practical/pastoral theologians further the well-being of religious communities and their members are their understandings really *(wirklich)* true.

Reformed Tradition: "The pastoral counseling relationship . . . is not itself relationship with God."

Gorsuch's exposition of the pastoral implications of the doctrine of revelation, with its frequent references to the Reformed tradition, offers a helpful means of comparison with Lutheranism. While these traditions share many similarities—full communion between the Evangelical Lutheran Church in America and various Reformed churches in the United States could not have been established recently otherwise—there have been classic differences between them that, this comparison suggests, may remain in their pastoral theologies and lived religion. Gorsuch begins her article with these words: "Revelation may be understood as an event of God's self-disclosure <u>and</u> our appropriation of it as such in faith."[31] For the purposes of my comparison, I find it illuminating to read Gorsuch's three subsequent views of revelation as efforts to relate the divine on one side of her underlined conjunction, "and," with the human on its other side. They are related, first, by experience as a medium that bridges both the special revelation of God's saving work and natural knowledge of God; second, by the collision of narratives between God's story for an individual and that individual's self understanding; and third, by divine revelation itself and a pastoral counselor's communications through which a counselee may experience divine revelation.

However, even as Gorsuch conjoins the divine and the human, she is careful to keep them separate. For example, while she upholds the importance of general revelation and human experience, as noted above, she also quickly cautions that neither be too immediately identified with the divine. Similarly, in her third view of revelation as "interpersonal communication," Gorsuch first conjectures that her witness of a "beneficent presence" to a depressed person, Raymond, may have revealed something to him about God. But then she remarks, "God's revelation is surely not dependent on a care-giver." Thus, while Gorsuch hopes that Raymond's "experience becomes revelation—that he comes to understand and appropriate 'compassionate presence' in a way that moves toward fuller relationship with God," she does not identify her ministry with God's revelation: "The pastoral counseling relationship itself offers an experiential referent for cooperative labor in relationship to a problem and good interpersonal relationship, *but is itself not relationship with God*" [emphasis added].[32]

Gorsuch's care to maintain a separation between things divine and things human contrasts with the Lutheran proclivity for a more direct, less cautious connecting of the divine and human in all its theology, including its theology of consolation. As an example, it is helpful to compare Luther's ministry with the apparently depressed Matthias Weller to Gorsuch's description of her pastoral care with the depressed Raymond. Luther believed that God's revelation to Weller came directly through human care: "God has commanded men to comfort their brethren, and it is God's will that the afflicted should receive such consolation as God's very own."[33] Also, Luther believed that the ministry *was itself* Weller's relationship to God: "It is most certainly God's word, coming to you according to God's command through others, that comforts you."[34] Both these citations evince the "other emphasis" of the theology of consolation noted at the conclusion of chapter two. "God alone," one must say along with Gorsuch (and the Lutheran Gerhard Ebeling). But "God only in very finite and interpersonal means," one must say in the Lutheran tradition.

As noted earlier, most of the co-researchers testified about the ways in which consolation was located in finite means and interpersonal relationships. For Ruth, scripture had a "narrative" that "charged her up" by connecting her with the lives of other struggling saints; it was "as alive for me as another person." Charles pointedly refrained from referring to God in God-self and spoke instead about how the mercy of God was something that was handed on to him, that handled him and that he himself could handle. For Julia, the church sanctuary— the scene where holy acts are performed—offered her "sanctuary" by providing her the place to hear the promise of new life. Allison's ecclesial existence was oriented not only to God but to the people who conveyed the presence of God in the midst of her tragedy.

This conjoining of things divine and human that seems less cautious and more direct than that of the Reformed tradition, as Gorsuch has presented it, is epitomized in the Lutheran assertion that "the finite can bear the infinite." Contrary to what they called the *extra Calvinisticum*—"that because of the property of the human nature it is impossible for Christ to be present at the same time in more than one place, still less to be present with his body everywhere"—for pastoral purposes early Lutherans proposed that God is fully present in the humanity of Jesus.[35] Out of apparent empathy, Jenson attempts to articulate traditional Calvinist concerns about this claim. "Is there not an idolatrous blurring of the differences between God and creatures? From their viewpoint, they [the Calvinists] were right: so long as God is defined by timelessness, and creaturehood is understood as inwardly akin to 'materiality' the Lutheran Christological innovations were indeed intolerably paradoxical."[36]

The pastoral intent of this paradoxical doctrine, however, has been to guide not only those with troubled consciences but all who suffer away from speculations about God in Godself and toward trust in God's embodied goodwill for humanity. In accord with the Lutheran perspective that the infinite may be born "in, with, and under" the most finite forms of consoling ministries, the Lutheran perspective on consolation is that pastoral care is itself the revelation of God.[37]

"Clothed in Nothingness"

The meaning of the Lutheran perspective on consolation may be further elaborated by returning to the citation with which this book began and exploring some of its implications for care, consolation, theology, and theological anthropology.

> Therefore our life is simply contained in the bare Word; for we have Christ, we have eternal life, eternal righteousness, help and consolation. But where is it? We neither possess it in coffers nor hold it in our hands, but have it only in the bare Word. Thus has God clothed his object in nothingness.

"The Word is a transient thing"

There are several ways to interpret this saying by Luther about consolation, and some are not very consoling. As noted earlier, for many persons the term *consolation* itself connotes a very thin gruel for physical and spiritual hungers. It is, finally, nothing more than a tantalizing collection of bare words that do not perform what they promise. In a seemingly similar manner, Luther here says consolation is nothing more than a word. God gives us consolation through that which, laid bare, is nothing.

As also noted in the introduction, Luther constructed his theology of consolation using the theory and practice of certain elements of late-medieval mysticism. Accordingly, one may also read this Luther citation as promoting a strong-willed "letting go" of the will at best and a melancholic surrender to nothingness at worst. Luther here seems to epitomize a Lutheran way of being in the world on which Charles commented: "We sort of expect, like Calvinists sort of expect predestination of certain things that happen, that things are not going to be rosy. Things can get screwed up. People can be mean. And things can be bad. People always said this is Lutheran pessimism or Lutheran realism."

Perhaps even more painful than resigning oneself to death and hell is experiencing God as eerily absent at those painful moments. During the terrors of her troubled marriage and afterward, Ruth said simply, "God is frightening." God frightened Ruth not so much by lashing out at her but by leaving her in the lurch: "Lord, you know you've brought me this far and we're out here in the wilderness." Nothing may be more disconsoling than to encounter nothing from God. And yet, in a way, that is what Luther says: The consolation of God comes in the form and matter of nothing that lasts. Nothing provokes more anxiety than peering into the abyss between being and nothingness, as Paul Tillich repeatedly did in his writings and life.[38]

However, the above interpretations of Luther's remarks are not the only plausible ones. There is another that incorporates all of their frightening features but moves beyond them. Reflecting on this citation of Luther, Jane Strohl emphasizes that God's consolation is located precisely in the "evanescent" quality of "the bare word."[39] That is, God has entrusted God's most precious gift in that which is finite, frail, and human—God has mixed Godself up with that which is nothing: "The word is a transient thing. It strikes the ear and is gone. You don't get more elemental than this: to use speech and hearing, sound waves and air as the medium by which God brings consolation." According to Strohl, therefore, some terror is indeed attached to the consolation of God: "The word has to keep happening to be real." Strohl notes Luther's great fear that God would fall silent because the word might not be spoken. Such a silence would have been the final sign of God's abandonment of God's people. Therefore, Strohl continues, "Luther felt it is important beyond measure that we keep those promises of God sounding." To say this another way, if these promises are not articulated, then people would hear words of God's love from "no-body."

However, along with his concern about the future of this consoling word, Luther trusted that it would be handed on. Looking at some current instances of Lutheran lived religion, his trust seems to have been warranted. For example, Strohl describes the hope she herself received from this evanescent something at a time when God had seemed absent—when, as her troubled marriage was ending, she received communion only hours before the birth of her daughter, and several weeks later presented that daughter for baptism. Referring to both occasions, Strohl simply says, "I had never been so hungry or desperate before." Her lifelong faith and seminary-informed theology did not sustain her: "I could not keep a file on the Gospel. I could not store it up, hold it in my hands, or possess it in a coffer." How then did she receive consolation? "Because a community of Christians came together for communion, because a community of Christians came together for a baptism, the Word was there for me. Yes, it was the old *LBW* *[Lutheran Book of Worship]*, nothing unusual. But it worked. They were doing what they do naturally. They could have done it to a cha-cha and it would have worked."

For the consolation she received for her fright following the disso-lution of her marriage, Ruth seems similarly graced and thankful: "But I have this baptism; I have this Christ."

As I often tell students, in Lutheranism, it is only through that which is here today and gone tomorrow that God is heard today and tomorrow. In this tradition and lived religion, the consolation of God is contained in an infinite number of finite human acts and created elements. Thus, because there were those who hauled rock under the deck of Allison's house, because of the rock itself, because there were those who nurtured Oscar at his church, because someone baked bread and someone else brought that bread to Robert for commu-nion and then said a number of bare words—for these reasons and for countless others—these people received the consolation of God. All these acts and elements have passed away or will pass away. Thus has God clothed God's consolation in nothingness.

Pastoral Care and Theology Clothed in Nothingness

The Lutheran tradition has long been noted for its paradoxical—intol-erably paradoxical, for some—theological proposals. Lutheranism's theology of consolation may be one of these proposals: One finds God not by looking for God, but by looking in the least likely places. Even the designated, and therefore most likely, means of consola-tion—Word, Sacrament, and the priesthood of all believers—are made up of the least likely components—sound waves, water, bread, wine, and sinners. Even more ironically, God may be found outside these components. Thus, Julia emphasizes that she received consolation from the "context" of a sanctuary: that is, in what she pointedly does not relate to Word and Sacrament and the priesthood, but is the scene where the word is proclaimed, the sacraments are administered, and the priesthood is brought into being. Similarly, Charles understands the solace of a generically spiritual, nonbiblical gift book as confirmation of what has been handed to him in the theology of the cross: "To search for God means you are not going to find him." The theology of consolation expresses the paradox found in the theology of the cross, whereby God often appears under the form of opposites.

What does this theology of consolation mean for pastoral care? It means that what are frequently portrayed as the most distinctively pastoral of ministries—counseling and other specialized forms of care—may not always be the primary means of bringing consolation. To be sure, they may do so, and therefore pastors and laity may find good reasons to direct more of their time and talents toward such ministries. The care afforded by such ministry was beneficial to Robert and Charles through hospital chaplaincy, and to Julia through the care of her pastoral psychotherapist. However, from the perspective of theology of the cross, one may discern the consolation of God in the most common church practices—preaching and administering the sacraments. From this viewpoint, one also may encounter the consolation of God in the most ordinary of means—like the hauling of rock for Allison and the performance of a Bach cantata for Ruth.

What place is there for theology in this theology of consolation? The following opinions, from Forde and Solberg respectively, suggest there seems to be none: "Theology, no matter how sweetly done, does not cure tribulation."[40] "Knowledge of God does not and never has come through theology!"[41] Why are these very different theologians of the cross alike in saying such bad things about theology? I believe they are alike in doing so precisely for the sake of human consolation and theology itself.

Of course, theology as a discipline of study may cure tribulation and, in fact, has done so. That is, people have been comforted by insights afforded through the field throughout the centuries. For example, I hypothesize that a previous generation of pastors and laity once found solace in Tillich's ruminations—and that some in this generation may still. My hypothesis is supported by the fact that my colleague in pastoral theology at Vanderbilt Divinity School, Bonnie Miller-McLemore, routinely assigns Tillich's *The Courage to Be* when she teaches the school's introductory pastoral care course. However, throughout the centuries people have received consolation by many means other than theology, through a host of practices that are equally efficacious. Forde's point is that when theology is for proclamation and thereby speaks to the human condition, it is truly sweet and cures tribulation.

Many theologians would concur with Forde that there is often an unfortunate distinction between knowledge of God and the discipline of theology. However, I read Solberg's rather truculent, almost outlandish remark to mean that knowledge of God comes neither through this discipline nor even from anything remotely resembling it. Luther said something similar: "Experience alone makes a theologian. . . . It is by living—no, rather it is by dying and being damned that a theologian is made, not by understanding, reading, or speculating."[42] Of course, saving and consoling knowledge of God may come through the discipline of theology. But from Solberg's perspective as a theologian of the cross, not only is theology inherently no more capable of doing so than any other practice, but because of its prestige and power, it may be less likely to do so.

In the lived religion of the Lutheran co-researchers, some, like Charles, experienced a continuity between their theology and lived religion while others, like Robert, experienced a series of jolting disjunctions. Within the history of Lutheranism, the relationship between theology and lived religion has been a source of tremendous concern and even controversy—especially between the orthodox (echoed today by Charles) who did not separate them and the Pietists who claimed that they should not be separated but often are. The Pietists often argued that, between theology and lived religion, there may be a gap big enough for even God to fall into. Be that as it may, I await proposals that are more irenic than those I have cited—and yet are unmistakably Lutheran—on how theology and lived religion may inform one another for the care and consolation of suffering souls. I look forward to the development of Luther's claim that the suffering of the theologian, brought on by the disparate realities of a sinful, suffering world and a righteous God, is the distinguishing mark of knowledge of God. Furthermore, I look forward to the development of theologies that overcome the division between theology and lived religion by noting that all theology is "theologizing," that is, a practice carried out in the lived religion of various people, and that all lived religion is informed by various forms of theologizing.

Clothed in Nothingness: Humanity Constituted and Consoled by Bare Words

In sketching the history of consolation in Christianity in chapter one, I noted that Hodgson compared the theology of the semi-fictional lay Methodist preacher Dinah Morris in Eliot's *Adam Bede* with Hegel's theology in which God becomes God by becoming what is not God. "'God himself is dead,' it says in a Lutheran [Good Friday] hymn, expressing an awareness that the human, the finite, the fragile, the weak, the negative are themselves a moment of the divine, that they are within God's very self, that finitude, negativity, otherness are not outside of God and do not . . . hinder unity with God."[43]

Luther himself never quite said that God died on the cross, but did locate the majesty of God precisely in God's presence in that ungodly scene and the transcendence of God in God's being hiddenly present in that unjust suffering.

Earlier, I asked whether finite and fallible practices may obscure the providence of God and at the same time be the means of God's consolation. In Lutheranism, those practices are the very means—the only means—by which God does God's business. This relatively unreserved conjoining of divine and human elements may propose a radically different understanding of the divine-human relationship than that of theologians in Luther's time as well as in our own time, such as Kathryn Tanner. She states: "Replacing the divine with the human or confusing the human with the divine threatens, therefore, to make a Christian way of life an idol. Even in Christ, the human never approximates the divine by way of alteration of its own properties."[44]

However, Tanner's understanding of the *communicatio idiomatum* does not match either that of orthodox Lutheranism or recent readings by Finnish Lutheran scholars. For the former, this doctrine is rendered as a "happy exchange," whereby humanity, though sinful, is granted all of the goodness of God.

> I am a sinner, but I am borne by his righteousness, which is given to me. I am unclean, but his holiness is my sanctification, in which I ride gently. I am an ignorant fool, but his wisdom carries me forward. I deserve condemnation, but I am set free by his redemption, which is a safe wagon for me.[45]

The latter group has advanced plausible arguments that Luther frequently and boldly proclaimed the divinization of humanity as the primary effect of this exchange: "For it is true that a man helped by grace is more than a man; indeed, the grace of God gives him the form of God and deifies him, so that even the Scriptures call him 'God' and God's son."[46]

There is another way in which Tanner's comment contrasts with, and thereby highlights, certain features of consolation in Lutheran tradition and lived religion. One may argue that in Lutheranism it makes no sense to refer, as Tanner does, to human properties except as they are affected by the divine-human relationship.

> The doctrine of justification by faith alone implies that human reality is not a substance given prior to all community. Rather, humanity happens in the event of communication, in the speaking and hearing of the word. The word—the actual, ordinary human word—is the active initiation of human reality. What I am is not defined in advance by some set of timelessly possessed attributes; it is being defined in the history of address and response in and by which you and I live together. . . . The doctrine of justification will be secure only when the ontology so sketched is worked out.[47]

Here Jenson proposes an anthropology that derives from a theology. That is to say, he maintains that what it means to be a human is what it means to be in relationship with God. Furthermore, the latter part of the above quotation suggests that a human being is constituted by relationship with other persons. The doctrine of justification requires a "working out" of this relational ontology.

I believe that my analysis of consolation in the early Lutheran tradition has offered *prima facie* evidence that such a relational ontology is central to the tradition: ". . . humanity has no essence and only a disconsolate existence apart from a right relationship with God. God does not bestow this consoling relationship directly on any of us but offers it to all of us only through the ministrations of others" (see page 44). Furthermore, I believe that my analysis of the lived religion of seven Lutherans shows that it was the quality of their human relationships that brought consolation to some and tribulation to others. When they experienced grace, many of them paradoxically experienced it as coming both from God alone and yet also from what they received from others. The relational theological anthropology of the Lutheran tradition means that "humanity" comes into being only through human communication and care. That is, humanity is constituted and consoled by that which is clothed in nothingness.

To be sure, there is some terror attached to this anthropology. Unlike Stoicism, Lutheranism teaches that there is nothing in us by which we are capable of willing ourselves into the peace of God. We have seen examples of this in Lutheran lived religion beyond that of the co-researchers. Strohl, in her dread, "could not keep a file on the Gospel." For Martin and Katherine Luther, in their grief, even the death of Christ was "unable to drive out sorrow from our innermost depths." Along with the terror, however, there is the promise of communities like the ones that brought consolation to Strohl and the Luthers, and there is the promise itself that those communities bring regarding the God who wills life for God's people.

Consolation Clothed in Nothingness: Practices and Tradition

> She [Dinah Morris] provided comfort without consolation; by her sympathetic deeds and truthful speech, she manifested God's presence in the world.[48]

Why comfort without consolation? Because, Hodgson believes, Dinah did not merely make truth-claims about a good God but made that God present through careful speech and deeds. Therefore, the connection between her actions and the divine will was immediate:

"The quiet ministry of Dinah Morris *is* providence at work, and her deep conviction was simply that God is our ever-constant friend who gives us strength by sharing in the joys and sorrows of this mortal life."[49] Like many theologians of the cross, Dinah was not concerned with God in Godself but with God as God is good for humanity. Like some theologians of the cross, she proclaimed a God who suffers when humanity suffers. Like theologian of the cross Solberg and Wesleyan theologian Couture, her focus was on merciful practices. From my perspective as a theologian of the cross, the comfort Dinah Morris brought was thereby the very consolation of God. From this perspective, it is not possible to distinguish the consolation of God from the ministry of humanity.

Luther frequently highlighted our powerlessness to console ourselves or others, because the power to do so comes from God alone. At the same time, he wrote about the importance of the efforts of the consoler in bringing about that consolation.[50] On the one hand, the promise of God's consolation is unconditional. On the other hand, that promise is dependent on its being made. More to the point, that promise is dependent on there being persons who make the promise to others. That is, in this tradition, the consolation of God is dependent on tradition—with all of its problematics. Or to say this even more accurately, consolation is dependent on traditioning—handing on what is good and godly.

For some of the co-researchers, their experience of receiving tradition may be summarized in Charles's words: "You handle it, you let yourself be handled by it, and it works." How does it work—or fail to work—for millions of other Lutherans handling and being handled by their tradition? How does it work for believers within other religious traditions? These are questions worthy of exploration.[51]

Excursus
Some Reflections on Atonement Theologies in Tradition and Lived Religion

⇒•⇐

While I agree with Leanne van Dyk that atonement theologies do not necessarily lead to abuse or neglect, I am confronted with the reality of their doing so in some lived religion. Such an encounter occurred recently when one of my students, who is investigating a variety of religious education programs for parents, shared with me the contents of a curriculum developed and marketed by a mega-church. This curriculum advises loving parents to demonstrate their love for their toddlers by "turning their backs" to their needy cries, just as God turned God's back to the cries from the cross of God's beloved son.

In a number of the co-researchers' stories, I did not have to strain to hear disturbing appropriations of teachings from Luther's Small Catechism and from related atonement theologies. Rather, hearing these stories strained me.

> I love and fear God. And you can't have that tension in a relationship. You can't be afraid of someone and also trust them deeply. You can accept discipline from someone that you love and be in fear of their anger and their wrath and not also really, really trust them. Because if they're just random in their anger, it makes you crazy. It can make you nuts. That's what abused

women go through. They love this man who any Friday night could come home with flowers or a gun. . . . I love the way the catechism contemplates God, because it is exactly my experience. . . . I think that some of how God is revealed to us through the suffering of Jesus isn't without our suffering.

Ruth's account is strikingly similar to the title of a work by Anne Marie Hunter in which she looks for theological sources for women's abuse: "Fear, Respect, and Love: Divine and Human Bonds of Connection and Control." Hunter links these women's conflicted attachments of fear/love for their abusers to those atonement theologies that teach that one must love the God who sends unjust suffering both to God's son and to the abused. Darby Ray summarizes Hunter's concerns this way: "In most communities, there exists a confusion among love, respect, and fear, and this confusion carries over to the way we think about and relate to God. . . . Battered women find themselves with 'a tormentor they love, not one they hate.'"[1]

When I shared with a Lutheran colleague the citation above, in which Ruth links her fear and love of God to her parallel feelings for her abusive husband, that colleague remarked, "That's not what fear and love of God means for Luther. She's just wrapping the tradition around her experience." My response then, and now, is not only that she is certainly doing so, but that we all do so. Of course, one solution to such "wrapping around" may be better education in the tradition. However, other solutions have been proposed by theologians such as Tanner.

Thus contemporary white feminist and womanist theologians often question the propriety of saying that Jesus's death was saving in itself; saying so might appear to validate the suffering of the innocent as a remedy for the faults of their oppressors. Nothing is served by arguments over how far such a suggestion strayed from past Christian practice of talking about the atonement; everything depends on the relative plausibility of their respective construals of how past and present Christian materials hang together. If atonement theories do threaten to justify suffering in contemporary times, would that be harder to integrate with the way these Christian practices hang together than if one were to drop such theories instead?[2]

Reflections on whether atonement theologies, and related theologies about fear/love of God, produce unnecessary suffering is a seemingly unending source of concern. Many, such as Darby Ray and J. Denny Weaver, believe that the Anselmian proposal that God sought "satisfaction" for God's righteous wrath through the violent death of God's son may lead to only more wrath and death. Both Denny and Ray have adopted Gustav Aulen's appropriation of patristic Christus Victor theology in a way they believe avoids the criticisms of Brown and Bohn.[3] In particular, Ray eschews Anselmian proposals that Jesus' death was "satisfaction for sin" and Abelardian proposals that it modeled self-sacrifice and love.[4]

A number of Lutheran theologians, the most prominent being Gerhard Forde, have also joined the chorus of those who spurn the concept of satisfaction or self-sacrifice in atonement theologies. However, in doing this, they have also done something much more: Just as they call on the faithful to avoid speculation about God in Godself, they enjoin them to avoid any concern with God's wherewithal or wishes in the crucifixion of Jesus.

Forde contends that when Luther contemplates the cry of Jesus from the cross, Luther does not attempt to justify God's ways to humanity because he understood that no one can set this passage right. All attempts to get "behind the scene" to the mind of its divine author are bound to be fruitless at best and sanctimonious or smug at worst.[5] In other words, there is nothing compensatory or fulfilling in this particularly unjust act: "Such things as payment and satisfaction are not immediately evident in looking at the cross."[6] Atonement between God and humanity cannot be "accomplished by heavenly transactions between Jesus and God."[7] No attempt is made to understand how God is reconciled by the death of Christ, but only how persons may be brought to faith in God's power through the means of consolation.[8] God is "satisfied" only when certain fruits of the crucifixion and resurrection are manifest—when "theology is for proclamation" and when sacraments are administered to the faithful in their need. In other words, in Luther's understanding of the atonement, there has been a "reversal of directions." No longer should our concern be about God's relationship to Godself in this event, but rather it should be about what God's bearing sin and suffering means for humanity.[9]

We have seen in the lived religion of Ruth, Allison, and Robert that they appropriated the tradition in ways that added to their suffering. Is there any evidence that the experience of other co-researchers differed from that of these three and, in that difference, reflected an understanding like that articulated above by Forde and others? In their avoidance of speculation about the will of God, it does seem that both Charles and Julia articulated something like a "reversal of directions." As he suffered many ills, Charles carefully avoided the kind of concern Ruth expressed: "God is more the environment in which I live rather than someone who is playing tricks on me or jerking me around this way or the other." To be sure, Charles believes that God is involved in all things but does not try to figure out that involvement: "My measure of faith is to say I'll let God figure these things out and I'll ask Him when I get there." Rather than focusing on God in Godself, he focuses on the "handling" given him through many forms of care. Similarly, Julia articulated a theology of the cross focusing on what God had done for her, not for any suffering she should consequently endure: "Christ's suffering in life and on the cross is related to a gift of grace from God. It has nothing to do, in my mind, with the suffering that would happen to a human being because of our relationships or illness or whatever. God's will is not for the divorce. God's will is not for suffering."

Both Charles and Julia have carefully concluded that it is a bad business to concern themselves with the "why" of God. Still, I wonder whether all persons who work with the elements of atonement theologies can or will assemble them the way Charles and Julia have. It is noteworthy that these two are clergy—persons professionally trained in the tradition—while two of the persons who expressed the most tribulation related to those teachings were laywomen—that is, persons who are the objects of most concern surrounding atonement theologies. And it is noteworthy that one clergy person, Robert, held beliefs about the wrath of God that "even though . . . not a part of [his] theology," could not be dispelled by that theology.

While I hold to an atonement theology like that of Charles and Julia—one that eschews efforts to explain suffering on the cross and elsewhere—I am aware that not all people seem to do so. Nor can I dismiss those who hold theologies like those of Ruth and Allison as ill-formed members of the tradition because, as I noted earlier, Luther clearly taught what they and many other Christians believe: "A theologian of the cross (that is, one who speaks of the crucified and hidden God) teaches that punishments, crosses, and death are the most precious treasury of all and the most sacred relics which the Lord of this theology has consecrated and blessed."[10] At the same time, it is not clear to me what it would mean to "drop" atonement theologies, as Tanner indicates may be possible. For what does one drop: The cross? The cry of Jesus from the cross? The silence of God in the face of that cry? The problem with such dropping may be not so much that constitutive parts of a tradition might disappear (an unnecessary worry if tradition is not constituted by parts from the past but by the use of those parts in the present and therefore may be always disappearing) but that a series of experiences that resonate with much of human experience might be removed (a somewhat Schleiermachian understanding of doctrine).

Tanner seems to have a criterion for such dropping or not dropping: "The determination of rightness is a matter of fit."[11] Some other Christians hold similar criteria. For example, reflecting on his experience of the Lutheran tradition, Charles claimed that it "works." The "working" of Charles and the "fitting" of Tanner are akin to a kind of pragmatism that one may *judge* the worth of the idea by its fruits. However, there are other pragmatisms—like that of C. S. Peirce—that emphasize not so much that one may judge as *understand* an idea by its fruits.[12] Peirce laid out this philosophical principle—as clearly as he ever laid out anything—in his famous Pragmatic Maxim: "Consider what effects, which might conceivably have practical bearings, we conceive the object of our conception to have. Then, our conception of these effects is the whole of our conception of the object."[13] Accordingly, for purposes of understanding the ways in which atonement theologies work, one may revise the Pragmatic Maxim this way: "Consider how atonement theologies have practical effects in lived religion, and how the object of atonement theologies—the death and resurrection of Jesus Christ—are understood to be related to these practical effects. Then, our understanding of these effects—that is, an understanding of how atonement theologies bear on lived religions—is the whole of the concept of atonement."

As I noted earlier, Van Dyk suggests that, to a degree, the question of the abusive quality of atonement theology for men as well as women calls not only for theoretical discussion but also for empirical inquiry. That is to say, her remarks suggest that we must investigate the relationship between theologies of atonement and the lived religion of those who have appropriated those theologies. Following the precepts of my revision of Peirce's Pragmatic Maxim, I propose, therefore, that a "consideration" of atonement theologies may come through quantitative and qualitative empirical studies of the beliefs and practices of those who hold various "conceptions" of atonement theology and how their lived religion reforms those "conceptions." I envision such studies conducted primarily by a community of ecclesial inquirers who wish to understand more about the shape of ecclesial existence—the kind of inquiry Schleiermacher called for in his practical theology. Of course, the results of such studies cannot produce certain knowledge of the practical effects of atonement theologies—only in their wildest imaginings do empirical researchers think that certain knowledge of religious beliefs and practices is possible—but it may result in probable knowledge of how those theologies "work." Accordingly, I believe that it would be worthwhile to inquire into how it has worked for other Lutherans—and members of other religious traditions—to have handled and been handled by atonement theologies. The initial focus of this inquiry would not be on judging the worth of these theologies based on their practical effects in lived religion but simply would seek to understand those effects. However, given the probable knowledge that might show itself to the hearts and minds of an ecclesial community of inquirers, I also envision that judgment might follow.

Notes

⨠·⨞

Preface

1. Bonnie J. Miller-McLemore, "The Subject and Practice of Pastoral Theology as a Practical Theological Discipline: Pushing Past the Nagging Identity Crisis to the Poetics of Resistance," in *Liberating Faith Practices: Feminist Practical Theologies in Context,* ed. Denise M. Ackermann and Riet Bons-Storm (Leuven: Peeters, 1998), 179.

2. The Constructive Theology Workgroup was organized in the mid-1970s to promote collaborative work in constructive Christian theology, and most of its efforts have been directed toward preparing textbooks for introductory courses including Peter C. Hodgson and Robert H. King, *Christian Theology: An Introduction to Its Traditions and Tasks* (Minneapolis: Fortress Press, 1994). The group was reconstituted in the late 1990s with a new and expanded membership, with funding from the Wabash Center for Teaching and Learning in Theology and Religion, and with the mission of preparing a new textbook.

3. Amy Plantinga Pauw, "Reflections on the Structure of the Workgroup on Constructive Theology" (unpublished paper for the Constructive Theology Workgroup, Nashville, 2001), 3.

4. Joerg Rieger, "Structuring a Textbook on Constructive Christian Theology" (unpublished paper for the Constructive Theology Workgroup, Nashville, 2001), 7.

5. I have focused directly on this issue in "Pietism of a Higher Order? A Look at Contemporary Practical Theology," *Covenant Quarterly* (August 2002): 2–20.

6. Mark U. Edwards, "Characteristically Lutheran Leanings in Pedagogy" (unpublished paper for the Association of Teaching Theologians,

Department for Theological Education, Division for Ministry, Evangelical Lutheran Church in America, 2001), 13.

7. "Darumb ist unser leben schlects ynn das blosse wort gefast, Denn wir haben ja Christum, wir haben das ewige leben, ewige gerechtickeit, huellf und trost. Aber wo ists? wir sehen nicht, wir haben nicht ynn dem kasten noch henden, sondern allein ynn dem blossen wort. Also gar hat Gott sein ding ynn das nichts gefast" (*D. Martin Luther's Werke: Kritische Gesamtausgabe*, 65 vols. [Weimar: Böhlau, 1883–1993], 32:123, 25–29). Translation by Jane Strohl, "Luther's Eschatology: The Last Times and the Last Things," (Ph.D. diss., University of Chicago, 1989), 120. I have changed Strohl's translation of *Trost* as "comfort" to "consolation" in keeping with my translation of that term throughout this book. However, I have kept her insightful translation of *gefast* as "clothed."

1. Backgrounds and Orientations

1. Edward Farley offers a thoughtful exploration of the relationship between tradition and traditioning in *Ecclesial Reflection: An Anatomy of Theological Method* (Philadelphia: Fortress Press, 1982).

2. Adolf von Harnack, *What Is Christianity?* trans. T. B. Saunders (New York: Harper & Row, 1957), 55.

3. Ibid., 298.

4. For recent Catholic investigations of tradition, see John E. Thiel, *Sense of Tradition: Continuity and Development in Catholic Faith* (Oxford: Oxford University Press, 2000), and Terrence W. Tilley, *Inventing Catholic Tradition* (Maryknoll, N.Y.: Orbis, 2000). For an analysis of the mutual misunderstandings between von Harnack and Loisy, see Stephen Sykes, *The Identity of Christianity: Theologians and the Essence of Christianity from Schleiermacher to Barth* (London: SPCK, 1984), 123–47.

5. Kathryn Tanner, *Theories of Culture: A New Agenda for Theology* (Guides to Theological Inquiry; Minneapolis: Fortress Press, 1997), 129.

6. Ibid., 163.

7. Richard Handler and Jocelyn Linnekin, "Tradition, Genuine or Spurious," *Journal of American Folklore* 97, no. 385 (1984): 276.

8. David D. Hall, ed., *Lived Religion in America: Toward a History of Practice* (Princeton, N.J.: Princeton University Press, 1997), viii.

9. In *Lebensgeschichte und gelebte Religion von Frauen* (Life-history and lived religion of women) (Stuttgart: Kohlhammer, 1998), Regina Sommer details how Christian socialist women struggle with their triple identity. See also Wolf-Eckart Failing and Hans-Gunter Heimbrock, eds., *Gelebte Reli-*

gion wahrnehmen: Lebenswelt, Alltagskultur, Religionpraxis (Noticing lived religion: life-world, daily culture, and the praxis of religion) (Stuttgart: Kohlhammer, 1998).

10. Philip Jacob Spener, *Pia Desideria,* ed. and trans. Theodore G. Tappert (Philadelphia: Fortress Press, 1964), 95.

11. "I argue that if there is to be an authentic religious and philosophical reclamation of Hegel, it is necessary to continue the attempt to view more accurately the man and his work over against the spiritual horizon of his time. This horizon is Pietism—and it is this horizon, I argue, that both haunts and nurtures Hegel throughout his life and even beyond it." Alan Olson, *Hegel and the Spirit: Philosophy as Pneumatology* (Princeton, N.J.: Princeton University Press, 1992), 37.

12. Ibid., 45.

13. Ibid., 27.

14. "Seen in historic perspective, pastoral consolation serves to relieve one's sense of misery by bringing the sufferer into an understanding of his still belonging to the company of hopeful living." William A. Clebsch and Charles R. Jaekle, *Pastoral Care in Historical Perspective* (New York: J. Aronson, 1975), 45. "Consolation serves . . . by helping to relieve the disconsolate person from his sense of misery, even while acknowledging that the damaging or robbing experience that initiated disconsolation remains irreparable in and of itself." Ibid., 47.

15. Thomas C. Oden, *Pastoral Theology: Essentials of Ministry* (San Francisco: Harper & Row, 1982), 226–48.

16. "Nun ist unbestritten, daß im mittelalterlichen und frühneuhochdeutschen Sprachgebrauch 'Trost' einen weiteren semantischen Horizont hatte, als uns vertraut ist, aber auch als dies bei Luther der Fall war" (It is not disputed now that in the standard German usage of the medieval and early modern periods, consolation ['Trost'] had a broader semantic horizon than that with which we are familiar, but also than was the case for Luther). Gerhard Ebeling, *Luthers Seelsorge: Theologie in der Vielfalt der Lebenssituationen an seinen Briefen Dargestellt* (Luther's pastoral care: theology depicted in his letters amidst the diversity of life-situations) (Tübingen: Mohr, 1997), 31.

17. "Dabei ist zu beachten, daß dieses Wort im Gegensatz zum modernen Gebrauch für Luther keinen pejorativen Beiklang hat" (Furthermore, it must be noted that, in contrast to modern usage, this word "Trost" did not have a pejorative ring to it for Luther). Martin Treu, "Trost bei Luther: Ein Anstoß für die heutige Seelsorge" (Consolation according to Luther: an

impetus for today's pastoral care), *Pastoraltheologie* 73, no. 1 (1984): 92. Treu argues that in Luther's thought one is not simply consoled "by" various things but "for" various things—it has an active sense usually not captured in today's usage.

18. John T. McNeill, *A History of the Cure of Souls* (New York: Harper & Row, 1951), 26–36.

19. Lucius Annaeus Seneca, "Consolation of Helvia" in *The Stoic Philosophy of Seneca: Essays and Letters of Seneca,* ed. and trans. Moses Hadas (New York: Norton, 1958), 111–12.

20. Clebsch and Jaekle, *Pastoral Care,* 123.

21. Cyprian, "On Mortality," in *Ante-Nicene Christian Library: Translations of the Writings of the Fathers, The Writings of Cyprian,* vol. 8, ed. Alexander Roberts and James Donaldson (Edinburgh: T. & T. Clark, 1870), 467–68.

22. Ute Mennecke-Haustein, *Luthers Trostbriefe* (Luther's letters of consolation) (Gütersloher: Gerd Mohn, 1989).

23. Jeremy Taylor, "The Rule and Exercise of Holy Dying" in Clebsch and Jaeckle, *Pastoral Care,* 267.

24. George Eliot, *Adam Bede* (London: Penguin, 1985), 155.

25. Ibid., 495.

26. Ibid., 374.

27. Peter C. Hodgson, *The Mystery beneath the Real: Theology in the Fiction of George Eliot* (Minneapolis: Fortress Press, 2000), 17.

28. Georg Wilhelm Friedrich Hegel, *On the Philosophy of Religion: Volume III, The Consummate Religion,* trans. R. F. Brown, P. C. Hodgson, and J. M. Stewart, ed. Peter C. Hodgson (New York: Oxford University Press), 326.

29. Carter Lindberg, "The Lutheran Tradition" in *Care and Curing: Health and Medicine in the Western Religious Traditions,* ed. Ronald L. Numbers and Darrel W. Amundsen (New York: Macmillan, 1986), 173.

30. Gerhard Ebeling, *Luther: An Introduction to His Thought,* trans. R. A. Wilson (Philadelphia: Fortress Press, 1970), 32.

31. Lindberg, "The Lutheran Tradition," 176.

32. See Robert Benne, "The Lutheran Tradition and Public Theology" in *Lutheran Theological Seminary Bulletin* 75 (Fall 1995): 15–26. Also see Philip Hefner, "Living Together under the Gospel: Resources and Needs in the Lutheran Tradition," in *Trinity Seminary Review* 19 (Summer 1997): 19–25.

33. Günther Gassmann and Scott Hendrix, *Fortress Introduction to the Lutheran Confessions* (Minneapolis: Fortress Press, 1999), 180.

34. Epitome 2 and Solid Decoration 3, "Formula of Concord," in *The Book of Concord: The Confessions of the Evangelical Lutheran Church*, ed. Robert Kolb and Timothy J. Wengert, trans. Charles Arand et al. (Minneapolis: Fortress Press, 2000).

35. For some recent reviews of the Lutheran hermeneutical circle, see John Reumann, ed., *Studies in Lutheran Hermeneutics* (Philadelphia: Fortress Press, 1979), especially Horace D. Hummel, "The Influence of Confessional Themes on Biblical Interpretation." For a convincing argument about the central place of "justification" in the New Testament canon, see John Reumann, *Righteousness in the New Testament* (Philadelphia: Fortress Press, 1982). While I believe that Reumann's argument stands or falls independently of his religious tradition, I also find it hard to imagine anyone other than a Lutheran New Testament scholar making his argument.

36. "Wir hoffen, daß mit dieser Veröffentlichung der Vorträge über das so wichtige Thema rechter Seelsorge nach reformatorischem Verständnis einem breiten Leserkreis neue und hilfreiche Anregungen für die Seelsorge vermittelt werden." Joachim Heubach, ed., *Luther als Seelsorger* (Luther as a carer of souls), Veröffentlichungen der Luther Akademie, V. Ratzeburg, vol. 18 (Erlangen: Martin-Luther Verlag, 1991), 7. Throughout the book, I have translated "Seelsorge" as "pastoral care," while I have translated "Seelsorger" as "pastor." I find translations of "Seelsorger" as "carer of souls," "pastoral-care giver," or "pastoral counselor" to be misleadingly suggestive that the function of a Seelsorger is substantially different from that of a "pastor."

37. Gassmann and Hendrix, *Lutheran Confessions*, 180.

38. Martin Marty, *Health and Medicine in the Lutheran Tradition: Being Well* (New York: Crossroad, 1983), 17.

39. Carter Lindberg, "The Lutheran Tradition" in *Care and Curing*, 174.

40. The degree to which all the unaltered forms of the "Symbolical Books" of the Book of Concord are normative for Lutherans has been the source of sometimes dispiriting and sometimes enlivening controversy in the centuries that followed its publication. For a summary of the history and theology of the Book of Concord itself, see Eric W. Gritsch and Robert W. Jenson, *Lutheranism: The Theological Movement and Its Confessional Writings* (Philadelphia: Fortress Press, 1976), 16–33. See also Gassmann and Hendrix, *Lutheran Confessions*, 35–47.

41. Friedrich Schleiermacher, *Christian Caring: Selections from Practical Theology*, trans. James O. Duke (Philadelphia: Fortress Press, 1850/1988), 101.

42. "Postmodernism suggests that those studying religion are seldom, if ever, able to extricate themselves from specific faith commitments of various

kinds. All scholars, not just feminists, must assess the particular biases and advocacies that shape their understandings" (Bonnie J. Miller-McLemore, "Feminist Theory in Pastoral Theology," in Bonnie J. Miller-McLemore and Brita L. Gill-Austern, eds., *Feminist and Womanist Pastoral Theology* (Nashville: Abingdon, 1999), 93.

43. Henning Luther, "Praktische Theologie als Kunst für Alle: Individualität und Kirche in Schleiermachers Verständnis Praktischer Theologie" (Practical theology as an art for everyone: Individuality and the church in Schleiermacher's understanding of practical theology), *Zeitschrift fur Theologie und Kirche* 84:3 (1987): 371–93.

44. Pamela D. Couture, *Blessed Are the Poor? Women's Poverty, Family Policy, and Practical Theology* (Nashville: Abingdon, 1991).

45. Pamela D. Couture, "Feminist, Wesleyan, Practical Theology and the Practice of Pastoral Care," in Ackermann and Bons-Storm, *Liberating Faith Practices,* 44.

46. Thomas C. Oden, *Pastoral Theology: Essentials of Ministry* (New York: Harper & Row, 1982).

47. "Historical objectivism . . . conceals the involvement of the historical consciousness itself in effective history. . . . [h]istorical objectivism resembles statistics, which are such an excellent means of propaganda because they let the facts speak and hence simulate an objectivity that in reality depends on the legitimacy of the questions asked." Hans-Georg Gadamer, *Truth and Method,* trans. Garrett Barden and John Cumming (New York: Seabury, 1975), 268.

48. Ellen T. Charry, *By the Renewing of Your Minds: The Pastoral Function of Christian Doctrine* (New York: Oxford University Press, 1997), 5.

49. Ibid., 17.

50. Andrew Purves, *Pastoral Theology in the Classical Tradition* (Louisville: Westminster John Knox, 2001).

51. Ibid., 115.

52. Anton Boisen, *The Exploration of the Inner World: A Study of Mental Disorder and Religious Experience* (New York: Harper & Row, 1936).

53. Bonnie J. Miller-McLemore, "The Living Human Web: Pastoral Theology at the Turn of the Century," in *Through the Eyes of Women: Insights for Pastoral Care,* ed. Jeanne Stevenson Moessner (Minneapolis: Fortress Press, 1996).

54. Sharon G. Thornton, *Broken Yet Beloved: A Pastoral Theology of the Cross* (St. Louis: Chalice, 2002); Richard C. Eyer, *Pastoral Care under the Cross: God in the Midst of Suffering* (St. Louis: Concordia, 1994).

55. Jane E. Strohl, "Suffering as Redemptive: A Comparison of Christian Experience in the Sixteenth and Twentieth Centuries," in *Remembering the Past: Prospects in Historical Theology*, ed. Mary. P. Engel and Wayne E. Wyman Jr. (Minneapolis: Fortress Press, 1992), 110.

56. Marcia J. Bunge, "The Restless Reader: Johann Gottfried Herder's Interpretation of the New Testament" (Ph.D. diss., University of Chicago, 1986), 17.

2. Consolation in the Early Lutheran Tradition

1. Kathryn Tanner, *Theories of Culture: A New Agenda for Theology* (Guides to Theological Inquiry; Minneapolis: Fortress Press, 1997), 129.

2. Treu argues this point throughout his writings: "Luther bildet aus ihnen kein starres System einander zugeordneter Lehraussagen, sondern er versucht, in immer neuen Anläufen mit ihnen die Vorbedingungen des Trostes zu umschreiben. Das ist insofern verständlich, als es Luther nicht um die Darlegung abstrakt dogmatischer Lehrinhalte geht, sondern um die theologisch reflektierte Erfahrung des Menschen in seiner Verlorenheit coram Deo; nicht zuletzt sind solche Aussagen immer wieder von Luthers eigenen Erfahrungen geprägt" (Luther does not fashion from those concepts ["suffering" "tribulation," and "conscience"] teachings that are placed one next to the other in a rigid system, but attempts to rewrite the pre-conditions of consolation in ever new encounters with those concepts. That is understandable, because what is at stake for Luther is not the abstract presentation of dogmatic matters, but, rather, the experience—reflected on theologically—of humanity in its forlorn state before God. Not least of all, Luther's teachings are repeatedly stamped with his own experience). Martin Treu, "Die Bedeutung der Consolatio für Luthers Seelsorge bis 1525" (The significance of consolation for Luther's pastoral care until 1525), *Luther-jahrbuch* 53 (1986): 18–19.

3. John Thomas McNeill, *A History of the Cure of Souls* (New York: Harper and Brothers, 1951), 163. Similarly, Ebeling contends that the pastoral intent of the Reformation movement "wird deutlich dokumentiert durch die bekannten Tatsachen der Genese von Luthers Theologie" (has been clearly documented in the events known to have been involved in the genesis of Luther's theology). Thus, Luther's reforming insight has important pastoral implications: "Die sogenannte reformatorische Grundentdeckung stellt sich als eine theologisch-exegetische Einsicht von hohem seelsorgerlichen Rang dar" (The so-called fundamental discovery of the Reformation stands as a theological and exegetical insight of the highest

pastoral rank). Gerhard Ebeling, *Luthers Seelsorge: Theologie in der Vielfalt der Lebenssituationen an Seinen Briefen dargestellt* (Luther's pastoral care: Theology depicted in his letters amidst the diversity of life-situations) (Tübingen: Mohr, 1997), 474–75.

4. For summaries of the practice and of Luther's response to it, see Heiko O. Oberman, *Luther: Man between God and the Devil*, trans. E. Walliser-Schwarzbart (New Haven: Yale University Press, 1989), 187–97; Carter Lindberg, *The European Reformations* (Oxford, U.K.; Cambridge, Mass.: Blackwell, 1996), 73–79.

5. Walter Koehler, *Dokumente zum Ablassheit von 1517* (Documents regarding the controversy about indulgences of 1517) (Tübingen: Mohr, 1934), 32:132.

6. Gassmann and Hendrix briefly but helpfully summarize some of the many concomitant social and political forces that aided in the birth and growth of the Lutheran movement. Günther Gassmann and Scott Hendrix, *Fortress Introduction to the Lutheran Confessions* (Minneapolis: Fortress Press, 1999), 1–5.

7. *Luther's Works*, American ed., 55 vols. (St. Louis: Concordia and Philadelphia: Fortress Press, 1955–86), 31:231.

8. Ibid., 297.

9. Ibid., 298.

10. Steiger explores the consoling features in this teaching in Luther. Johann Anselm Steiger, "Die communicatio idiomatum als Achse und Motor der Theologie Luther: Die 'fröhliche Wechsel' als hermeneutischer Schlüssel zu Abendmahlslehre, Anthropologie, Seelsorge, Naturtheologie, Rhetorik und Humor" (The exchange of properties as the axis and motor of Luther's theology: the "happy exchange" as the hermeneutical key to teachings on the Last Supper, anthropology, pastoral care, natural theology, rhetoric, and humor), *Neue Zeitschrift für Systematische Theologie und Religionsphilosophie* 38, no. 1 (1996): 1–28.

11. Apparently, part of the tract's success lay in its consoling message: "The quick and widespread acceptance of this tract attests to the inner needs of the common people." Martin Bertram, introduction to *Luther's Works*, 42:5.

12. Jane Strohl reads this treatise as a straightforward application by Luther of his new understanding of justification: "This true consolation, like the righteousness of faith, is wholly God's gift." Jane E. Strohl, "Luther's 'Fourteen Consolations,'" *Lutheran Quarterly* 3 (1989): 181. Similarly, Appel notes the centrality of the concept that the image of Christ who promises the end of suffering through the resurrection is the source of true

consolation. Helmut Appel, *Anfechtung und Trost in Spätmittelalter und bei Luther* (Tribulation and consolation in the later middle ages and according to Luther) (Leipzig: M. Heinfius, 1938), 121.

13. *Luther's Works,* 42:105.

14. Ibid., 108–9.

15. David Terry notes that, in distinction from Staupitz, Luther called for the dying to focus not on their sins but on the Sacrament. David Terry, "Martin Luther on the Suffering of the Christian" (Ph.D. diss., Boston University, 1990), 205. Similarly, Jared Wicks argues that while Luther maintained a late-medieval concern to make sacraments "the final drama of personal salvation," he nevertheless believed that "one's worthiness and disposition is a marginal matter, perhaps a snare, for what matters is to believe true what God declares and shows forth in sign." Jared Wicks S.J., "Applied Theology at the Deathbed: Luther and the Late-Medieval Tradition of the *Ars Morieni,*" *Gregorianum* 79, no. 2 (1998): 365. Wicks contends that Luther differs from Gerson, Peuntner, and Geiler by focusing on one fact: "The sacraments reveal and apply, not Jesus' offering to God, but God's astounding gift to individual believers." Ibid., 366. Appel contends that for Luther the dying person is less one who struggles to achieve consolation, and more one over whose righteousness God and the devil wage war (Appel, *Anfechtung und Trost,* 134). In a way that seems contrary to Appel, Strohl contends that Luther maintained vestigial concerns to appease the wrath of God at the hour of death: "Here Luther has not progressed beyond the view of medieval Christendom. . . . While proclaiming faith to be a gift, Luther still holds the dying person responsible for remaining constant in the conviction that he is saved by grace alone. Justification is God's work alone, given whole and complete to the believer in this life, but it is not possessed irrevocably until God's trustworthiness has been tested in the hour of one's death and found not wanting." Jane E. Strohl, "The Hour of Death: The Touchstone of the Evangelical Gospel," in "Luther's Eschatology: The Last Times and the Last Things" (Ph.D. diss., University of Chicago, 1989), 165.

16. Treu focuses much of his writings on consolation on this fact: "Zugespitzt kann daher gesagt werden: Luthers Trosttheologie ist der spezifische poimenische Aspekt seiner Rechtfertigungslehre sola fide" (It can be said pointedly: Luther's theology of consolation is the specifically pastoral aspect of his teaching that one is justified by faith alone). Martin Treu, "Trost bei Luther: Ein Anstoß für die heutige Seelsorge" (Consolation according to Luther: an impetus for today's pastoral care), *Pastoraltheologie* 73, no. 1 (1984): 96.

17. "The Augsburg Confession: German Text" in *The Book of Concord: The Confessions of the Evangelical Lutheran Church,* ed. Robert Kolb and Timothy J. Wengert, trans. Charles Arand et al. (Minneapolis: Fortress Press, 2000), 4.1–4.3.

18. "Apology of the Augsburg Confession (September 1531)" in *The Book of Concord,* 4.9, 4.20, 4.61, 4.64.

19. Ibid., 4.8.

20. Ibid., 4.19.

21. Ibid., 4.62.

22. Ibid., 4.40, 4.49, 4.56, 4.72, 4.78, 4.249, 4.305.

23. "The Smalcald Articles (1537)" in *The Book of Concord,* 2.1, 5.

24. Eric W. Gritsch and Robert W. Jenson, *Lutheranism: The Theological Movement and Its Confessional Writings* (Philadelphia: Fortress Press, 1976), 42–43.

25. Friedrich Mildenberger, *Theology of the Lutheran Confessions,* trans. E. Lueker (Philadelphia: Fortress Press, 1986), 37.

26. Harold Grimm, "Introduction to the Heidelberg Disputation" in *Luther's Works,* 31:37. While Staupitz may have misjudged the depth of Luther's theological concerns, he appears to have had an important influence on Luther's own theology of *Seelsorge.* See Markus Wriedt, "Staupitz und Luther, Zur Bedeutung der seelsorgelichen Theologie Johanns von Staupitz für den jungen Martin Luther" (Staupitz and Luther: toward the significance of the pastoral theology of Johannes von Staupitz for the young Luther), Joachim Heubach, ed., *Luther als Seelsorge,* Veröffentlichungen der Luther Akademie, V. Ratzeburg, vol. 18 (Erlangen: Martin-Luther Verlag, 1991).

27. In his theology of the cross, Luther introduced a paradigm shift away from the scholastic theology in which he had been trained. This shift is summarized neatly in Jürgen Moltmann's assertion that the theology of the cross introduced "a new principle of theological epistemology. . . . Luther does not consider theological theory in itself, its subject-matter and its method, but theory in connection with its use by human beings." Jürgen Moltmann, *The Crucified God: The Cross of Christ as the Foundation and Criticism of Christian Theology,* trans. R. A. Wilson and J. Bowden (New York: Harper & Row, 1974), 208. Martin Marty contends that there are pastoral implications of this shift: "The meaning of the cross does not disclose itself in contemplative thought but only in suffering experience. The real theologian makes discoveries not in the study or classroom but in the sickroom." Martin Marty, *Health and Medicine in the Lutheran Tradition* (New York: Crossroad, 1983), 59.

28. Some contend that Luther invariably connected physical and social suffering with these spiritual tribulations: Galen Tinder, "Luther's Theology of Christian Suffering and Its Implications for Pastoral Care," *Dialog* 25, no. 2 (Spring 1986): 109; Martin Treu, "Bedeutung der Consolatio," 13. Others maintain that he believed they may occur separately: Jane E. Strohl, "Luther and the Word of Consolation," *Lutheran Theological Seminary Bulletin* 67 (Winter, 1987): 23; Ebeling, *Luthers Seelsorge*, 397.

29. *Luther's Works*, 3:265.

30. Ibid., 31:129. See also 33:190.

31. Ibid., 14:31–32.

32. Ibid., 17:128.

33. Ibid., 33:139. Since Luther's time, a number of theologians have made the relationship between "God hidden" and "God revealed" their business. Von Loewenich summarized how various nineteenth-century Lutheran theologians accounted for this relationship in Walther Von Loewenich, *Luther's Theology of the Cross,* trans. Herbert J. A. Bouman (Minneapolis: Augsburg, 1976), 45–49. Brian A. Gerrish has done the same for twentieth-century theologians in "'To the Unknown God': Luther and Calvin on the Hiddenness of God" in *The Old Protestantism and the New: Essays on the Reformation Heritage* (Chicago: University of Chicago Press, 1982), 131–47. The list of theologians who concern themselves with this puzzle continues to grow.

34. Gerhard O. Forde, *Theology Is for Proclamation* (Minneapolis: Fortress Press, 1990), 16. Forde also provides the following description of the hidden God's eerie unresponsiveness: "God not preached is the God we can never get off our backs, the God who always comes back to haunt us when we think we have at last managed to escape by theological artifice, the God we invoke in curses even when we do not believe, the God about whose existence or nonexistence we argue in vain, the God whom we absolve from evil in our theodicies but in whose face we must shake our fist anyway, even the God to whom Jesus cried, 'Why have you forsaken me?' and received no answer." Ibid., 26.

35. I cannot here summarize the many complex and thoughtful readings of Luther and Calvin on God hidden, God revealed, and predestination. Some read Luther to have held to a kind of double predestination in his *Bondage of the Will.* Others have argued that Calvin and subsequent Reformed Confessions are careful not to ascribe the same level of agency to God in God's reprobation of the damned to that at work in God's election of the saved. R. C. Sproul, "'Double' Predestination," in *Sola Deo Gloria: Essays in Reformed Theology,* ed. R. C. Sproul (Philadelphia: Presbyterian and

Reformed Publishing Co., 1976). For an argument that strives to harmonize Luther's and Calvin's understanding of the hidden God and the revealed God, see Gerrish's "'To the Unknown God'" in *The Old Protestantism and the New,* 131–49.

36. "Formula of Concord" in *The Book of Concord,* S.D. 11.48.

37. For example, in a letter to one troubled by such matters, Luther wrote, "Your dear brother . . . has informed me that you are sorely troubled about eternal election. I am very sorry to hear this. May Christ our Lord deliver you from this temptation. Amen." Luther then observed that he himself knew "all about this affliction" and used his own experience to assist her. Believing that her doubts about whether God willed her eternal well-being actually came from the devil, Luther directed her away from meditating on such matters: "Now, such thoughts as yours are a vain searching into the majesty of God and a prying into his secret providence." *Martin Luther: Letters of Spiritual Counsel,* ed. and trans. Theodore G. Tappert (Philadelphia: Westminster Press, 1955), 115. Instead, she was enjoined to be consoled with God's revelation of God's good will for her: "He says, 'I am thy God.' This means, 'I care for you; depend upon me, await my bidding, and let me take care of you.'" Ibid., 116.

38. For example, a major controversy concerning predestination broke out at the end of the nineteenth century in the Midwestern United States. Eugene L. Fevold, "Coming of Age (1875–1900)," in *The Lutherans in North America,* ed. E. Clifford Nelson (rev. ed.; Philadelphia: Fortress Press, 1980), 313–25.

39. Gerrish ascribes this tension to the threat of the hidden God always looming behind the promises of the revealed God: "By a strange, circuitous route, Luther's argument ends up jeopardizing his own theological starting point. He insisted at the outset that he proclaimed nothing but 'Christ crucified.' But one of the doctrines that 'Christ crucified' brings with him [*sic*] finally forces us to acknowledge an inscrutable will of God behind and beyond the figure of Christ. We began from God's revelation in Christ as the only secure basis for a knowledge of God's gracious will; we end up by discovering that, after all, God wills many things that he does not show us in his Word" (Gerrish, "To the Unknown God," in *The Old Protestantism and the New,* 137). Strohl, a former student of Gerrish, makes a similar point in arguing that, even before the apocalypse, the God of wrath is always lurking somewhere behind Luther's God of grace: "For all Luther's emphasis on the cross as the only lens through which one can even begin to view the *Deus absconditus,* he does not succeed in neutralizing the fear that . . . drives the

sinner to flee to the hand of God." Jane E. Strohl, "Suffering as Redemptive: A Comparison of Christian Experience in the Sixteenth and Twentieth Centuries" in *Remembering the Past: Prospects in Historical Theology*, ed. M. P. Engel and W. E. Wyman Jr. (Minneapolis: Fortress Press, 1992), 104. Strohl contrasts Luther's position with that of his contemporary, the Anabaptist Hans Denck: "There is for Denck no gulf between what humanity knows of God through the revelation of the Word and what God knows of God's self. The divine will proclaimed publicly is not undermined at any time by some secret decree." Ibid., 103.

40. "The dialectic between the *opus alienum* and *opus proprium* leads Luther to assert that God's works are hidden 'under the form of their opposite.'" Alistair McGrath, *Luther's Theology of the Cross* (London: Blackwell, 1985), 155.

41. *Luther's Works,* 31:225.

42. Ibid., 42:183–84.

43. Ibid., 2:320, 3:5, 4:95, 42:74.

44. Ibid., 6:130f, 7:319, 4:326.

45. Ibid., 4:94.

46. Ibid., 6:376. See David Terry, "Martin Luther on the Suffering of the Christian" (Ph.D. diss., Boston University, 1990), 379–84, for a careful description of "The Game of God" in Luther's *Commentary on Genesis*. For an analysis of Luther's description of God's similar game with Jacob, see also Strohl, "Luther and the Word of Consolation," 24–26.

47. *Luther's Works,* 10:327.

48. Ibid., 30:16. Luther also remarked later, "God does not want us to search for misfortune and to choose it ourselves. Walk in faith and love. If the cross comes, accept it. If it does not come, do not search for it." Ibid., 109–10.

49. Ibid., 23:202.

50. Ibid., 23:205.

51. Ibid., 51:198.

52. Ibid., 14:152

53. Ibid., 24:14.

54. "Lutherans have understood Good Friday and Easter to mean that death and its various penultimate forms are not vanquished but strengthened by denial and repression." Carter Lindberg, "The Lutheran Tradition," in *Care and Curing: Health and Medicine in the Western Religious Traditions,* ed. R. L. Numbers and D. W. Amundsen (New York: Macmillan, 1986), 174.

55. "We do not offer his suffering in and for the world as if it were 'the answer' to human suffering in some doctrinal package. . . . We are part of the response of God to the massive suffering of God's world. In and through the church, visible and invisible, God provides in this world a representative—a priestly people . . . that they assume in concrete ways the concerns of their neighbors, their society, their world." Hall, *God and Human Suffering*, 141.

56. "Women nowadays are pointing out how deadly and paralyzing a wrong understanding of the cross can be, and with their protest they are calling to long-forgotten dimensions of the cross. In the last resort, the cross is a paradoxical symbol. This insight is strengthened by research into symbols: the cross is not just the guillotine or the gallows. Subconsciously it is also the symbol of totality and life and probably was able to survive as the central Christian symbol only with what was at the same time a subconscious significance." Elizabeth Moltmann-Wendel, "Is There a Feminist Theology of the Cross?" in *The Scandal of a Crucified World: Perspectives on the Cross and Suffering*, ed. Yacob Tesfai (Maryknoll, N.Y.: Orbis, 1994), 98.

57. "Finally, an epistemology of the cross, like its theological foundation, directs us to its hope in God's transformative solidarity with the world in its brokenness, and to the possibility that it may serve to guide our knowing and our doing so that [our] love may overflow more and more with knowledge and full insight to help [us] determine what is best." Mary M. Solberg, *Compelling Knowledge: A Feminist Proposal for an Epistemology of the Cross* (Albany, N.Y.: SUNY Press, 1997), 138.

58. Having surveyed a number of pertinent connections and rubs between some contemporary feminist theologians and Luther's theology, Thompson concludes, "Luther's conviction that God addresses human beings in a thoroughly concrete way, can be coupled with the feminist stress of God's presence in this world as leading to concrete reform at all levels of human relationships." Deanna Alice Thompson, "Theological Proximity to the Cross: A Conversation Between Martin Luther and Feminist Theologians" (Ph.D. diss., Vanderbilt University, 1998), 231.

59. Ibid., 81–82.

60. An earlier citation is exemplary: "A theologian of the cross (that is, one who speaks of the crucified and hidden God) teaches that punishments, crosses, and death are the most precious treasury of all and the most sacred relics which the Lord of this theology has blessed" (*Luther's Works*, 31:225). See also Gerhard Forde's recent work in which he analyzes Thesis 21 of the Heidelberg Disputation in a way that seems to connect the two hiddennesses (Gerhard O. Forde, *On Being a Theologian of the Cross: Reflections on Luther's Heidelberg Disputation, 1518* [Grand Rapids: Eerdmans, 1997], 81–90).

61. "The Augsburg Confession: German Text" in *The Book of Concord*, 5.1–4.

62. *Luther's Works*, 42:183. Word and Sacrament convey the unconditional gospel-promise: "So in our suffering we should act so that we give our greatest attention to the promise, in order that our cross and affliction may be turned to good, to something which we could never have asked or thought" (51:201).

63. Ibid., 24:18.

64. Ibid., 6:99–100.

65. Ibid., 3:291. In contrast, the true Christian may pray earnestly with the production of only a few words and in a short period of time. "We say without hesitation that he who contemplates God's sufferings for a day, an hour, yes, only a quarter of an hour, does better than to fast a whole year, pray a psalm daily, yes, better than to hear a hundred masses" (ibid., 42:11).

66. "It remains significant that before the Formula of Concord the Confessions have no special article on Holy Scripture" (Edmund Schlink, *Theology of the Lutheran Confessions*, trans. P. F. Koehneke and H. J. A. Bouman [Philadelphia: Fortress Press, 1961], 4). Schlink also contends that it is the promise contained in scripture that is the source of their authority for the Confessions: "This intense concern with the Gospel suggests that the Gospel is the norm in Scripture and Scripture is the norm for the sake of the Gospel" (ibid., 6). See also Gassmann and Hendrix, *Lutheran Confessions*, 52.

67. "The Large Catechism" in *The Book of Concord*, 4.52–53.

68. *Luther's Works*, 6: 356.

69. Ibid., 6:258.

70. Ibid., 6:364.

71. Ibid., 7:132.

72. Ibid., 4:96.

73. Ibid., 6:141. See also 6:356.

74. Luther referred to satisfaction as the "beginning, origin, door, and entrance to all the abominations of the late-medieval church" (*D. Martin Luther's Werke: Kritische Gesamtausgabe*, 65 vols. [Weimar: Böhlau, 1883–1993], 51:487, 29, in Gerhard O. Forde, "The Work of Christ," in *Christian Dogmatics*, 2 vols., ed. Carl E. Braaten and Robert W. Jenson [Philadelphia: Fortress Press, 1984], 2:49).

75. "The Smalcald Articles" in *The Book of Concord*, 3.6, 5.

76. "The Large Catechism" in *The Book of Concord*, 5.24.

77. Ibid., 5.72. Melanchthon also taught that the sacrament assisted the faithful in suffering: "[It] was instituted to console and strengthen terrified hearts when they believe that Christ's flesh, given for the life of the world, is

their food and that they come to life by being joined to Christ" ("Apology of the Augsburg Confession" in *The Book of Concord*, 12.10).

78. *Luther's Works*, 35:55.

79. Ibid., 35:50–51.

80. Ibid., 35:50. See also 35:58.

81. "The immeasurable grace and mercy of God are given to us in the sacrament to the end that we might put from us all misery and tribulation and lay it upon the community [of saints] and especially on Christ. . . . If I die, I am not alone in death; if I suffer, they suffer with me. All my misfortune is shared with Christ and the saints because I have a sure sign of their love toward me" (*Luther's Works*, 35:54).

82. "Apology of the Augsburg Confession" in *The Book of Concord*, 11, 12.

83. *Luther's Works*, 31:355.

84. Ibid., 35:54.

85. Ibid., 14:79.

86. Luther, *Letters of Spiritual Counsel*, 200. Similarly, "Do not be surprised if you must be assailed by the devil; but take comfort in the fact that you are not alone, but that there are more. They, too, must suffer this way. And bear in mind that your brothers help you fight" (*Luther's Works*, 30:142).

87. Luther, *Letters of Spiritual Counsel*, 41.

88. Ibid., 69.

89. Ibid., 89.

90. Ibid., 96.

91. Ibid., 97.

92. Ibid., 117.

93. *D. Martin Luther's Werke: Kritische Gesamtausgabe, Briefwechsel*, 18 vols. (Weimar: Böhlau, 1930–85), 10, NR. 3794, 20–29, 10.4080:20–29, in Strohl, "Luther and the Word of Consolation," 29.

94. "Apology of the Augsburg Confession" in *The Book of Concord*, 4.8.

95. In her careful study of Luther's letters of consolation, Ute Mennecke-Haustein argues that Luther adds something distinctive by connecting the power of the sacraments to console with God's presence in human discourse. She addresses the paradox that, while it is God alone who is the source of consolation, consolation comes through profane, visible, quite worldly means: "Der Grund für diese Verbindung von Ohnmacht und Vollmacht des Tröstenden ist die sakramentale Struktur der Sprache, in der dem äußeren, profanen Wort—sofern es freilich der Verkündung dienen soll—die Aufgabe zufällt, das innere Wirken des Geistes in der Dimension des sinnlich Erfahrbaren zum Ausdruck zu bringen und so vermittelnd dem

Consolandus in den Bereich des Inneren hinüberzuhelfen" (The basis for the connection of the consoler's powerlessness and powerfulness is the sacramental structure of language. Through the outward, profane Word [provided that it serves the task of proclamation without any impediments], language has the task of bringing the inner workings of the Spirit into the realm of sensate experience, and, correspondingly, of helping the one consoled over into the sphere of the inner Word). Ute Mennecke-Haustein, *Luthers Trostbriefe* (Luther's letters of consolation) (Gütersloher: Gerd Mohn, 1989), 274. I read her understanding of God's presence in that which seems removed from God to be a kind of theology of the cross: "Gott hat seine Heilzusage um der kreatürlichen Schwachheit des Menschen willen, dem es schwerfällt, an das Unsichtbare zu glauben, an ein äußerlich sichtbares und fühlbares Zeichen gebunden" (God has bound God's saving promises to a visible and tangible sign for the sake of humanity, which, in its creaturely weakness, has the difficult task of believing in what cannot be seen). Ibid., 272.

96. "The Large Catechism" in *The Book of Concord*, 1.21.

97. *Luther's Works*, 14:111. See also "Apology of the Augsburg Confession" in *The Book of Concord*, 4.170.

98. "The Large Catechism" in *The Book of Concord*, 1.27.

99. *Luther's Works*, 14:49.

100. Ibid., 14:50.

101. "Stop thinking about it and go to it right merrily. Your body demands it. God wills it and drives you to it. There is nothing that you can do about it" (Luther, *Letters of Spiritual Counsel*, 274).

102. "Except for theology, [music] alone produces what otherwise only theology can do, namely a calm and joyful disposition" (*Luther's Works*, 49:428).

103. Luther, *Letters of Spiritual Counsel*, 86.

104. In Luther's doing so, Mennecke-Haustein has argued that he specifically distinguishes him from the mystical teachings like those of Tauler: "Luther stellt hier der Tröstung durch das Wort Gottes die durch äußerlich-säkulare *delectatio* gegenüber, die 'auch gut' sei. . . . Aber er sieht in beiden Formen der Tröstung nicht, wie die Mystik, den unüberbrückbaren Gegensatz zwischen dem Trost Gottes und dem, den die Welt gibt" (Luther here contrasts the consolation conveyed by the word of God with that brought through external and secular delights, which are "also good." . . . However, unlike the mystics, he does not see in these two forms of consolation an unbridgeable opposition between the consolation of God and that which the world gives). Mennecke-Haustein, *Luthers Trostbriefe*, 271.

Mennecke-Haustein notes that, while many late-medieval pastoral instructors like Gerson believed the company of others to be a source of consolation, Luther further distinguished himself by adding various "worldly" pleasures to that company: "Doch in den meister Fällen verbindet er [Luther] die Mahnung zur *societas* mit der Empfehlung fröhlicher Unterhaltung in scherzhaften Gesprächen, Spielen und im Musizieren" (Yet, in most cases, he [Luther] connects the admonition to be in society with the recommendation of lighthearted entertainment through humorous conversation, games, and music). Ibid., 270. Despite the fact that, on one occasion, Luther attributes to Gerson a pastoral interest in things earthy and fleshly, Mennecke-Haustein also contends: "Gerade in dieser profunden Weltlichkeit ist der Rat, zu Verachtung des Teufels an *elegantes puellae vel chorae* zu denken, charakteristisch für Luther und nicht für Gerson" (Exactly in this profound worldliness is the advice to show contempt for the devil by recalling elegant women or dancing, characteristic for Luther and not for Gerson). Ibid., 271.

105. "Just look at your tools—your needle or thimble, your beer barrel, your goods, your scales and yardstick or measure—and you will read this statement inscribed on them . . . : 'Friend, use me in your relations with your neighbor just as you would want your neighbor to use his property in his relations with you.'" *Luther's Works*, 21:237. "Die in bezug auf Gott und sein Handeln geforderte Passivität im Trostgeschehen wird zum aktiven Handeln des Getrösteten in bezug auf den Nächsten" (The passivity required in relation to God and God's commerce changes into the active commerce of the consoled person in relation to the neighbor). Treu, "Bedeutung der Consolatio," 21. The freedom of the consoled Christian is the freedom to serve the neighbor: "Gegenüber allen Menschengeboten ist er frei, weil er nur an das Gebot der Nächstenliebe gebunden ist, aber die Erfahrung des göttlichen Trostes macht ihn frei zum Dienst am Nächsten, das heißt zur konkreten Bezeugung des göttlichen Trostes" (Christians are free from all human commandments since they are bound only to the commandment to love the neighbor. However, the experience of divine consolation makes them free for service to the neighbor, that is, for a concrete witnessing of divine consolation). Ibid., 22.

106. *Luther's Works*, 14:114–15.

107. *D. Martin Luther's Werke: Kritische Gesamtausgabe*, 65 vols. [Weimar: Böhlau, 1883–1993], 27:417, 13–418, 4 in Gerhard Ebeling, *Luther: An Introduction to His Thought*, trans. R. A. Wilson (Philadelphia: Fortress Press, 1970), 186.

108. Jenson provides a summary on this matter in Luther's Large Cate-chism this way: "We do not discover what is to be done 'before men' by special revelation, or by deduction from Scripture, or by 'praying about it' and obeying the next impulse from within. We discover what is to be done by rational consideration of the situation and of the neighbor's possibilities in it. . . . 'Reason' is the whole effort of man to deal with the circumstances of his life." Gritsch and Jenson, *Lutheranism*, 149–50.

109. Luther, *Letters of Spiritual Counsel*, 171.

110. Ibid., 250.

111. Giordano da Pisa, "Sermon of 1303/4" in Carter Lindberg, *Beyond Charity: Reformation Initiatives for the Poor* (Minneapolis: Fortress Press, 1993), 30.

112. Lindberg, *Beyond Charity*, 66.

113. "Because salvation is now perceived as the foundation of life rather than the goal and achievement of life, the energy and resources poured into acquiring other-worldly capital can be redirected to this-worldly activities. For Luther and his colleagues this meant that faith is to be active in service to the neighbor." Ibid., 97.

114. *Luther's Works*, 44:137, in Lindberg, *Beyond Charity*, 105.

115. "In tiefgreifendem Unterscheid zum 'Seelsorge' im antiken Ver-ständnis geht es nicht darum, sich selbst in die Hand zu bekommen, son-dern sich der Hand eines andern zu überlassen, der allein imstande ist, vor der Übermacht des Bösen zu bewahren" (In fundamental distinction from the classical understanding of pastoral care, it is not a matter of taking one-self by one's own hand, but of giving oneself over into the hand of another, who alone is able to protect one from the overwhelming force of evil). Ebel-ing, *Luthers Seelsorge*, 44.

116. The ancient tradition of *Menschenbildung* still obtains, but, through revelation one is presented with "ein Urteil und eine Hilfe . . . die nicht aus mir selbst entspringen, sondern gewissermaßen von außen mich kommen, allein so aber mein Innerstes zu treffen und zu bergen vermögen" (a judg-ment and a help . . . that does not originate out of myself but that, to some extent, comes from outside of me and is over me). Ibid., 44–45.

117. "Gott allein der Urheber des wahren Trostes ist (God alone is the author of true consolation)." Treu, "Trost bei Luther," 93.

118. "Lutherische Trosttheologie kann den Seelsorge selbst entscheidend entlasten und befreien" (The Lutheran theology of consolation can even decisively free and free up the pastor himself/herself). Ibid., 105. "Luther hat energisch betont, daß der Seelsorger weder der Urheber noch der Garant

des Trostes ist. Ein Satz wie 'Die Seelsorge ist der Träger der *Rechtfertigung Gottes*' wäre von Luther her anzulehnen, mich weil dies dem Pastoranden in seiner Situation nicht einmal so scheinen könnte, sondern weil solch ein Satz in der Gefahr steht, umfassend und ständig zu gelten, und damit den Seelsorger unter eine Art Erfolgszwang stellen würde" (Luther energetically emphasized that the pastor is neither the author nor the guarantor of consolation. Luther would have rejected a sentence such as "The pastor is the bearer of the *justification* of God" not because this might not seem to be the case to the one being pastored to, but because such an assertion stands in danger of being considered comprehensive and permanent, it would put the pastor under a kind of pressure to succeed). Ibid., 105.

119. Christian Möller, "Luthers Seelsorge und die neueren Seelsorgekonzept" (Luther's pastoral care and the new trends in pastoral care) in *Luther als Seelsorger: Veröffentlichungen der Luther Akademie E. V. Ratzeburg*, vol. 18, ed. Joachim Heubach (Erlangen: Martin-Luther Verlag, 1991), 113.

120. Luther, *Letters of Spiritual Counsel*, 89.

121. "Gott bindet sein Wort an menschlicher Wort und laßt seine Stimme in, mit, und unter menschlicher Stimme hören." Möller, "Luthers Seelsorge und die neueren Seelsorgekonzept," 113. Mennecke-Haustein, too, cites this same letter to von Stockhausen as illustrative of what is unique in Luther's theology of consolation: his mixing divine and human sources of solace, just as God mixes divine and human properties in the incarnation: "In der menschlichen Sprache als dem Medium der göttlichen Offenbarung verbinden sich als Innen-und Außenseite die Sphäre des göttlichen Wirkens durch den Heiligen Geist und die Sphäre des Menschlich-Kreatürlichen. Das Wort entspricht damit in seiner Grundstruktur dem Menschen, der ebenfalls zugleich *homo exterior*—kreatürliches Wesen—ist und *homo interior*—der Christenmensch, der im Glauben vor Gott steht" (With human language as the medium of divine revelation, the realm of the divine activity of the Holy Spirit and the realm of what is human/created combine both on the surface and inwardly. In its fundamental structure, the word thereby corresponds to humanity, which is simultaneously the outward person *[homo exterior]* and the inward person *[homo interior]*—the Christian who by faith stands before God). Mennecke-Haustein, *Luthers Trostbriefe*, 273. Somewhat in distinction from Treu, Mennecke-Haustein emphasizes the significance of a caregiver's style and rhetoric in communicating the consolation of God: "Doch die Erkenntnis der Ohnmacht des Predigers führt Luther nun nicht zu dem Schluß, daß es auf sein consolatorisches Bemühen gar nicht ankomme oder daß Form, Sprache und Inhalt seines Trostbriefs beliebig

seinen. Vielmehr betont er immer wieder seinen Willen, sich um den Consolandus zu bemühen, sein Bestes zu geben und alle seine Künste sprachlichen Überredens und Überzeugens, des Aufmunterns und Erheiterns, kurz, seine *rhetorica consolatrix* (vgl. S 19) einzusetzen" (Still the realization of the powerlessness of the preacher does not lead Luther to conclude that consolation does not really depend on his/her efforts to console or that the form, language and content of his letters of consolation are arbitrary. Rather he repeatedly emphasizes that it is his will to exert himself for the one being consoled, to give his best, and to employ his skills in persuading and convincing, in encouraging and cheering up—in short, his rhetoric of consolation). Ibid., 274.

122. Forde, *Theology Is for Proclamation,* 29.

123. Gerhard O. Forde, unpublished lecture, 1986. Cited with permission of author.

3. Significant Negative Events in Seven Lives

1. Kenneth Pargament, perhaps the leading researcher in this field, has recently suggested that religious coping in particular traditions is one of the new frontiers to be investigated. Pargament also indicates the helpfulness of such research for theology and pastoral theology: "Religion has much to gain by opening itself up to scientific psychological inquiry. Not that psychology can demonstrate the absolute truth of religious claims. . . . What psychology can offer are important insights into the footprints left by religion. These insights do not speak to religion's truth, but they do help us understand its manifestations and consequences" (Kenneth I. Pargament, *The Psychology of Religion and Coping: Theory, Research, Practice* [New York: Guilford, 1997], 10).

2. Readers interested in the methods and tools I used to gather data for that study, and this one, may refer to Leonard M. Hummel, "A Kind of Religious Coping: A Theoretical and Empirical Analysis of Consolation in the Lutheran Tradition" (Ph.D. diss., Boston University, 1999).

3. Quantitative research often involves control and manipulation of some of the data—independent variables—in order to determine if they have any significant relationship on other data—dependent variables. The analysis of the quantity of relationships between these data is what gives this method its name. Whereas pre-established metric norms of research are the tools of the quantitative researcher's trade, it is the researcher herself who is often described as the primary tool of qualitative research. Whereas the quantitative researcher first counts and then attempts to explain the data before him, the qualitative researcher first attempts to describe and then

understand the phenomenon before him. His methods of research are many—interviews (structured, semi-structured, or unstructured), the reading of documents, and sometimes actual participation in the data he is researching.

4. Kenneth I. Pargament et al., "A Qualitative Approach to the Study of Religion and Coping: Four Tentative Conclusions" (1990, unpublished manuscript cited with permission of the author), 3. Pargament also offers evidence that this method is especially useful in researching the experience of suffering in particular religious traditions. Having interviewed a Roman Catholic priest and a Christian Science practitioner, he found that for the former, "his tradition, constructed and filtered as it is, form[ed] the background to his religious life and personal coping efforts" (24), and for the latter that it was "impossible to disentangle [his] religious socio-cultural context from the way he came to terms with a critical event in his life" (26–27). Community psychologists find qualitative research useful in analyzing the social context of individual psychological processes, the relationship between individual experience and community, and the complexities of various group phenomena.

5. Don S. Browning, *Fundamental Practical Theology* (Minneapolis: Fortress Press, 1991), 12. Not all qualitative methods permit such give and take between the researcher and the researched. For example, Kruger lays out a series of intricate steps to "bracket out" preconceptions and to render data in a "scientific" language that may be alien to that of one's subjects. Dreyer Kruger, *An Introduction to Phenomenological Psychology* (Pittsburgh: Duquesne University Press, 1979), 130. Another researcher comments that this method involves "approach[ing] the phenomenon to be explored with no preconceived expectations or categories. The researcher is not seeking to validate any preselected theoretical framework. A phenomenological researcher has no preconceived operational definitions. The subject to be studied is approached naively; all data are accepted as given. The data gathered using this method is not limited to observable facts or objective empirical data. They include all available phenomena, including the subjective meanings that these phenomena or experiences had for the participants." Anna Omery, "Phenomenology: A Method for Nursing Research," *Advances in Nursing Science* (January 1983): 50. Kruger, Omery, and a number of other researchers presuppose that there can be research without presuppositions. Like the positivist philosophers before them, they believe that one may bracket one's existential concerns so that the nature of the objects studied may be clearly and distinctly revealed. All, therefore, are subject to

Habermas's, Gadamer's, and Bernstein's critiques of positivist social sciences. In contrast, Collaizzi's brand of phenomenological research, with its emphasis on "dialogic interviewing and imaginative listening, meditation rather than calculation, understanding rather than control" guides my own study here. Paul F. Collaizzi, "Psychological Research as the Phenomenologist Views It," *Existential Phenomenological Alternatives for Psychology,* ed. Ronald S. Vaile and Mark King (New York: Oxford University Press, 1978), 69.

6. William R. Shadish Jr., "Defining Excellence Criteria in Community Research," in *Researching Community Psychology: Issues of Theory and Methods,* ed. Patrick Tolan, Christopher Keys, Fern Chertok, and Leonard Jason (Washington, D.C.: American Psychological Association, 1990), 17.

7. Jane Rutledge, *Coping with Intimacy: A Problem for Single Adult Mormons* (Ph.D. diss., University of Denver, 1993). Pargament et al., "Qualitative Approach."

8. Kenneth I. Pargament and David S. Ensing et al., "God Help Me (I): Religious Coping Efforts as Predictors of the Outcomes to Significant Negative Life Events," *American Journal of Community Psychology* 18, no. 6 (December 1990): 793–824.

9. When using a semi-structured interview schedule, one reads the questions as written to each co-researcher but, if one comes to sense issues important to the subject not covered in the schedule, one may also ask questions not written there. Furthermore, subjects are permitted to ramble— that is, to talk about what they believe is relevant to their experience. The goal of administering semi-structured schedules, therefore, is to comprehend phenomena not solely "on the basis of the researcher's perspective and categories but from those of the participants in the situation studied." Joseph A. Maxwell, "Understanding and Validity in Qualitative Research," *Harvard Educational Review* 62, no. 3 (Fall 1992): 279–300, 289.

10. Peter C. Hill, "Indiscriminate Proreligiousness Scale," in *Measures of Religiosity,* ed. Peter C. Hill and Ralph W. Hood Jr. (Birmingham, Ala.: Religious Education Press, 1999), 123.

11. Regina Sommer, *Lebensgeschichte und gelebte Religion von Frauen* (Stuttgart: Kohlhammer, 1998). Wolf-Eckart Failing and Hans-Gunter Heimbrock, *Gelebte Religion Wahrnehmnen: Lebenswelt, Alltagskultur, Religionpraxis* (Stuttgart: Kohlhammer, 1998). Kristian Fechtner and Michael Haspel, *Religion in der Lebenswelt der Modern* (Stuttgart: Kohlhammer, 1998).

12. Regina Sommer, *Lebensgeschichte und gelebte Religion von Frauen* (Stuttgart: Kohlhammer, 1998), 110.

13. Walther von Loewenich, *Luther's Theology of the Cross,* trans. Herbert J. A. Bouman (Minneapolis: Augsburg, 1976), 114.

14. Tanner writes, "Particularly when it becomes clear that Christians have not always and everywhere believed and valued the same things, theologians often try to talk about Christian identity in terms of tradition." Kathryn Tanner, *Theories of Culture: A New Agenda for Theology* (Guides to Theological Inquiry; Minneapolis: Fortress Press, 1997), 128.

15. Ibid., 132.

16. Ibid., 133.

17. Ibid., 134.

4. Consolation in Lived Religion: Beliefs

1. A scholar of Charles Sanders Peirce states it this way: "Behind every deed, there is ultimately a thought. . . . Acting means that we believe something; believing something means that we are required to act." John E. Smith, *The Spirit of American Philosophy* (Albany, N.Y.: SUNY Press, 1983), 13.

2. In a number of significant ways, therefore, the solace these co-researchers describe differs from that described by the Mormon subjects of Mark Chamberlain's study, "The Role of Religion in Coping: A Qualitative Study of Eight Mormons" (Ph.D. diss., Brigham Young University, 1994), in which Chamberlain examines the religious beliefs and practices that young adult members of the Church of Jesus Christ of the Latter-Day Saints used to cope with a variety of stresses brought on by their grueling white-collar labor. For these Mormons, faith is something they consciously invoke to change from less godly ways to godlier ways. While Chamberlain did not indicate anything tradition-specific in this coping, my own study of the Mormon tradition strongly suggests to me that there was. For example, O'Dea's observation that "Mormonism had early embraced an extreme Arminianism and revival practices that are a part of this religious tradition, placing great emphasis upon the freedom of the human will," suggested why "change" might have been such a powerful "life-form" in their coping. Thomas O'Dea, *The Mormons* (Chicago: University of Chicago Press, 1957), 129. Furthermore, O'Dea's judgment that "Freedom, rationality, a world to conquer, a projection of the American continent to infinity" seems a fair summary of the coping efforts of these Latter-Day Saints (154). My thanks to my colleague at Vanderbilt, Kathleen Flake, for sharing her own impressions of these studies with me from her vast knowledge of and appreciation for Latter-Day Saint tradition and lived religion.

3. Robert Peel, *Health and Medicine in the Christian Science Tradition: Principle, Practice, and Challenge* (New York: Crossroad, 1998), 7.

4. David D. Hall, *Worlds of Wonder, Days of Judgment: Popular Religious Belief in Early New England* (New York: Knopf, 1989).

5. Timothy P. Weber is careful to note that attacks on tobacco use have been less common in the American South, while in other regions of the United States a sizeable number have "vehemently attacked tobacco and called on fellow believers to forsake it." Timothy P. Weber, "The Baptist Tradition" in *Caring and Curing: Health and Medicine in the Western Religious Traditions,* ed. R. L. Numbers and D. W. Amundsen (New York: Macmillan, 1986), 298.

6. John H. Leith, ed., *Creeds and Doctrines of the Church: A Reader in Christian Doctrine from the Bible to the Present* (Richmond, Va.: John Knox, 1973), 339.

7. Marcia J. Bunge, "Herder and the Origins of a Historical View of Religion" in *Revisioning the Past: Prospects in Historical Theology,* ed. Mary Potter Engel and Walter E. Wyman Jr. (Minneapolis: Fortress Press, 1992), 178. We shall revisit this claim in the conclusion.

8. For a thoughtful study of this concept in Tauler's thought, see Stefan Zekorn, *Gelassenheit und Einkehr: Zu Grundlage und Gestalt geistlichen Lebens bei Johannes Tauler* (*Gelassenheit* and Contemplation: Toward the Foundation and Form of the Spiritual Life according to Johannes Tauler) (Würzburg: Echter, 1993). Others in the late-medieval period made use of this term before Tauler, including Angelus Silenius and perhaps most notably Meister Eckhardt. See Udo Kern, ed., *Freiheit und Gelassenheit: Meister Eckhart Heute* (Freedom and *Gelassenheit:* Meister Eckhart Today) (Munich: Kaiser Verlag, 1980). For an examination of Martin Heidegger's later analysis of Eckhardt's thought in general and of *Gelassenheit* in particular, see John D. Caputo, *The Mystical Element in Heidegger's Thought* (Athens, Ohio: Ohio University Press, 1978), especially pages 118–26. For a recent appropriation of *Gelassenheit* as a tool in political struggles against evil, see Dorothee Soelle, *The Silent Cry: Mysticism and Resistance,* trans. Barbara and Martin Rumscheidt (Minneapolis: Fortress Press, 2001).

9. Carter Lindberg, *The Third Reformation? Charismatic Movements and the Lutheran Tradition* (Macon, Ga.: Mercer University Press, 1983).

10. William James, *The Varieties of Religious Experience* (New York: Random House, 1902). See especially pages 77–162.

11. Walter Klaassen, "The Anabaptist Tradition" in Numbers and Amundsen, *Caring and Curing,* 273–74. For another look at the centrality

of this concept in the Anabaptist tradition, see Robert D. Cornwall, "The Way of the Cross: The Anabaptist Concept of *Gelassenheit*," *Studia Biblica et Theologia* 17, no. 1 (1989): 33–54.

12. Luther's use of the concept is not as a human virtue but a Christian response to God's works of righteousness (Lindberg, *The Third Reformation?* 32). However, Lindberg further contends that the mystical roots of this teaching render its practice prone to work-righteousness, where "in spite of the role of grace in creating the sinner's receptivity for God, the burden of proof remains on the sinner to 'achieve' resignation and self-condemnation." Ibid., 36. Accordingly, Lindberg links *Gelassenheit* to a semi-Pelagian doctrine of justification whereby one does what one can to make oneself right with God—in this case, humbling oneself and forswearing one's desires. Christian Link argues that Luther gives a twist to a late-medieval distinction between the active life and the passive life, which ironically renders contemplative life—often thought to be a higher form of *Gelassenheit*—to be, in fact, the despised active life, and the active life of the justified sinner to be the passive, i.e., godly, way of being in the world. Christian Link, "Vita passiva: Rechtfertigung als Lebensvorgang" (The passive life: justification as a life-process), *Evangelische Theologie* 44/4 (1984): 315–51.

13. Gerhard wrote many pastoral treatises, a fact that belies the charge that the orthodox had no concern for the care of souls. Steiger has commented on the practical nature of Gerhard's work. Johann Anselm Steiger, "Seelsorge, Dogmatik und Mystik bei Johann Gerhard: Ein Beitrag zu Theologie und Frömmigkeit der Lutherischen Orthodoxie" (Pastoral care, dogmatics and mysticism in John Gerhard: A contribution to the theology and piety of Lutheran orthodoxy). *Zeitschrift für Kirchengeschichte* 106 (1995): 329–44.

14. "Die ihn leitende Frage war: Wie es möglich, die Weigelsche Frömmigkeit orthodox fruchtbar zu machen, ohne gegen die dogmatischen Grundsätze vor allem der CA und der Formula Concordiae zu verstoßen?" (The dominant question for him was whether it was possible to make Weigel's piety fruitful for orthodoxy without violating the dogmatic fundamentalism of the Formula of Concord and, above all, the Augsburg Confession). Ibid., 338.

15. "Ebenfalls in der Absicht, Mißverständnisse auszuschließen, hat Gerhard in der zweiter Auflage seiner, 'Schola Pietatis' das Taulersche Stichwort 'Gelassenheit' nicht mehr benutzt und sich in einem Brief an Balthasar Mentzer hierüber dahingehend geäußert, er habe unter 'Gelassenheit' nichts anderes verstanden als Luther, nämlich das Abstandnehmen des Menschen von seinem eigenen, natürlichen und sündigen Willen, wolle aber auf den

Gebrauch des Terminus verzichten, um nicht eine spiritualistische Interpretation zu evozieren" (Likewise, with the intention of ruling out misunderstandings, Gerhard no longer used the key-term Gelassenheit [employed by Tauler and his followers] in his second edition of the "The Scholar of Piety." Furthermore, in his letter to Balthasar Mentzer, Gerhard expresses in passing that he has no other understanding of Gelassenheit than that of Luther—Gelassenheit is the process whereby humanity renounces its own, natural sinful will—but that he wishes to renounce all use of the term in order to not evoke a spiritualist interpretation of his purpose). Johann Anselm Steiger, *Johann Gerhard (1582–1637): Studien zu Theologie und Frömmigkeit des Kirchenvaters der lutherischen Orthodoxie* (Studies on the theology and piety of the church fathers of Lutheran orthodoxy) (Stuttgart–Bad Cannstatt: Frommann-Holzboog Verlag, 1997), 79. Gerhard himself says the following:

> Vox Tauleriana, Gelassenheit, qua & Lutherus utitur, non alio a me acciptur sensu, quam eo, quem statim addo, videlicet, ut pro abnegatione nostri & resignatione voluntatis propriae accipiatur. . . . Nihilo tamen minus, cum intelligerem, hac vocula Enthusiastas abuti, eamque calumniae esse obnoxiam, submoui eam ex libris Scholae Eusebianae. absit enim a me, ut vel verbum proferre sciens velim, quod somnis fanaticorum istorum blandiatur.

> Tauler's term, *Gelassenheit,* which Luther also uses, I accept but only for the meaning that I here state: for the denial and resignation of our own proper will. . . . Nevertheless, since I recognize that the Enthusiasts abuse the word and that it is subject to unfair criticism, I have removed it from the books of the Eusebian School. Far be it from me, to want knowingly to put forward the slightest word that would encourage the dreams of those fanatics.

Erdmann Rudolf Fischer, *Vita Iohannis Gerhardi* (Leipzig, 1723), 301. My thanks to my colleague at Vanderbilt, J. Patout Burns, for his translation of the Latin.

16. Lindberg, *The Third Reformation?* 142.

17. Many Stoics taught that the ideal attitude in the face of suffering is indifference, and that one could will one's soul into such an apathetic state for, in Stoic anthropology "nothing is so tractable as the human soul." Epictetus, Disc 1.31 in Frederick Copleston, S.J., *A History of Philosophy:*

Volume 1, Part 2, Greece and Rome (Garden City, N.Y.: Image Books, 1962), 176. In a manner like the Stoics, the early Lutherans taught that it is a Christian's trust in God that enables one to endure suffering. Yet in the early Lutheran tradition, nothing is so *intractable,* so unable to set itself right when things go wrong, as the suffering soul. By all accounts, Luther did not display Stoic indifference during or after his daughter's death, but found consolation in his trust that others were praying for and with him.

18. "Gerhard führt Belege aus den Werken Ciceros, Horaz, Homers Senecas u. a. an, was veranschaulicht, wie viel Gerhard an einer Berücksichtigung der heidnisch-antiken Tradition im christlichen Kontext gelegen war" (Gerhard cites examples from the work of Cicero, Horace, Seneca, Homer, and so on, which illustrate the degree to which he located his work as a reconsideration of the classical [non-Christian] tradition in the context of Christianity). Steiger, *Johann Gerhard*, 35. As noted (p. 175, n. 115), Ebeling is concerned to show that Luther broke from this tradition.

19. He may be like a "twice-borner" not only in the Mennonite sense but also in the Jamesian sense. Though James regards Luther as having some once-born (i.e., optimistic and healthy) ways of confronting dangers, he most frequently portrays Luther as a typical twice-borner. Furthermore, James regards the Stoics as exemplary of a twice-born, gloomy-minded way of being religious but holds in high esteem a then newly gathered group of once-borners, the Christian Scientists—ironically, one of the groups with whom Michael identifies.

20. Kathryn Tanner, *Theories of Culture: A New Agenda for Theology* (Guides to Theological Inquiry; Minneapolis: Fortress Press, 1997), 108. Not that some people do not attempt to set up such boundaries. For example, Steiger strives to show that the "Orthodox reception of Mysticism [like the mysticism of Tauler and his use of *Gelassenheit*] did not take place slavishly (Die orthodox Beerbung der Mystik geschieht nicht sklavisch)." Steiger, "Seelsorge, Dogmatik, und Mystik bei Johann Gerhard," 338. That is, Steiger asserts that Gerhard maintained mastery over this non-Lutheran material. But how can Steiger prove this assertion? For just as one may claim that, for a time, Tauler was included in the circle of Gerhard's orthodox Lutheran thought, so one may claim that, for the same length of time, Gerhard was brought inside the fold of classical (but developing) Stoic thought and/or late-medieval mysticism such as Tauler's. I have similar concerns about Ebehard Winkler's contention that Meister Eckhardt employed his Christian belief in the unity of God to extract from Seneca "what appeared to him as true and useful (was ihm als wahr und brauchbar erscheint)." Eber-

hard Winkler, "Wort Gottes und Hermeneutik bei Meister Eckhart" (The Word of God and Hermeneutics according to Eckhard) in Kern, *Freiheit und Gelassenheit* (Freedom and *Gelassenheit*) (Munich: Kaiser, 1980), 177.

21. Barry Kendall Cunningham, "Religious Orientation as a Coping Resource among Black Americans" (Ph.D. diss., University of Michigan, 1984), 38.

22. Ibid., 78.

23. Laurence E. Jackson and Robert D. Coursey, "The Relationship of God Control and Internal Locus of Control to Intrinsic Religious Motivation, Coping, and Purpose in Life," *Journal for the Scientific Study of Religion* 27, no. 3 (September 1988): 399.

24. Ibid., 400.

25. Ibid., 407.

26. Nicholas C. Cooper-Lewter and Henry H. Mitchell, *Soul Theology: The Heart of American Black Culture* (San Francisco: Harper & Row, 1986), 14.

27. In "The Role of Religion in the Lives of Resilient, Urban, African-American Single Mothers," Anne E. Brodsky indicates that a variety of coping styles, including some like Ruth's but some very different from hers, were found among the subjects of her study. *Journal of Community Psychology* 28, no. 2 (2000): 199–219.

28. Moore maintains that studies of the contemporary African American church also should take into account the various traditions within that community: "The fact that there are a variety of churches which African-Americans attend suggests community diversity. . . . what values, beliefs, and behaviors do people share in a particular church? How would those values, beliefs, and behaviors compare with those of members from the same denomination, but not in the same church?" (Tom Moore, "The African-American Church: A Source of Empowerment, Mutual Help, and Social Change," in K. I. Pargament, K. I. Maton, and R. E. Hess, eds., *Religion and Prevention in Mental Health: Research, Vision, and Action* [Binghamton: Haworth, 1992], 253). Among the suggestions Cunningham offers for future study is one similar to that made by Moore—denominational and religious-tradition specific research in coping among black Americans. Barry Kendall Cunningham, "Religious Orientation as a Coping Resource among Black Americans" (Ph.D. diss., University of Michigan, 1984), 80. Like Moore and Cunningham, Jackson and Coursey close their study by calling for the examination of particular religious traditions and denominations within the African-American community: "The point, then, is that religious

beliefs, including perceptions of God control, are diverse, and this has significant implications regarding generalizing results from one religious sample [of African-Americans] to the next" (Jackson and Coursey, "Relationship," 409).

29. Walther von Loewenich, *Luther's Theology of the Cross,* trans. Herbert J. A. Bouman (Minneapolis: Augsburg, 1976), 114.

30. *Luther's Works,* American ed., 55 vols. (St. Louis: Concordia and Philadelphia: Fortress Press, 1955–86), 7:101.

31. Ibid.

32. Leanne Van Dyk, "Do Theories of Atonement Foster Abuse?" *Dialog* 35 (Winter 1996): 24.

33. *Luther's Works,* 6:376.

5. Consolation in Lived Religion: Practices

1. Robert's and Allison's questioning bear striking similarities to the quote of Luther cited in chapter three: "When such trials of 'Why' come, beware that you do not answer and allow these attacks to get control. Rather, close your eyes and kill reason and take refuge with the Word. Do not let the 'Why' get into your heart. The devil is too powerful; you cannot cope with the situation." *Luther's Works,* American ed., 55 vols. (St. Louis: Concordia and Philadelphia: Fortress Press, 1955–86), 17:128.

2. See chap. 2, n. 95, for Ute Mennecke-Haustein's proposal that the tangibility of the sacraments is a central feature of Luther's sacramental theology.

3. See chap. 2, n. 123, on Christian Möller.

4. Martin Luther, "The Large Catechism" in *The Book of Concord,* 1.27.

5. Their ability to do so also correlates with the teaching in Article 18 of the Augsburg Confession in the Book of Concord that human will, while bound in its relationship with God, has a degree of freedom in other areas: "[Human] will has some freedom for producing civil righteousness and for choosing things subject to reason. . . . In Book III of his *Hypognosticon* Augustine says this in just so many words: 'We confess that all human beings have a free will that possesses the judgment of reason. It does not enable them, without God, to begin—much less complete—anything that pertains to God, but only to perform the good or evil deeds of this life. By "good deeds" I mean those that arise from the good in nature, that is, the will to labor in the field, to eat and drink, to have a friend, to wear clothes, to build a house, to marry, to raise cattle, to learn various useful skills, or to do whatever good pertains to this life'" ("The Augsburg Confession," Latin version, 18.1–5 in *The Book of Concord*).

6. Jane Rutledge, "Coping with Intimacy: A Problem for Single Adult Mormons" (Ph.D. diss., University of Denver, 1993).

7. Abigail R. Evans, *Redeeming Marketplace Medicine: A Theology of Health Care* (Cleveland: Pilgrim, 1999). A helpful summary of these problems, and very helpful suggestions for their remedy, are presented in *Our Ministry of Healing: Health and Health Care Today* (Chicago: Evangelical Lutheran Church in America, 2001).

8. Pamela D. Couture, *Blessed Are the Poor? Women's Poverty, Family Policy and Practical Theology* (Nashville: Abingdon, 1991), 37.

9. Susan Dunlap, *Counseling Depressed Women* (Louisville: Westminster John Knox, 1997), 7.

10. For an analysis of the interpersonal discord and role transitions that are associated with depression, see Myrna M. Weissman, John C. Markowitz, and Gerald L. Klerman, *Comprehensive Guide to Interpersonal Psychotherapy* (New York: Basic Books, 2000), 75–101. For a summary of recent research on the strong association between marital discord and depression, with a focus on the experience of women, see Jennifer Christian Herman, K. Daniel O'Leary, and Sarah Avery Leaf, "The Impact of Severe Negative Events in Marriage on Depression," *The Journal of Social and Clinical Psychology* (Spring 2001). For a look at the epidemiology of women and depression, see S. I. Wolk and M. M. Weissman, "Psychiatric Problems of Women," in *Current Practice in Medicine*, ed. R. C. Bone (New York: Churchill Livingstone, 1999), 121–28.

11. Robert Coles, "Dickens and Little Dorrit," in *That Red Wheelbarrow: Selected Literary Essays* (Iowa City: University of Iowa Press, 1988), 25.

6. "Clothed in Nothingness"

1. For example, see Merton P. Strommen, Milo L. Brekke, Ralph C. Underwager, Arthur L. Johnson, *A Study of Generations* (Minneapolis: Augsburg, 1972). This investigation, subtitled *A Report of a Two-Year Study of 5,000 Lutherans Between the Ages of 15–65: Their Beliefs, Values, Attitudes, Behavior,* revealed much about these four dimensions among this sample and, with a high degree of statistical probability, in the population they represented. While dated, its results indicate what those who study popular religion and lived religion—and those in close contact with both—have concluded by other means: while official theology may be one thing, what the laity believe and practice, though not completely different, may be significantly different. For a more recent study that arrives at what seems to be a similar conclusion, see "Religious Commitment in the Evangelical Lutheran

Church in America: Findings from the *Faith Practices Survey.*" Kenneth W. Innskeep, Department for Research and Evaluation, Evangelical Lutheran Church in America, July 23, 2001. (http://www.elca.org/re/reports/faith-prac.pdf). The following citation is illustrative: "It [the survey] shows that Lutherans are committed and that they believe and practice their faith routinely, but the ELCA is remarkably diverse when it comes to how its members approach beliefs and practices" (2).

2. Brooks Hays and John E. Steely, *The Baptist Way of Life* (Macon, Ga.: Mercer University Press, 1981).

3. Using Bordieu's notion of *habitus,* Peter Stromberg examined the ways members of a Swedish pietist congregation experience grace through their communal life and concludes that it is not a cultural consensus about the symbols of grace that binds this community, but their commitment to shared worship and life together. See Peter G. Stromberg, *Symbols of Community: The Cultural System of a Swedish Church* (Tucson: University of Arizona Press, 1986).

4. Kathryn Tanner, *Theories of Culture: A New Agenda for Theology* (Guides to Theological Inquiry; Minneapolis: Fortress Press, 1997), 122.

5. Ibid., 132.

6. Ibid., 116.

7. Ibid., 133.

8. David D. Hall, *Lived Religion: Toward a History of Practice* (Princeton, N.J.: Princeton University Press, 1997), x.

9. Ibid., xii.

10. Marcia J. Bunge, "Herder and the Origins of a Historical View of Religion," in *Revisioning the Past: Prospects in Historical Theology,* ed., Mary Potter Engel and Walter E. Wyman Jr. (Minneapolis: Fortress Press, 1992), 178.

11. Ibid., 178.

12. Tanner, *Theories of Culture,* 78.

13. Frederick Barnard, "Culture and Civilization in Modern Times," in *The Dictionary of the History of Ideas: Studies of Selected Pivotal Ideas,* vol. 1 (New York: Scribner, 1973), 620–21.

14. Bunge, "Herder and the Origins of a Historical View of Religion," 178.

15. Pamela Couture, "Revelation in Pastoral Theology: A Wesleyan Perspective," *The Journal of Pastoral Theology* 9 (1999): 21–34. Nancy J. Gorsuch, "Revelation and Pastoral Theology: Cooperation, Collision, and Communication," *The Journal of Pastoral Theology* 9 (1999): 35–48.

16. Couture, "Revelation in Pastoral Theology," 22.

17. Ibid., 26.

18. Gorsuch, "Revelation and Pastoral Theology," 36.

19. Ibid., 38.

20. Ibid., 44.

21. Couture, "Revelation in Pastoral Theology," 27.

22. Mary Solberg, *Compelling Knowledge: A Feminist Proposal for an Epistemology of the Cross* (Albany: SUNY Press, 1997), 17.

23. Ibid., 118.

24. Marcia J. Bunge, "The Child in German Pietism," in *The Child in Christian Thought* (Grand Rapids: Eerdmans, 2000), 252.

25. Couture, "Revelation in Pastoral Theology," 28.

26. Solberg, *Compelling Knowledge,* 11.

27. Sharon G. Thornton, *Broken Yet Beloved: A Pastoral Theology of the Cross* (St. Louis: Chalice, 2002), 117.

28. Ibid., 152.

29. Ibid., 187.

30. Alan Olson, *Hegel and the Spirit: Philosophy as Pneumatology* (Princeton, N.J.: Princeton University Press, 1992), 27.

31. Gorsuch, "Revelation and Pastoral Theology," 35.

32. Ibid., 44.

33. Martin Luther, *Letters of Spiritual Counsel,* ed. and trans. Theodore G. Tappert (Philadelphia: Westminster Press, 1955), 96.

34. Ibid., 89.

35. "Formula of Concord," Epitome 8, *The Book of Concord: The Confessions of the Evangelical Lutheran Church,* ed. Robert Kolb and Timothy J. Wengert, trans. Charles Arand et al. (Minneapolis: Fortress Press, 2000), 513.

36. Eric W. Gritsch and Robert W. Jenson, *Lutheranism: The Theological Movement and Its Confessional Writings* (Philadelphia: Fortress Press, 1976), 108.

37. In fact, some believe Calvin taught a theology as incarnational as that of Luther. See Brian A. Gerrish, *Grace and Gratitude: The Eucharistic Theology of John Calvin* (Minneapolis: Fortress Press, 1993).

38. At various places in the first volume of his *Systematic Theology* and throughout *The Courage to Be,* Tillich grappled with what he regarded to be the "nothingness" of human existence [See *Systematic Theology,* 3 vols. (Chicago: University of Chicago Press, 1951–63); *The Courage to Be* (New Haven: Yale University Press, 1952)]. In the conclusion of his autobiographical reflections, Tillich extends to all humanity his observations about

his own long, complicated life: "The man [*sic*] who stands on the many boundaries experiences the unrest, insecurity, and inner limitation of existence in many forms. He knows the impossibility of attaining serenity, security, and perfection. This holds true in life as well as in thought, and may explain why the experiences I have recounted are rather fragmentary and tentative." Paul Tillich, *On the Boundary: An Autobiographical Sketch* (New York: Scribner, 1966), 97–98.

39. This citation from Strohl and the ones that follow in this section are taken from a videotape of her public address "Evangelism and the Congregation" at the New England Synod Assembly, Evangelical Lutheran Church in America, Sturbridge, Mass., June 2, 1994. I make these citations with the author's permission.

40. Gerhard O. Forde, *Theology Is for Proclamation* (Minneapolis: Fortress Press, 1990), 29.

41. Solberg, *Compelling Knowledge*, 99.

42. *Luther's Works*, 54:7; *D. Martin Luther's Werke: Kritische Gesamtausgabe*, 65 vols. [Weimar: Böhlau, 1883–1993], 5:163, 28, in Solberg, *Compelling Knowledge*, 57.

43. Georg Wilhelm Friedrich Hegel, *On the Philosophy of Religion: Volume III, The Consummate Religion*, trans. R. F. Brown, P. C. Hodgson, and J. M. Stewart, ed. Peter C. Hodgson (New York: Oxford University Press, 1985), 326.

44. Tanner, *Theories of Culture*, 126.

45. *Luther's Works*, 42:164.

46. *Luther's Works*, 51:58. For relevant works by Finnish scholars or on their scholarship, see Risto Saarinen, "The Presence of God in Luther's Theology" *Lutheran Quarterly* (Spring 1994): 3–13, and Carl Braaten and Robert Jenson, eds., *Union with Christ: The New Finnish Interpretation of Luther* (Grand Rapids: Eerdmans, 1998).

47. Gritsch and Jenson, *Lutheranism*, 68.

48. Peter C. Hodgson, *The Mystery beneath the Real: Theology in the Fiction of George Eliot* (Minneapolis: Fortress Press, 2000), 17.

49. Ibid., 55.

50. As I indicated in chap. 2, n. 95, Ute Mennecke-Haustein argues that, for Luther, God alone is the source of consolation, but that consolation is located in that which is finite and fallible.

51. In the excursus that follows, I describe some of the problematics around consolation, tribulation, and atonement theologies that could be a part of such exploration.

Excursus

1. Darby K. Ray, *Deceiving the Devil: Atonement, Abuse, and Ransom* (Cleveland: Pilgrim), 42, 43. The citation is from Anne Marie Hunter's work, which was written for the American Academy of Religion in 1992. As she did for Darby Ray, Hunter very kindly let me review the entire manuscript of her presentation. Anne Marie Hunter, "Fear, Respect, and Love: Divine and Human Bonds of Connection and Control" (paper presented at the annual meeting of the American Academy of Religion, 1992), 18.

2. Kathryn Tanner, *Theories of Culture: A New Agenda for Theology* (Guides to Theological Inquiry; Minneapolis: Fortress Press, 1997), 162.

3. J. Denny Weaver, *The Nonviolent Atonement* (Grand Rapids: Eerdmans, 2001). Ray, *Deceiving the Devil*, 1998. Joanne C. Brown and Carole A. Bohn, eds., *Christianity, Patriarchy, and Abuse: A Feminist Critique* (New York: Pilgrim, 1989).

4. Ibid., 36.

5. Forde employs the distinction between primary and secondary discourse to critique atonement theories: "A construct, for instance, like vicarious satisfaction, taken to mean that God in the abstract is somehow moved objectively to change from an attitude of wrath to one of mercy or love by the sacrifice of Jesus on the cross, always creates more problems than it solves" (Gerhard O. Forde, *Theology Is for Proclamation* [Minneapolis: Fortress Press, 1990], 119). Forde does not explore another frequently employed solution—that God was not involved in this act, nor in any other form of human suffering. He does not do so, it seems to me, because that would render God to be eerily absent and therefore effectively wrathful.

6. Ibid, 119.

7. Gerhard Forde, in *Christian Dogmatics,* 2 vols., ed. Carl Braaten and Robert Jenson (Philadelphia: Fortress Press, 1984), 2:51.

8. Ibid., 50.

9. Ibid., 50. Forde's themes have been picked up among some Lutheran liberationist and feminist theologians. In his work of liberation theology and the theology of the cross, Alberto García claims, "Luther is not attempting to set up a 'theory of atonement' as Anselm did. To begin with Luther does not attempt to provide a mere theoretical answer to the question: Why did God become man?" Alberto L. García, "Theology of the Cross: A Critical Study of Leonardo Boff's and Jon Sobrino's Theology of the Cross in Light of Martin Luther's Theology of the Cross as Interpreted by Contemporary Luther Scholars" (Th.D. diss., Lutheran School of Theology at Chicago, 1987), 268. "Luther's stress on the incarnational humanity of God as a

means of our discerning God's divinity sets our sights on God's solution. It is not a question of God, but rather a question of God's answer to humanity. It is a concrete and real demonstration of God's eternal love for us." Ibid., 270. Similarly, Deanna A. Thompson proposes, "The message of Christ on the Cross is that 'God comes to us.' God changes our situation, because we, not God, are the ones who need to be changed. If a theology of the cross is going to hold on to some version of Luther's understanding of the depth of human sinfulness, then humanity must be viewed as incapable of reaching back toward God. The radical message of the cross for Luther, then, was that God offers Godself to us as a gift." Deanna A. Thompson, "Theological Proximity to the Cross: A Conversation between Martin Luther and Feminist Theologians" (Ph.D. diss., Vanderbilt University, 1998), 193. I would welcome elaborations of these works by these authors.

10. *Luther's Works*, American ed., 55 vols. (St. Louis: Concordia and Philadelphia: Fortress Press, 1955–86), 31:225.

11. Tanner, *Theories of Culture*, 77.

12. See John E. Smith, *The Spirit of American Philosophy* (Albany, N.Y.: SUNY Press, 1983), 13–14.

13. Charles Sanders Peirce, "How to Make Our Ideas Clear," in *Peirce on Signs*, ed. James Hoopes (Chapel Hill: University of North Carolina Press, 1991), 169. I read the following remark by Tanner to convey a similar notion: "One does not know what Christians mean by God without also knowing what they mean by Christ or by human existence lived religiously." Tanner, *Theories of Culture*, 77.

Select Bibliography

Appel, Helmut. *Anfechtung und Trost in Spätmittelalter und bei Luther* (Tribulation and consolation in the late Middle Ages and according to Luther). Leipzig: Heinfius, 1938.

Browning, Don S. *Fundamental Practical Theology.* Minneapolis: Fortress Press, 1991.

Bunge, Marcia J. "The Child in German Pietism." In *The Child in Christian Thought.* Edited by Marcia J. Bunge. Grand Rapids: Eerdmans, 2000.

———. "Herder and the Origins of a Historical View of Religion." In *Revisioning the Past: Prospects in Historical Theology.* Edited by Mary Potter Engel and Walter E. Wyman Jr. Minneapolis: Fortress Press, 1992.

Charry, Ellen T. *By the Renewing of Your Minds: The Pastoral Function of Christian Doctrine.* New York: Oxford University Press, 1997.

Clebsch, William A., and Charles R. Jaekle. *Pastoral Care in Historical Perspective.* New York: Aronson, 1975.

Couture, Pamela D. *Blessed are the Poor? Women's Poverty, Family Policy, and Practical Theology.* Nashville: Abingdon, 1991.

———. "Feminist, Wesleyan, Practical Theology and the Practice of Pastoral Care." In *Liberating Faith Practices: Feminist Practical Theologies in Context.* Edited by Denise M. Ackermann and Riet Bons-Storm. Leuven: Peeters, 1998.

———. "Revelation in Pastoral Theology: A Wesleyan Perspective." *The Journal of Pastoral Theology* 9 (1999): 21–34.

Dunlap, Susan. *Counseling Depressed Women.* Louisville: Westminster John Knox, 1997.

Ebeling, Gerhard. *Luther: An Introduction to His Thought.* Translated by R. A. Wilson. Philadelphia: Fortress Press, 1970.

———. *Luthers Seelsorge: Theologie in der Vielfalt der Lebenssituationen an seinen Briefen Dargestellt* (Luther's pastoral care: theology depicted in the diversity of life-situations in his letters). Tübingen: Mohr, 1997.

Engel, Mary P., and Walter. E. Wyman Jr. *Remembering the Past: Prospects in Historical Theology.* Minneapolis: Fortress Press, 1992.

Failing, Wolf-Eckart, and Hans-Gunter Heimbrock. *Gelebte Religion Wahrnehmnen: Lebenswelt, Alltagskultur, Religionpraxis* (Observing lived religion: life-world, daily culture, and the praxis of religion). Stuttgart: Kohlhammer, 1998.

Farley, Edward. *Ecclesial Reflection: An Anatomy of Theological Method.* Philadelphia: Fortress Press, 1982.

Forde, Gerhard O. *On Being a Theologian of the Cross: Reflections on Luther's Heidelberg Disputation, 1518.* Grand Rapids: Eerdmans, 1997.

———. *Theology Is for Proclamation.* Minneapolis: Fortress Press, 1990.

Gadamer, Hans-Georg. *Truth and Method.* Translated by Garrett Barden and John Cumming. New York: Seabury, 1975.

Gassmann, Günther, and Scott Hendrix. *Fortress Introduction to the Lutheran Confessions.* Minneapolis: Fortress Press, 1999.

Gerrish, Brian A. *Grace and Gratitude: The Eucharistic Theology of John Calvin.* Minneapolis: Fortress Press, 1993.

———. *The Old Protestantism and the New: Essays on the Reformation Heritage.* Chicago: University of Chicago Press, 1982.

Gorsuch, Nancy J. "Revelation and Pastoral Theology: Cooperation, Collision, and Communication." *The Journal of Pastoral Theology* 9 (1999): 35–48.

Gritsch, Eric W., and Robert W. Jenson. *Lutheranism: The Theological Movement and Its Confessional Writings.* Philadelphia: Fortress Press, 1976.

Hall, David D., ed. *Lived Religion in America: Toward a History of Practice.* Princeton: Princeton University Press, 1997.

Hodgson, Peter C. *The Mystery beneath the Real: Theology in the Fiction of George Eliot.* Minneapolis: Fortress Press, 2000.

Hummel, Leonard M. "A Kind of Religious Coping: A Theoretical and Empirical Analysis of Consolation in the Lutheran Tradition." Ph.D. diss., Boston University, 1999.

———. "Pietism of a Higher Order? A Look at Contemporary Practical Theology." *Covenant Quarterly* (August 2002): 2–20.

Hunter, Anne Marie. "Fear, Respect and Love: Divine and Human Bonds of Connection and Control." Paper presented at the Annual Meeting of the American Academy of Religion, San Francisco, 1992.

Innskeep, Kenneth W. *Religious Commitment in the Evangelical Lutheran Church in America: Findings from the Faith Practices Survey.* Chicago: Department for Research and Evaluation, Evangelical Lutheran Church in America, July 23, 2001. http://www.elca.org/re/reports/faithprac.pdf.

Kolb, Robert, and Timothy J. Wengert, eds. *The Book of Concord: The Confessions of The Evangelical Lutheran Church.* Translated by Charles Arand et al. Minneapolis: Fortress Press, 2000.

Klaassen, Walter. "The Anabaptist Tradition." *Caring and Curing: Health and Medicine in the Western Religious Traditions.* Edited by Ronald L. Numbers and Darrel W. Amundsen. New York: Macmillan, 1986.

Lindberg, Carter. *Beyond Charity: Reformation Initiatives for the Poor.* Minneapolis: Fortress Press, 1993.

———. *The European Reformations.* Cambridge, Mass.: Blackwell, 1996.

———. "The Lutheran Tradition." In *Care and Curing: Health and Medicine in the Western Religious Traditions.* Edited by Ronald L. Numbers and Darrel W. Amundsen. New York: Macmillan, 1986.

———. *The Third Reformation? Charismatic Movements and the Lutheran Tradition.* Macon, Ga.: Mercer University Press, 1983.

Luther, Henning. "Praktische Theologie als Kunst für Alle: Individualität und Kirche in Schleiermachers Verständnis Praktischer Theologie" (Practical theology as an art for everyone: individuality and the church in Schleiermacher's understanding of practical theology). *Zeitschrift fur Theologie und Kirche* 84, no. 3 (1987): 371–93.

Luther, Martin. *Letters of Spiritual Counsel.* Edited and translated by Theodore G. Tappert. Philadelphia: Westminster, 1955.

Marty, Martin. *Health and Medicine in the Lutheran Tradition.* New York: Crossroad, 1983.

McNeill, John T. *A History of the Cure of Souls*. New York: Harper & Row, 1951.

Mennecke-Haustein, Ute. *Luthers Trostbriefe* (Luther's letters of consolation). Gütersloher: Gerd Mohn, 1989.

Mildenberger, Friedrich. *Theology of the Lutheran Confessions*. Translated by E. Lueker. Philadelphia: Fortress Press, 1986.

Miller-McLemore, Bonnie J. "The Living Human Web: Pastoral Theology at the Turn of the Century." In *Through the Eyes of Women: Insights for Pastoral Care*. Edited by Jeanne Stevenson Moessner. Minneapolis: Fortress Press, 1996.

———. "Feminist Theory in Pastoral Theology." In *Feminist and Womanist Theology*. Edited by Bonnie J. Miller-McLemore and Brita L. Gill-Austern. Nashville: Abingdon, 1999.

Möller, Christian. "Luthers Seelsorge und die neueren Seelsorgekonzept" (Luther's pastoral care and the new attempts in pastoral care). In *Luther als Seelsorger* (Luther as Pastor), volume 18. Edited by Joachim Heubach. Erlangen: Martin-Luther Verlag, 1991.

Moltmann-Wendel, Elizabeth. "Is There a Feminist Theology of the Cross?" In *The Scandal of a Crucified World: Perspectives on the Cross and Suffering*. Edited by Yacob Tesfai. Maryknoll, N.Y.: Orbis, 1994.

Numbers, R. L., and D. W. Amundsen, eds. *Care and Curing: Health and Medicine in the Western Religious Traditions*. New York: Macmillan, 1986.

Oden, Thomas C. *Pastoral Theology: Essentials of Ministry*. New York: Harper & Row, 1982.

Olson, Alan. *Hegel and the Spirit: Philosophy as Pneumatology*. Princeton, N.J.: Princeton University Press, 1992.

Pargament, Kenneth I. *The Psychology of Religion and Coping: Theory, Research, Practice*. New York: Guilford, 1997.

Peel, Robert. *Health and Medicine in the Christian Science Tradition: Principle, Practice, and Challenge*. New York: Crossroad, 1998.

Peirce, Charles Sanders. "How to Make Our Ideas Clear." In *Peirce on Signs*. Edited by James Hoopes. Chapel Hill: University of North Carolina Press, 1991.

Purves, Andrew. *Pastoral Theology in the Classical Tradition*. Louisville: Westminster John Knox, 2001.

Ray, Darby K. *Deceiving the Devil: Atonement, Abuse, and Ransom.* Cleveland: Pilgrim, 1998.

Schleiermacher, Friedrich. *Christian Caring: Selections from Practical Theology.* Translated by James O. Duke. Philadelphia: Fortress Press, 1850/1988.

Schlink, Edmund. *Theology of the Lutheran Confessions.* Translated by P. F. Koehneke and H. J. A. Bouman. Philadelphia: Fortress Press, 1961.

Seneca, Lucius Annaeus. "Consolation of Helvia." In *The Stoic Philosophy of Seneca: Essays and Letters of Seneca.* Edited and translated by Moses Hadas. New York: Norton, 1958.

Solberg, Mary M. *Compelling Knowledge: A Feminist Proposal for an Epistemology of the Cross.* Albany: SUNY Press, 1997.

Sommer, Regina. *Lebensgeschichte und gelebte Religion von Frauen* (Life-history and lived religion of women). Stuttgart: Kohlhammer, 1998.

Spener, Philip Jacob. *Pia Desideria.* Edited and translated by Theodore G. Tappert. Philadelphia: Fortress Press, 1964.

Steiger, Johann Anselm. "Die communicatio idiomatum als Achse und Motor der Theologie Luther: Die 'fröhliche Wechsel' als hermeneutischer Schlüssel zu Abendmahlslehre, Anthropologie, Seelsorge, Naturtheologie, Rhetorik und Humor" (The exchange of properties as the axis and motor of Luther's theology: the "happy exchange" as the hermeneutical key to teachings on the Last Supper, anthropology, pastoral care, natural theology, rhetoric, and humor). *Neue Zeitschrift für Systematische Theologie und Religionsphilosophie* 38, no. 1 (1996): 1–28.

————. *Johann Gerhard (1582–1637): Studien zu Theologie und Frömmigkeit des Kirchenvaters der lutherischen Orthodoxie* (studies on the theology and piety of the Church-fathers of Lutheran Orthodoxy). Stuttgart-Bad Cannstatt: Frommann-Holzboog, 1997.

————. "Seelsorge, Dogmatik und Mystik bei Johann Gerhard: Ein Beitrag zu Theologie und Frömmigkeit der Lutherischen Orthodoxie" (Pastoral care, dogmatics and mysticism according to Johann Gerhard: a contribution to the theology and piety of Lutheran Orthodoxy). *Zeitschrift für Kirchengeschichte,* vol. 106 (1995): 329–44.

Strohl, Jane E. "Luther and the Word of Consolation." *Lutheran Theological Seminary Bulletin* 67 (Winter 1987): 23–34.

————. "Luther's Eschatology: The Last Times and the Last Things." Ph.D. diss., University of Chicago, 1989.

————. "Luther's 'Fourteen Consolations.'" *Lutheran Quarterly* 3 (1989): 169–82.

————. "Suffering as Redemptive: A Comparison of Christian Experience in the Sixteenth and Twentieth Centuries." In *Remembering the Past: Prospects in Historical Theology*. Edited by Mary. P. Engel and Wayne. E. Wyman Jr. Minneapolis: Fortress Press, 1992.

Strommen, Merton P., Milo L. Brekke, Ralph C. Underwager, and Arthur L. Johnson. *A Study of Generations*. Minneapolis: Augsburg, 1972.

Tanner, Kathryn. *Theories of Culture: A New Agenda for Theology*. Guides to Theological Inquiry. Minneapolis: Fortress Press, 1997.

Terry, David. "Martin Luther on the Suffering of the Christian." Ph.D. diss., Boston University, 1990.

Thompson, Deanna Alice. "Theological Proximity to the Cross: A Conversation Between Martin Luther and Feminist Theologians." Ph.D. diss., Vanderbilt University, 1998.

Thornton, Sharon G. *Broken yet Beloved: A Pastoral Theology of the Cross*. Saint Louis: Chalice, 2002.

Treu, Martin. "Die Bedeutung der Consolatio für Luthers Seelsorge bis 1525" (The significance of consolation for Luther's pastoral care until 1525). *Lutherjahrbuch* 53 (1986): 7–25.

————. "Trost bei Luther: Ein Anstoß für die heutige Seelsorge" (Consolation according to Luther: an impetus for today's pastoral care). *Pastoraltheologie* 73, no. 1 (1984): 91–106.

von Loewenich, Walther. *Luther's Theology of the Cross*. Translated by Herbert J. A. Bouman. Minneapolis: Augsburg, 1976.

Weaver, J. Denny. *The Nonviolent Atonement*. Grand Rapids: Eerdmans, 2001.

Weber, Timothy P. "The Baptist Tradition." In *Caring and Curing: Health and Medicine in the Western Religious Traditions*. Edited by R. L. Numbers and D. W. Amundsen. New York: Macmillan, 1986.

Wicks, Jared. "Applied Theology at the Deathbed: Luther and the Late-Medieval Tradition of the *Ars Moriendi*." *Gregorianum* 79, no. 2 (1998): 345–68.

Index

❯❯·❮❮

107203

CPSIA information

260546BV